Detroit:

City of Race

and Class

Violence

GREAT LAKES BOOKS

Detroit:

City of Race and Class Violence

Revised Edition

MI
305.8
WIDI
C.1

by B. J. Widick

Foreword by Horace L. Sheffield, Jr.

WAYNE STATE UNIVERSITY PRESS
DETROIT   1989

Library of Congress Cataloging-in-Publication Data

Widick, B.J.
    Detroit: city of race and class violence.

    Bibliography: p.
    Includes index.
    1. Detroit (Mich.)—Race relations.   2. Detroit (Mich.)—Politics
and government.   3. Violence—Michigan—Detroit—History—
20th century.   I. Title.
F574.D49A28 1989   305.8'009774'34   88-33761
ISBN 0-8143-2104-6

For Wade H. McCree, Jr.

Contents

Foreword

Horace L. Sheffield, Jr.

FOR MANY of us who spent a lifetime of activity and struggle in Detroit, the reissue and updating of B. J. Widick's provocative book highlighting the city's history of race and class violence will unquestionably evoke some bittersweet personal memories about the men, the institutions, and the turbulent events that shaped our destinies and the character of the city and its people. For younger generations, Widick's book will be a lively story and a useful analysis. It should help them grasp what the people of Detroit went through in recent decades. It shows the trends that got us where we are today and what forces are molding our future.

Listing a few of the topics included in this book suggests what rich material awaits the reader: the industrial tyranny and plantation politics of the 1920's; the impact of the Great Depression and the rise of the CIO; blacks in the unions and plants; wartime Detroit and the 1943 riot; the 1967 riot and its shattering effects; the attempts at post-riot reconstruction; and finally the emergence of a dominant black political power base that still lacks economic clout.

Unlike some writers who rely on either personal experiences or academic studies and research, Widick brings

ix

to his book an invaluable combination of both sources of knowledge. I know this from our long personal relationship which began in 1948 when he was a chief steward in Local 7 of the UAW. Widick was an early and ardent supporter of the Trade Union Leadership Council (TULC) and an active member of its executive board when our demands for greater black representation in all levels of UAW leadership were not exactly the most popular within the union.

In 1949 he and Irving Howe wrote the *UAW and Walter Ruether,* which pulled no punches in raising issues involved in the hard road to equality within as well as outside the union movement.

Along with leaders like Brendan Sexton, Guy Nunn, Leonard Woodcock, and Douglas Fraser, Widick was always available for hard work and offered public support through his writings. We were in a lot of good fights together—from helping Jerry Cavanagh upset machine politics to become mayor of Detroit to helping A. Philip Randolph force George Meany and the AFL-CIO leadership to accept the establishment of the Negro American Labor Council.

Whether it was in the Chrysler Jefferson plant where Widick spent fifteen years or in his careers as a UAW staff member and a professor at Wayne State University and Columbia University, my friend earned a reputation for "telling it like it is." This was obviously manifest in the first edition of *Detroit: City of Race and Class Violence,* published in 1972, and in his writings on labor and Detroit which appeared in *Nation* magazine for more than two decades. His reputation for candor also won him a distinguished teaching award in 1972 from the Graduate School of Business of Columbia University.

The second edition of this book includes a new chapter that examines the social, political, and economic forces that have deeply affected the city from 1967 to 1987. Widick's critical mind has not lost any of its sharpness. *Detroit: City of Race and Class Violence* makes for a controversial book, but as I write this foreword I am reminded that his pessimistic views on discrimination are not unlike those set forth by the strategic planning committee, which used the term "apartheid" to describe discriminatory patterns in Detroit. Widick is not off target from the latest findings of the national Urban League report.

Preface to
Great Lakes Books Edition

IN THE ORIGINAL edition I argued that the most acute past and present problems of modern American society were inherent in Detroit. Furthermore, I maintained that the city's experiences had significant national repercussions. Detroit's fate was a harbinger of America's future. The book warned that the devastating social explosion of July 1967 shattered the conventional belief that Detroit was the model of a large industrial city working out its race and class problems.

Notwithstanding the riot's grim aftermath, I projected an essentially optimistic future. Detroit would be different than other "inner cities." I envisioned a powerful black community, having a strong economic, social, and political base. It would contain a growing black middle class and an influential black industrial union movement.

It didn't work out that way. I did a three-year study to review what has happened in Detroit since 1967, why it has happened, and what it signifies. The results of my study are published in the epilogue in this edition. To be sure, city politics did become dominated by black political power. Mayor Coleman Young was easily reelected three times since his first triumph in 1973. But the loss of 100,000 manufacturing jobs gutted the industrial base of the city. The high-paying auto jobs disappeared as plants closed or moved to the suburbs or to other states and countries. Demographic changes resulting from population shifts to the suburbs helped shrink the city: Detroit lost 600,000 people, and the drain continues.

Meanwhile, metropolitan Detroit saw the creation of boomtowns—suburbs whose affluence is comparable to any area in the United States, a fact often overlooked. By confusing metropolitan Detroit with the city of Detroit, the vast gap between the affluent suburbs and the depressed city frequently is obscured. The ordeals that Detroit residents have endured during the structural changes—above all, unemployment and dislocations—are the source of many poignant stories and crises. Is it a wonder that Detroit has developed a poor image problem in this context? Or that frustration levels are always high? As a consequence of these turbulent changes, the city's destiny remains in the grip of two overwhelming forces—social and economic—that victimize its shrinking population and make living a nightmare and the future bleak. I have concluded on the basis of my study that, "One social force, like an incurable cancer, is the persistence of racism, manifested in black frustration and rage and white fears, which prevents healthy race relations."

My second judgment is more controversial. It suggests who is responsible for this situation. "Above all, there is a reticence to analyze the second powerful force—besides the race issue—which negatively affects Detroit. It is the impact of the decisions of the power structure—the auto industry leaders, the big merchandisers, and the real estate investors—to shift the bulk of its plants, stores, investments, and activities outside the city." Surely, unless these forces are recognized as primary determinants in molding Detroit's condition, efforts to alleviate if not cure the city's ills seem likely to end up as exercises in shadowboxing with realities.

This analysis of the city's distress obviously casts a heavy cloud on the rosy scenario in which conservative America has basked during the Reagan era. But much of America has problems similar to those plaguing Detroit. In many respects this book supports the masterful study by the brilliant sociologist William J. Wilson. His book, *The Truly Disadvantaged: The Inner City, the Underclass and Public Policy,* presents persuasive evidence that explodes the myths in liberal and conservative orthodoxies about blacks. A new spectre haunts us: a different, socially isolated underclass, unreachable by liberal or conservative panaceas. This is the great challenge.

Since leaving Wayne State University for Columbia University I have written and lectured extensively in the United States and abroad about the United Auto Workers Union, the auto industry, and Detroit. I have returned to Detroit many times over the years to visit friends, discuss ideas, and keep up with events. This has been an invaluable stimulant. Two personal friends, however, do deserve special thanks for their contributions. Oscar Paskal of the UAW educational department has shared his experiences and knowledge with me since we both worked at Chrysler after World War II. Paskal became an outstanding educator and is recognized as such by his peers. And I am much in debt to Merle Henrickson, the long-time director of the Detroit Board of Education Planning and Building Division, formerly a member of the city planning commission. His lifetime activities in the city and his knowledge of it are remarkable. Henrickson's continuous analysis of the city's trends are a gold mine of data and information.

Preface to Great Lakes Books Edition

I am deeply grateful to Phil Mason, editor of the Great Lakes Books Series, for his interest in reprinting *Detroit: City of Race and Class Violence,* and to Paulette Petrimoulx for her invaluable assistance in the editing of the updated portions of this book. Needless to say, only I am responsible for the results of my work.

June 1988   B. J. WIDICK

Preface

As DETROIT goes, so goes the country. Name the acute problems, past or present, of modern American society and the auto capital of the world has confronted them, with an impact felt by the entire nation. Many of these problems emerged when the lure of high profits and high wages drew hundreds of thousands of European immigrants, Southern white workers, dispossessed blacks, and the extraneous rural population of the Midwest into the factory complex of Detroit. In conventional wisdom the city has been regarded as a melting pot. In reality Detroit has served the function of a pressure cooker, often exploding in racial and class conflict.

The industrial complex absorbed people of different races, creeds, and ethnic and class origins for its manpower requirements, but did not eliminate the divisive factors inherent in the social composition of the city. In 1971 the differences were, if anything, more visible than during any other period since World War I.

Until now, the city of Detroit has survived its racial and class conflicts, but at painful cost; the outlook for the 1970's is hardly reassuring. At every stage of its history Detroit has been a battleground where attempts to modify the status quo—whether it be institutional arrangements, power relationships, or social attitudes—have met with vigorous resistance. This violent reaction to new ideas or ways of doing things, as campus reformers and radicals learned recently, seems endemic to the entire American scene.

In broad terms, society generally responds to new challenges with reform, repression, or sometimes a mixture of both; if these prove inadequate, it may move toward a revolutionary crisis. Each policy finds its advocates, generates its activists, and gains some measure of support in the nation. The 1970's began in an atmosphere of national crisis, with fear of violence on the campus and in the streets heightened by a growing racial polarization—perhaps the major problem now confronting American society.

As usual, the debate over issues in critical times becomes shrill and emotion-packed. Extremism flourishes. In an earlier period of Detroit's history, it was the powerful voice of Rev. Charles Coughlin, representing to labor and the liberal community the threat of "fascism from the right" which frightened many people and gained fanatic supporters. Before that, it was the campaign of the Ku Klux Klan to win a mayoralty election in 1924—a campaign which almost succeeded. The ideology of the KKK left its permanent mark on Detroit; its heritage provides the climate for the modern George Wallaces.

On the industrial front, the repressive conditions in the auto plants led to the protest of labor in the sitdown strikes of the 1930's. When management continued to resist the idea of unionism, the workers reacted by seizing the plants, notably in the General Motors empire. It is interesting that the attempted repression in the name of "law and order" or "management's rights" was followed not by revolution, but by reform in the establishment of the trade unions.

xviii

Detroit was a focal point of class conflict in the turbulent thirties. The citadel of anti-unionism became the scene of John L. Lewis' first major victories for industrial unionism. As a consequence, Detroit became the power base for the world's two largest unions, the auto workers and the teamsters, and gave Walter Reuther and James Hoffa national influence.

Each moment of crisis brought the inevitable fear of "communist plots" and "totalitarianism of the Left." To put these fears in perspective—for there were indeed radicals on the Left active in all protest actions—one must look at Detroit's past. Along with the hardships of the Depression, the brutal treatment of the workers and unemployed made many of them radicals, just as intolerant attitudes toward youthful protesters — lumping them all together and ignoring their complaints—serve to radicalize many college students. The internal impact of an international event like war on Detroit and the nation has also been underestimated.

War brutalizes men and society, often acting as a catalyst for violent outbursts. World War II brought thousands of blacks and whites to Detroit, creating a keg of social dynamite; the 1943 race riot was inevitable, and the occasion was a time for "killing niggers" by whites and police. The Korean war aroused passions which led to mob violence against suspected radicals in a Detroit inflamed by McCarthyism.

Currently, the violence of the disastrous war in Indo-China has permeated the thinking of most Americans with terrifying effect. Four students were killed at Kent State with little evidence of national remorse, except among the young. The Black Panthers "are getting what they deserve"; one hears that at every level of American society.

Such attitudes denote a society living in fear and frustration, once again looking for scapegoats rather than root causes. The contrast of these attitudes with the Victorian optimism in Detroit during the 1960's is remarkable. Nowhere in the nation were there more illusions about an affluent society and significant social progress, with the national press singling out Detroit's way as the future of America. The fabulous success of the auto industry, the rich contracts of the UAW with the industry's leaders, the emergence of a brilliant young political figure, Mayor Jerome P. Cavanagh — these appeared to be manifestations of a new era of social peace.

The 1967 riot shattered these illusions. Its destruction was far greater in terms of human relations than in the obvious physical damage. The legacy of racial hatred, *de facto* segregation in the community and schools, and the revival of class tension hung over the city like storm clouds.

At each point in time the Establishment—the complex of power structures and leadership—has been unwilling or unable to understand the coming crises. In the 1920's and 1930's it was primarily the white working people who insisted that they be treated as human beings equal in stature to their economic peers. They achieved integration in our society mainly through the institution of unionism. One has only to see their homes in the suburbs to realize their present stake in society. Their problems today are quite different from those of the harsh past they still remember.

One minority was never given the opportunities for economic and social progress which were available to the immigrants and the uprooted whites of America. A successful black physician could not become part of the community like an Italian or Polish or Serbian doctor. Blacks learned that in 1924 from the Ossian Sweet case. They were kept on the fringes of industrial Detroit.

(The Ford Motor Company was a notable exception, with its policy of hiring about 10 per cent of its local work force from the ghettos). Not until a labor market shortage and the protests of workers during World War II did Detroit Negroes enter the industrial scene in visible numbers. The extraordinary difficulties Negroes had to overcome to be accepted as human beings is a totally different story in Detroit from the history of the immigrants. Blacks always faced both race and class discrimination. Immigrants faced irritating prejudices and class bias, but they were accepted as whites and therefore superior in status to the black man.

The alienation of the black man, and to a lesser degree of some poor whites, was the underlying cause of the 1967 riot—a protest against a society which, if it did not totally exclude the black man, clearly considered him undesirable. The 1967 riot was not blacks versus whites, as in 1943, but blacks and *some* whites against the power structure, the landlord, the merchant, and the hated police.

Given these assumptions, the subsequent campaigns to rebuild the city of Detroit were foredoomed to failure. Once again the solution to a social crisis was viewed primarily in terms of the reestablishment of "law and order," and public support listed heavily in the direction of repression. Reform has been so slight that it resembles Bandaids; they stop the bleeding but don't cure the wound. Social solutions on a local or state scale are minuscule compared to the needs. Yet current national priorities preclude any significant redress of social ills.

The violence of public debate in this context will undoubtedly continue to provoke violent reactions among differing segments of the population.

What makes Detroit distinctly important and what is new here is the emergence of a black community possessing a powerful economic, social, and political base. In this respect it is unlike other inner cities in urban areas which seem doomed to become wastelands of human and material resources. All trends suggest that Detroit, the city, is destined to become a black metropolis—not just a slum or a ghetto, though these do exist, but a municipality with a strong black middle class and, perhaps more significantly, a powerful black unionized working class. This black community has already demonstrated its strength, viability, and leadership on both political and union fronts. It is moving toward domination of the city and challenging the white suburbs in every area of public controversy. It is too early to foretell the outcome of the racial and class conflicts. But we can see definite trends in the successes and failures of the past and the present. My aim here has been to better define certain social issues by placing them in the larger context of such trends, both urban and national. Until this is done, any true solutions are impossible.

Many individuals have contributed to this book by way of discussion and suggestions, and by making its publication possible. Emmanuel Geltman, editor at Quadrangle Books, helped shape its focus and assured its publication. Gene Brook, co-director of the Institute of Labor and Industrial Relations, University of Michigan–Wayne State University (Labor Division), and director of Wayne State's labor college, contributed a critical analysis of the manuscript. As a long-time writer and associate of Guy Nunn's UAW *Eye Opener* radio and TV programs, Brook's knowledge of the city is difficult to equal. The early chapters were edited by my friend Albert Fried, the historian, and our numerous discussions were of invaluable assistance to me.

Anthony Ripley of the *New York Times,* a former Detroit newspaperman and confidential assistant to

Mayor Jerome P. Cavanagh, reviewed the material on the 1960's. The former mayor was also quite candid with me in his discussion of those days. James Keeney, a Ph.D. candidate at Columbia University who spent three years in Detroit, was very generous in allowing me to use his material and research on Detroit's race and housing problems. My former colleagues in the UAW and the men and women whom I know in the auto plants kept me well informed over the years on events in the plants and in the city. Wilbur Thompson, the urban economist from Wayne State University, provided the original impetus for this study in the form of a grant from the Urban Institute of that school while I was teaching there. Additional funds were made available by the faculty research committee of the Graduate School of Business, Columbia University. Assignments from Carey McWilliams, editor of the *Nation,* and from Irving Howe, editor of *Dissent,* enabled me to return more frequently to Detroit than I would otherwise have been able to do.

Many thanks are also due Mrs. Bonnie De Athos of Wayne State University, Mrs. Sonya Whynman, and Mrs. Dolores Nichols of the Graduate School of Business, Columbia University, for the typing of the manuscript and for the patience so indispensable to an author. And, most of all, gratitude goes to my wife Barbara and my son Marshall Jason, who make my life and work such a real pleasure.

July 1971   B. J. WIDICK

Detroit:

City of Race and Class Violence

The Legacy of the KKK

1

I N 1924–1925 the Ku Klux Klan mounted a campaign to dominate Detroit—the fourth largest city in the United States and the symbol of American industrial success. Its appeal, simple and direct, was based on anti-Catholicism and white superiority.

As an organization, the KKK was destroyed on these issues. But it left a legacy of prejudice more visible than ever today. In a city of 350,000 Catholics out of a total population of nearly 1,000,000, the KKK program overreached itself. A proposal to outlaw parochial schools in Michigan was defeated by a vote of 610,699 to 353,817. However, in the September 1924 primary in Detroit, the KKK mayoralty candidate was defeated only by technical rulings which invalidated 17,000 votes.

The remarkable thing about the KKK political campaign was that its candidate was a write-in. Charles Bowles received 106,679 votes, excluding the 17,000; John W. Smith, backed by Catholic and Negro voters, had 116,807; and Joseph Martin, who was on the ballot against Smith, totaled 84,929.

John W. Smith, who was elected, denounced the Klan for seeking to "establish a dictatorship" in Detroit when it took to the streets and provoked violence. But in a sense the KKK also won when the mayor, elected with Negro votes, accepted the Klan's view that black men ought to stay in their place.

> . . . I must say that I deprecate most strongly the moving of Negroes or other persons into districts in which they know their presence may cause riot or bloodshed.
>
> I believe that any colored person who endangers life and property, simply to gratify his personal pride, is an enemy of his race as well as an incitant to riot and murder. These men, who have permitted themselves to be tools of the Ku Klux Klan in its effort to fan the flames of racial hatred into murderous fire, have hurt the cause of their race in a degree that can not be measured.[1]

The language may have been softened somewhat at times, but essentially this was, and generally still is, the attitude in Detroit toward the efforts of blacks to become equal citizens in all respects. The KKK has long been dead as a strong organization in Detroit, but most whites still hold Smith's view.

In view of what happened in 1925 in the Motor City, Smith's policy was tragic—one of the many instances of white racism which frustrated Negroes and aroused their anger.

The red glare of fiery crosses and men marching in white hoods were common sights in Detroit in those days. In July 1925, the frenzy of the KKK became more ominous. An audience of ten thousand cheered KKK speakers who urged the 100 per cent Americans "to keep the niggers in their place." Blacks were beginning to break out of the ghetto, and the time for direct action was now.

The uprooted Southern "hillbillies" and "red-necks" responded enthusiastically. They were already deeply disturbed by what was happening to their America: too many Jews were running stores; too many politicians with funny foreign names were winning office; and the Pope's followers were gaining influence everywhere.

Following a report that a "smart nigger" had bought a house in an all-white neighborhood, the Klan ended its Saturday night rally with a call to organize "neighborhood improvement associations," particularly on the east side of Detroit.

One man, more than anyone else in Detroit, knew what this rally portended. He was black and he had purchased a house outside the ghetto in an all-white neighborhood on the east side.

Dr. Ossian H. Sweet, the home purchaser, had all the attributes which American society demands that a black man have to be accepted. He was middle class, educated, a man of culture; his enemies were ignorant, racist, and proletarian. His ordeal became a test for Detroit, and a preview of American society's dilemmas and agonies for the next four decades.

The subsequent maelstrom of events almost destroyed Dr. Sweet. In the long run they led to his suicide. More immediately, he was put in jail with his wife, Gladys, a university graduate; his brother Otis, a dentist; another brother who was a student at Wilberforce College; John Latting, a former Army captain; William Davis, a federal narcotics officer; and five businessmen.

For a white man had been killed, probably by a black man, and these eleven prisoners were charged with first-degree murder. They were held without bail pending trial before an all-white jury.

This was the stark background to the "Sweet case" which commanded world attention in 1925. It also illuminated the soul of Detroit.

A stroke of good fortune, and the influence of the National Association for the Advancement of Colored People, made a lynch trial impossible, though the white community was filled with cries for Negro blood in the name of "law and order."

It happened that the presiding judge, recently appointed to the state bench, was a brilliant young liberal, Frank Murphy, the man who later rose to become mayor of Detroit, governor of Michigan, Attorney General, and finally Justice of the United States Supreme Court.

The NAACP convinced Clarence Darrow, defender of unpopular causes and recent opponent of William Jennings Bryan in the Tennessee "monkey trial," to take the Sweet case. W.E.B. DuBois, the Negro writer, said of Darrow: "He was absolutely lacking in racial consciousness and one of the few white folks with whom I felt quite free to discuss matters of race and class."[2] Only a lawyer of Darrow's stature, and with his understanding of the underlying issues, could really help the defendants, and Darrow accepted the challenge. He was assisted by Arthur Garfield Hays, the noted civil libertarian; Walter Nelson, a prominent and courageous Detroit lawyer; and a working staff of anonymous local Negro lawyers who kept in the background so as not to further inflame public opinion.

The overwhelming difficulty faced by the defense was the white community's conviction that the Negroes had to be guilty. And numerous witnesses, the testimony of the police, the tactics of the prosecution—all reinforced that conviction.

What happened when Ossian Sweet moved into his new home depended on what version one believed, and, more important, what one *wanted* to believe. It would take the consummate skill of Clarence Darrow to piece together the story from the accounts of all the participants, the police, and the witnesses, to explain what motivated men like Dr. Sweet, and to expose the depths of racism in the city.

As far as the white community and the prosecution were concerned, the facts of the case were clear enough:

a shooting had taken place and a white man had been killed. What more was needed except the identity of the killers, and that too was known. Arthur Garfield Hays accurately described the prosecution's version of events: It was "a warm summer evening in a quiet, neighborly community. The Sweet house stood on a corner. Diagonally across was the high school with a spacious yard. Opposite and along the street were small frame houses owned and occupied by simple, kindly people—the men mostly mechanics, the women housewives, dutifully caring for broods of children. People were sitting on their porches enjoying the cool air after dusk, visiting and chatting. A few sauntered casually along the street. Some were on their way to a corner grocery. Here and there a car was parked. Of course, the fact that Negroes had moved into the corner house was of interest, but peace and quiet was assured by a half dozen policemen who stood guard at various places, keeping people away from the sidewalk in front and on the side of the Sweet house. Suddenly, unexpectedly and without provocation, a fusillade of shots rang out from the rear, sides and front of the house, and Leon Breiner, chatting with a group on the porch of the Dove home opposite, was killed. His pipe was still in his mouth when he was carried away. Another man in the group was wounded.

"After painting this picture, the prosecutor cried 'Cold-blooded murder!' and the newspapers, of course, echoed his cry: 'Another murder by Negroes. They are becoming a menace to the community!' "[3] Simple justice required that the Negroes be found guilty of first-degree murder and appropriately punished.

The defense did not dispute the bare facts. It did seem clear that Breiner had been killed by a shot from the house. It was true that ten men had gathered there with provisions, guns, and ammunition to withstand a possible siege and that the shooting had come from various windows. (Moreover, there had been extensive police presence, and the arrested blacks had made conflicting statements, almost confessions, about firing guns.) But if one related what happened on the night of September 9, 1925, when Breiner was killed, to what had been, and was then, happening in Detroit, the white man's version of the event was badly distorted. As Clarence Darrow said at one point during the trial:

> I insist that there is nothing but prejudice in this case; that if it was reversed and eleven white men had shot and killed a black while protecting their home and their lives against a mob of blacks, nobody would've dreamed of having them indicted. I know what I am talking about, and so do you. They would have been given medals instead. Ten colored men and one woman are in this indictment, tried by twelve jurors, gentlemen. Everyone of you are white, aren't you? At least you all think so. We haven't one colored man on this jury. We couldn't get one. One was called and he was disqualified. You twelve men are trying a colored man on race prejudice.

Emphasizing his point, Darrow added, "Now let me ask you whether you are not prejudiced. I want to put this square to you, gentlemen. I haven't any doubt but that every one of you is prejudiced against colored people."[4]

Immediately preceding Dr. Sweet's purchase of the $18,500 two-story house, Detroit had seen a wave of anti-Negro violence which received little attention in the daily press. In April 1925, a Negro woman with a five-week-old baby had purchased a home in a white neighborhood. She was menaced by a crowd of whites and the home was stoned. Threatened again by the mob, she took a shotgun and fired it over their heads. A white neighbor then swore out a warrant for her arrest. That same month Dr. Sweet had witnessed what happened to a friend of his, Dr. Fred Turner, who had bought a house on Spokane Avenue in Detroit. "Turner," commented Dr. Sweet in his testimony, "always had the greatest confidence in the word of white people; he felt that they belonged to a race superior to his own. Consequently, when they wanted to enter his house, to rob him, it wasn't necessary to break down the door. It was far simpler to deceive him. One of the leaders simply knocked and, when Dr. Turner came to the door, said, 'Open, Turner, I'm your friend.' Dr. Turner believed him and opened the door. The next moment he was dough in the hands of the mob."[5] Dr. Sweet said he would never forget the picture of the leader of the mob accompanied by a few followers, with one or two policemen standing by, trying to talk the Turners into selling the property and getting out. Mrs. Turner refused to sign the deed. Later there were police in the basement of the house and, with their consent, Negroes were allowed to arm and stand guard upstairs. But the situation was impossible and Dr. Turner eventually left.

There were other incidents of this kind, but the most portentous of them took place on July 11, when over ten thousand Ku Klux Klanners listened to men advocating a law that would compel Negroes to live in certain quarters of the city. But until the passage of such a law, they announced, "neighborhood improvement associations" would be organized. More particularly, a meeting would be held in Howe school yard at the corner of Garland and Charlevoix, which all people in the neighborhood were ordered to attend "in self-defense." At this meeting, around the corner from where the Sweets' recently purchased home was located, some six to seven hundred persons organized an improvement association and thus prepared to keep the Sweets from moving into their home.[6]

Dr. Ossian Sweet knew that he faced danger in moving into the all-white neighborhood. He had told his brother Otis, "I have to die a man or live a coward." He was determined not to suffer the fate of Dr. Turner. So when he moved in on Tuesday morning, September 8, with two small vans of furniture, he also brought arms and ammunition, and made arrangements for a number of his friends to stay with him.[7] It was quiet the first night, but on September 9 the mood changed. Though nearly 71 witnesses, including police officers, testified that all was calm and normal, the defense did find two white people who were willing to talk freely about the events of that evening. Philip Adler, a general reporter for the *Detroit News,* said he was driving with his family down St. Clair to Charlevoix when he noticed an unusual gathering of people all along the block. He thought there must have been an accident, since policemen were diverting traffic. He himself was not allowed to proceed to Charlevoix. Adler circled around and cut through an alley to Garland, an adjoining street, where he parked his car. Having a nose for news, he went down toward the Sweet house. The people on Garland, he testified, seemed to be mostly men in their shirt sleeves, with a general look of belonging to the community, and they were quite different from the 500 or so on the Charlevoix side of the street. That crowd was in a belligerent mood. When he asked what this was all about, he was told that "Some nigger family had moved in there and the people were trying to get rid of them." Meanwhile he heard stones hitting the house.[8] Adler's account corroborated Otis Sweet's. Sweet stated that when he arrived on the evening of September 9 with Walter Davis, an ex-Army captain, "The street was a sea of humanity. The crowd was so thick you couldn't see the street or the sidewalk. Just getting to the front door was like running the gauntlet. I was hit by a rock before

I got inside. The stone throwers were yelling, 'Let's get the Niggers.' "[9]

Mrs. Sweet vividly recollected the events of that night. She told about looking out the window and seeing the school yard full of people, and also the space near the grocery store. People were in the alley and on the porches of flat houses opposite. Cars were coming and parking two deep. The mob was thick. She heard the stones fly. She talked about two young Negroes who came near the house, intending to help the Sweets. But they fled under a barrage of stones, coals, rocks, and bricks. She remembered the chant of the crowd: "Niggers, they're niggers—Get the damn niggers!"[10] It was this cry that Dr. Sweet heard as he opened the door for his brother and Davis.

> When I opened that door to let them in, I realized that for the first time in my life I stood face to face with the same mob that has haunted my people throughout its entire history. I knew that my back was against the wall, that I was black and that because I was black and had found the courage to buy a home, they were ready to wreak their vengeance upon me. The whole thing, the whole situation filled me with an appalling fear—a fear that no one could comprehend but a Negro, and that Negro one who knew the history behind his people.[11]

Under oath, Detroit police testified to a story that had little if any relation to what the Negroes had been describing as the actual events outside the Sweet home. For example, in the interrogation of Inspector Norton M. Schucknecht, in charge of the eleven-men police detail at the house when the shooting occurred, there was this exchange:

> QUESTION: There was no one there when you got there? The time of your arrival was about 7:30?
> ANSWER: There were people on the street but they were walking up and down and there was no congregating. He said he had instructed his office Dr. Sweet could

11

live there if we had to take every man in the station to
see that he did.

QUESTION: Did you see anyone armed with clubs or
other weapons?

ANSWER: Not at any time.

QUESTION: What happened about 8:15?

ANSWER: Suddenly a volley of shots was fired from the
windows of Dr. Sweet's home.

QUESTION: How many shots?

ANSWER: About fifteen or twenty.

Of course the police could not explain why reserves
had been called, why traffic had been stopped, and why
they had ordered people to move on. Inspector Schucknecht's testimony was supported by that of Lt. Paul Shel-
lenburger:

QUESTION: Did you see an unusual number of automobiles in the district while you were there that night?

ANSWER: I should say not.

QUESTION: Were you present when Deputy Superintendent Sprott instructed Schucknecht to direct traffic
off of Garland Avenue?

ANSWER: I was.

QUESTION: Did you participate in the discussion about
the number of machines that were coming into that immediate neighborhood?

ANSWER: I did not.

QUESTION: Did you know where the automobiles went
after leaving Garland Avenue?

ANSWER: I do not.

QUESTION: Do you know how many automobiles were
parked just before this, that is before the shooting, on
any side of the side streets east and west of Garland
Avenue?

ANSWER: I do not.

QUESTION: Or where the occupants of those cars went?

ANSWER: I do not.

QUESTION: You do not know whether they came back,
walked back to the corner of Charlevoix and Garland,
do you?

ANSWER: I do not.

12

QUESTION: Isn't it true now, officer, that it was because there were so many machines coming into Charlevoix and Garland, that you officers determined you would divert the traffic off of Garland so as to keep them coming up there?

ANSWER: No, sir.

QUESTION: Then why did you not stop the traffic from coming up St. Clair and Bewick? [The streets to the right and left of Garland and parallel to it.]

ANSWER: Because it was not necessary.

QUESTION: Why wasn't it necessary?

ANSWER: I think the streets are wider and can accommodate more cars.

QUESTION: Tell us how many feet wider Bewick Avenue is than Garland Avenue.

ANSWER: I couldn't tell you. I don't think there is any difference in the width at all.

QUESTION: How many feet wider is St. Clair than Garland?

ANSWER: [By this time the officer's face was a dull red.] I don't think there is any difference in the width at all.

QUESTION: Then, why didn't you stop automobiles from going to Bewick?

ANSWER: Why should I?

QUESTION: Well, you did at Garland, did you not?

ANSWER: Yes.

QUESTION: Why did you do that at Garland?

ANSWER: Because we did not want any cars in the vicinity, only what belonged there.

QUESTION: Were there any persons coming in that vicinity in automobiles who did not belong in that neighborhood?

ANSWER: Not after the traffic was diverted.

QUESTION: Were they before?

ANSWER: Yes.

QUESTION: Who were they?

ANSWER: I do not know.

QUESTION: Was traffic getting heavy?

ANSWER: It appeared to me that people were getting curious, more so than anything else, and there was an unusual amount of traffic.

QUESTION: Then there was an unusual amount of automobile traffic there wasn't there?
ANSWER: There was.

Many witnesses summoned by the prosecution seemed to support the testimony of the police officers and the prosecutor's general description of the situation. However, in cross-examination the defense was able to bring out the real purpose of the Water Works Improvement Association and the real purpose of the mass meeting that had been announced at the Ku Klux Klan rally. One witness, asked when the association started, replied, "A long time ago."

QUESTION: When did you first hear that the Sweets were moving into the neighborhood?
ANSWER: That was a long time ago, too.
QUESTION: Did that have anything to do with your joining the club?
ANSWER: Possibly.
QUESTION: Did it?
ANSWER: Yes.
QUESTION: You joined the club to aid in keeping that a white district?
ANSWER: Yes.
QUESTION: At the meeting, was any reference made to keeping the district free from colored people?
ANSWER: Yes.
QUESTION: How many people were present at the meeting?
ANSWER: Seven hundred.

Other witnesses indicated the same concerning the policy of the Water Works Improvement Association. In cross-examination Darrow was able to pin down one prosecution witness:

QUESTION: Did the speaker talk about "legal means"?
ANSWER: I admitted to you that this man was radical.
QUESTION: Answer my question. Did he talk about legal means?

ANSWER: No.

QUESTION: He talked about driving them out, didn't he?

ANSWER: Yes, he was radical. I admit that.

QUESTION: You say you approved of what he said and applauded it, didn't you?

ANSWER: Part of his speech.

· QUESTION: In what way was he radical?

ANSWER: Well, I don't—I myself do not believe in violence.

QUESTION: I didn't ask you what you believe in. I said in what way was he radical? Is there more that you want to say [about] what you mean by radical, that he advocated violence?

ANSWER: No, I don't want to say any more.

QUESTION: You did not rise in the meeting and say, "I myself don't believe in violence," did you?

ANSWER: No; I had a fine chance with six hundred people there!

QUESTION: What? You would have caught it yourself, wouldn't you? You wouldn't have dared to do it at that meeting?

Before he could reply, the prosecuting attorney exclaimed in much excitement, "Don't answer it!" Adding, as he turned to the judge, "I object to it as very, very improper," to which Judge Murphy returned in a calm voice, "The objection is sustained." Then, knowing very well how neatly the prosecutor's interruption had underscored the moment, Darrow resumed:

QUESTION: What did you mean by that?

ANSWER: You imagine I would have made myself heard with six hundred people there? I wasn't on the platform.

QUESTION: What did you mean by saying that you would have had a fine chance in that meeting where six hundred people were present to make the statement that you said?

ANSWER: I object to violence.

QUESTION: Did anybody—did anybody in that audi-

15

ence of six hundred people protest against advocating violence against colored people who moved into the neighborhood?

ANSWER: I don't know.

QUESTION: You didn't hear any protests?

ANSWER: No.

QUESTION: You only heard applause?

ANSWER: There was—as I stated, this meeting was in the school yard.

QUESTION: You heard nobody utter any protest; and all the manifestation you heard was applause to what he said?

ANSWER: Yes, that is all.

In reexamination by the prosecutor, the same witness was asked, "Did he [the speaker] *advocate* violence?" The reply was, "I said the man was radical." "I know you did," persisted the prosecutor. He repeated the question. "Did he advocate violence?" There was silence and then the witness replied, "Yes."

Clearly, the defense was uncovering an organized movement willing to use any means to keep Negroes from breaking out of the ghetto. The contradictory testimony of witnesses and police officers established this beyond much doubt. However, it was strange that another major aspect of Detroit's racial discrimination was not pursued. The police department's reputation for being anti-Negro was seldom questioned. It was a notorious fact that in 1925 the police department sent an officer to the South to recruit new personnel. Furthermore, in 1924–1925 over forty Negroes had been killed by policemen. There were no investigations even though the mayor himself had warned against the use of excess force by policemen.

Obviously, Dr. Ossian Sweet's determination to protect his family and property indicated a lack of confidence in the city's police; it was a prudent act in view of previous Negro experience. His decision to move into a white neighborhood, and then to defend himself with the aid of his friends and with weapons if necessary, suggests strong motivation and feelings that were somewhat unusual in the successful middle-class Negro. In both his testimony and interviews with reporters Dr. Sweet explained why he refused at all costs to capitulate or surrender to a white mob. As a boy in Polk County, Florida, he had once seen the ashes, still smoking hot, from which the charred remains of a lynched Negro had been removed. As a young boy he had also seen, near Bartow, Florida, a crowd of some 5,000 white racists lynch a Negro youth whose name was Fred Rochelle. The terrified child saw the whites pour gasoline over Rochelle and set fire to him. He heard the shrieks and groans of the victim, and he watched the white crowd turn the whole occasion into a Roman drinking bout. He saw them taking pictures of the frightful scene and then picking pieces off the burned bones and flesh to take home as souvenirs.

Later Dr. Sweet witnessed the race riot in Washington, D.C., when Negroes were hunted through the streets like animals. He also described to the jury and the press the violence of the Chicago race riots which began when a white mob killed a young Negro boy who, while swimming, had accidentally drifted to a white beach. He recounted the incident in which five Negroes were shot to death in Roseville, New Jersey, and eighteen Negro homes and a Negro church burned after World War I; that of the lynching in Arkansas of the four Johnson brothers, who had been taken off a train by a mob; and that in which a Negro doctor, after trying to protect his home from a mob, was murdered by police when he surrendered. Dr. Sweet was conscious of the fact that over 3,000 Negroes had been lynched within one generation. He could have added that there had been no arrests, or

17

indictments, or convictions. Self-defense, he concluded, was the only justice a Negro could know.

The emotional climax of the trial came when Darrow called Ossian Sweet himself to the stand. Sweet described the menacing events of September 9, and his response to them.

Frightened, after getting a gun I ran upstairs. Stones were hitting the house intermittently. I threw myself on the bed and lay there a short while—perhaps fifteen or twenty minutes—when a stone came through the window. Part of the glass hit me.

"What happened next?" Darrow asked.

Pandemonium—I guess that's the best way to describe it—broke loose inside my house. Everyone was running from room to room. There was a general uproar. Somebody yelled, "Here's niggers. Get them! Get them!" As my brother and Davis rushed inside my house a mob surged forward, 15 or 20 feet. It looked like a human sea. Stones kept coming faster. I was downstairs. Another window was smashed. Then one shot, then eight or ten from upstairs. Then it was all over.

Then came Darrow's key question: "What was your state of mind at the time of the shooting?"
Sweet answered:

When I opened the door and saw the mob, I realized I was facing the same mob that had hounded my people through its entire history. In my mind, I was pretty confident of what I was up against. I had my back against the wall. . . . I was filled with a peculiar fear, a fear of one who knows the history of my race. I knew what mobs had done to my people before.

In his appeal to the jury after the Sweet testimony, Darrow questioned whether or not it was possible for any twelve white men, no matter how hard they tried, to try a Negro fairly. He pointed out that the Sweets spent their first night in their new home afraid to go to bed. The next night they spent in jail.

Now the state wants them to spend the rest of their lives in the penitentiary. The state claims there was no mob there that night. Gentlemen, the state has put on enough witnesses who said they were there, to make a mob. There are persons in the North and South who say a black man is inferior to a white and should be controlled by the whites. There are also those who recognize his rights and say he should enjoy them. To me this case is a cross section of human history. It involves the future and the hope of some of us that the future will be better than the past.[12]

Judge Murphy instructed the jury to remember that a man's home was his castle and that no one had a right to invade it. He also made it quite clear that a man had the right to shoot if he had reasonable ground to fear that his life or property was in danger. And that right, Murphy emphasized, belonged to Negroes as well as to whites. The jury deliberated for 46 hours, during which time the arguments were so loud and violent they could be overheard from outside the jury room.

Finally the jury came out and announced that it had been unable to reach a verdict. The district attorney, however, did not give up, and a second trial was held the next spring. This time there was only one defendant, Henry Sweet, the youngest brother of Ossian. The state maintained that Henry Sweet had shot Breiner because he alone had admitted firing his gun. In most respects the trial was similar to the first one. The testimony remained almost unchanged. The big difference in the second trial was Darrow's remarkable seven-hour summation; it ranks as one of his greatest speeches.

In it he came back to the theme of his first summation. It was, he argued, an all-white jury. No Negro was being allowed on it because of the prosecution's challenges. He further contended that anti-Negro prejudice lay buried deep down in each of the jury members. And rising to the full measure of his eloquence, Darrow declared:

> Gentlemen, lawyers are very intemperate in their statements. My friend, Moll, said that my client here was a coward. A coward, gentlemen. Here, he says, were a gang of gunmen, and cowards—[they] shot Breiner through the back. Nobody saw Breiner, of course. If he had his face turned toward the house, while he was smoking there, waiting for the shooting to begin—it wasn't our fault. It wouldn't make any difference which way he turned. I suppose the bullet would have killed him just the same, if he had been in the way of it. If he had been at home, it would not have happened. Who are the cowards in this case? Cowards, gentlemen! Eleven people with black skins, eleven people, gentlemen, whose ancestors did not come to America because they wanted to, but were brought here in slave ships, to toil for nothing, for the whites—whose lives had been taken in nearly every state in the Union—they have been victims of riots all over this land of the free. They have had to take what is left after everybody else had grabbed what he wanted. The only place where he has been put in front is on the battlefield. When we are fighting we give him a chance to die, and the best chance. But, everywhere else, he has been food for the flames, and the ropes, and the knives, and the guns and the hate of the white, regardless of law and liberty, and the common sentiments of justice that should move men. Were they cowards?
>
> No, gentlemen, they may have been gunmen. They may have tried to murder. But they were not cowards. Eleven people, knowing what it meant, with the history of the race behind them, with a knowledge of shooting and killings and insult and injury without end, eleven of them go into a house, gentlemen, with no police protection, in the face of a mob, and the hatred of a community, and take guns and ammunition and fight for their rights and for your rights and for mine, the rights

of every being that lives. They went in and faced a mob seeking to tear them to bits. Call them something besides cowards. The coward curs were in the mob gathered there with the backing of the law. A lot of children went in front and threw the stones. They stayed for two days and two nights in front of this home, and by their threats and assault were trying to drive the Negroes out. Those were the cowardly curs and you know it. I suppose there isn't any ten of them that would come out in the open daylight against those ten. Oh no, gentlemen, their blood is too pure for that. They can only act like a band of coyotes baying some victim who has no chance. And then my clients are called cowards.

These black people were in the house with the black man's psychology, and with the black man's fear, based on what they had heard and what they had read and what they knew. I don't need to go far. I don't need to travel to Florida, I don't even need to talk about the Chicago riots. The testimony showed that in Chicago a colored boy on a raft had been washed to a white bathing beach, and men and boys of my race stoned him to death. A riot began, and some one hundred and twenty were killed. I don't need to go to Washington or to St. Louis. Let us take Detroit. I don't need to go far either in space or time. Let us take this city. Now, gentlemen, I am not saying that the white people of Detroit are different from the white people of any other city. I know what has been done in Chicago. I know what prejudice growing out of race and religion has done the world over, and all through time. I am not blaming Detroit. I am stating what has happened, that is all.[13]

Many Negroes and liberal commentators like David Lilienthal viewed the outcome of the Sweet trials as a milestone in the progress of America—a step forward in breaking down the pattern of housing discrimination. This interpretation proved wrong. It took the most brilliant courtroom lawyer in the nation and a most unusual judge to get justice for the defendants—and these two elements were to be rare indeed in the coming decades.

21

In the 1970's the white noose still hangs around the neck of black Detroit, and there has never been any remorse about the trial and anguish of Dr. Sweet and his friends.

As if to emphasize this point, forty years after the trial the assistant prosecutor had this to say:

> The case had come to the attention of our office twenty-four hours before the actual shooting. Phone threats to the Sweets had been reported and a police guard had been posted on the street. The following night, shots were fired simultaneously from six or seven windows in the Sweet home. Mr. Breiner was hit while on the porch of a house across the street. A young man was wounded. The shooting appeared to follow a prearranged signal from within the Sweet house. We interviewed police officers who were in agreement that the crowd out in front was not numerous and that there was no threat of violence. Based on these conversations, we issued a warrant on the theory that the shots were fired without provocation. . . . I think we had a good case, there was no skullduggery nor any attempt to railroad the defendants. As we saw the case, there was some premeditation because of the guns in the home. It simply is not so that there was a crowd of several thousand outside. There was no battering ram, no tar and feathers. The crowd out in front was 35 to 40 persons, at most. There was no violence. I would take my oath on that. A careful search of the house revealed only one broken pane of glass. The prosecution argued that the men inside shot "because of their pent-up excitement."[14]

"Decent" Detroit has learned little from its experiences.

The Twenties: Industrial Tyranny and Plantation Politics

2

IN THE 1920's, Detroit gained its reputation as the dynamic auto center of the world. Its symbol of success was Henry Ford, whose rise to power resembled an Horatio Alger story-come-true.

The Ossian Sweet case was soon forgotten—submerged by the new wave of industrial success. The black ghetto was there, but not really there for the white world. The focus was on new cars. For the Polish immigrants, the largest ethnic group among the 320,000 foreign born, the independent municipality of Hamtramck was like an extension of the homeland. For white southern migrant workers, Detroit was a terrifying industrial complex—the big and ugly city where a country boy felt lost. For the new rich, and the increasing number of millionaires, it was a gold mine for making money, lots of it.

Detroit, in a word, was the kind of American city writers liked to describe as a melting pot. More accurately, it was a caldron seething with ethnic, racial, and class tensions and hatreds: a social and political jungle with little to recommend it but the opportunities it offered—to some—for economic gain.

For there were always two Detroits—black and white. The city prides itself on its history as an underground station for runaway slaves. Only recently did it acknowledge that it had been the scene of a major anti-Negro riot in 1833.

This was precipitated by the Negroes' outrage at the arrest of Thornton Blackburn and his wife, who had run away from their master in Louisville, Kentucky. They arrived in Detroit in 1830, and in 1833, when an agent for the Kentucky owner of Blackburn came to Detroit, the runaways were delivered into the custody of Sheriff John M. Wilson and placed in jail. Mrs. Blackburn escaped by changing clothes with a free Negro, Mrs. George French, who was released when her identity was established, then later arrested as an accomplice and forced to flee to Canada. Blackburn himself, as he was being taken from the jail for delivery to the South, was rescued by a group of Negroes and whites. In the struggle attending the rescue, one Negro was shot and the sheriff was almost killed.

White resentment over the escape exploded into mob violence. Nearly all Negro homes were burned, any Negroes found were beaten, and only when Governor John R. Williams brought in troops did the terror cease. As usual, it was the Negroes who were arrested and kept in jail until "things quieted down."[1]

Another anti-Negro riot occurred during the Civil War. Its cause is an all too familiar story in American history. A Negro by the name of William Faulkner had been accused of assaulting a little girl. He was arrested, and on his way back to jail on the day of his trial, he was knocked down by a white mob. The next day he was convicted and sentenced to life in prison. On his way to jail, a mob attempted to lynch him, but they were stopped when the sheriff killed one of them. In retaliation the white mob roamed the streets of Detroit, beat, stoned, and shot Negroes and set their homes on fire. As a consequence, most Negroes fled to Canada, where they remained for some time. Seven years later, Faulkner was declared innocent.²

A new chapter seemed to open in 1870 when Michigan granted Negroes the right to vote. But this gain in political freedom had no impact on Detroit or Michigan politics, for the number of Negroes then living in the state was inconsequential. By 1910, only a little more than 1 per cent of Detroit's population was Negro: 5,741 out of 465,766. The Negro migration from the South was still a trickle, despite the prevalent belief that the North was less prejudiced than the South. Negroes were reluctant or unable to leave the South because they were too poor to move; as tenant farmers or sharecroppers they were almost always in debt. Moreover, the manpower needs of the North were filled by European immigrants. And when Negroes did find work, they were discriminated against by both employers and unions. White industrial society, then, simply closed its doors to them. Most Negroes were forced into menial domestic and personal service or restricted to odd jobs as unskilled laborers.³

Prior to World War I, white industrialists extended "opportunities" to Negroes by hiring them as strikebreakers. In the early 1880's they were imported to help break steel strikes in Pittsburgh. They were employed as strikebreakers in Kansas and Illinois coal mines. They were used to break the strike of the Chicago meat-packing plants in 1894 and also in the great steel strike of 1919.⁴

The Lackawanna mills, employing only 72 Negroes before the strike, were operated chiefly by Negro labor. Eight thousand Negro strikebreakers were used at Chicago. Here the companies did no importing. Their agents were able to get all they wanted on State Street. Most of them lost their jobs when the contest was over. Thousands were imported into the bituminous coal fields of

Pennsylvania during the coal strike of 1922. When the strike was over, 8,000 remained in the Pittsburgh district alone. Negroes were used in the railway shopmen's strike of 1922 and gained permanent places in the shops of several systems. The Detroit Urban League furnished Negro labor to break a strike in the metal trades in 1921; the Urban League of Newark assisted in breaking a brickmaking strike in Sayerville, New Jersey, in 1923; and the New York League supplied material to break several strikes in Connecticut cities. This propensity to scab intensifies race feeling.[5]

Henry Ford's policy of hiring approximately 10 per cent of his work force from among the Negroes was a rare and notable exception in American industrial practice.

On January 5, 1914, he announced that he would pay wages of five dollars a day to all workers. This marked the beginning of a northward migration of both white and Negro workers which continued until the depression of 1920. "I was twelve years old," Joe Louis later recalled, "when Pat Brooks heard about the money Ford was paying. He went up first, then brought us up to Detroit. We moved in with some of our kin in MacComb Street. It was kind of crowded there, but the house had toilets indoors and electric lights. Down in Alabama we had outhouses and kerosene lamps. My stepfather got a job with Ford, and we got a place of our own in a frame tenement in Catherine Street."[6]

In the immediate postwar period Detroit was one of the few large cities that had no major race riot. St. Louis, Chicago, Cleveland, Philadelphia, Kansas City, Scranton, and Seattle were among the American cities that experienced violent race conflicts, largely the result of a white effort to keep Negroes from improving their social status.

Perhaps the reason Detroit was "different" right after

World War I was that, thanks to the acute labor shortage, Negroes held some jobs. A canvass of the twenty largest urban Detroit firms in 1917 showed a total of 2,874 Negro workers. In 1919 the number had increased to about 11,000, of whom 6,000 were employed at the River Rouge Plant of the Ford Motor Company. It was estimated that another 4,000 Negroes were employed at Ford's Highland Park Plant. Needless to say, most of these workers in both plants were employed in a foundry or steel plant, and at heavy labor. Employment in the booming auto industry continued to rise for both Negroes and whites until 1929, when Negroes comprised roughly 40,000 out of about 450,000 blue-collar workers. In most plants they represented about 3 per cent of the work force. The white-collar work force remained almost totally white.[7] At this time, there were slightly less than 120,000 Negroes in Detroit out of a total population of about one and a half million.

The exodus to the North was not confined to Negroes. Poor whites in masses began moving to Detroit from Arkansas, Kentucky, Tennessee, Alabama. They too had heard the good news that one could make a decent living up north. The auto industry itself sent recruiters to many areas in its search for cheap and docile labor (a practice that continued until recent times). By 1948, almost half a million inhabitants of Detroit were Southerners who brought their prejudices, customs, and language with them. A black man was a "nigger." In a sense, the South was transplanted into the North, its poor people placed in the new and turbulent context of the industrial city. The Ku Klux Klan was indeed "at home" in that environment.

The Polish community was able to resist the ridicule of the Anglo-Americans and the antagonism of the KKK because it had a social, political, and economic base in

Hamtramck. There the language of the mother country enjoyed equal status with English. Bilingual signs and restaurants were necessary. And the Polish vote was an increasingly important political factor. While anti-Semitism was a heritage from the old country, the Polish had to be taught to hate the black man, and on that score the KKK *did* leave a permanent imprint on the immigrants.

> Before the masses of Polish immigrants had become naturalized, the Negroes, as native citizens, considerably influenced Hamtramck politics. A Negro was elected to the city's first common council, and Negroes have been appointed since to various administrative posts.[8]

Using the odious term "niggers" gave the foreign-born worker (mainly Polish) a sense of identity with white society, and by throwing the spotlight of prejudice on the Negro, he turned it away from himself.

Arthur Wood, in his definitive study of the Polish community of Hamtramck, pointed out that "The newspapers, vaudeville and other agencies in Detroit have built a stereotype of Hamtramck as a community redolent with crime, vice and political corruption." The author claims that "This is a grossly unfair appraisal of Hamtramck, whose people are generally decent and hard-working [and anti-Negro—B.J.W.]. The fact seems to be that the community is used as a kind of scapegoat on which to unload the sins of Detroit itself. Thus, when a serious crime is committed in Detroit, the newspapers will shout: 'Police Seek Gangsters in Hamtramck Hideout,' despite the lack of evidence that Hamtramck or its citizens are involved."[9]

Even the "poor white trash" from the South could join in this scorn of the foreigner. If, in turn, the "foreigner" looked down on the black man, it was only a normal reaction, an attitude fostered by this ugly factory city. The Anglo-Americans who ran Detroit were the source of another form of racism. The anti-Semitic ravings of

28

the *Dearborn Independent* were financed not by some crackpot outfit, but by none other than Detroit's first citizen, Henry Ford. As a definitive history of Ford states:

> It would have been better had Ford never entered journalism either. The *Dearborn Independent* of May 22, 1920, featuring on its front cover an unsigned article, "The International Jew: The World's Problem," began an anti-Semitic campaign which was to place on Henry Ford's career its darkest blot. The total losses of the Dearborn Publishing Company from its origin until its dissolution in 1930 aggregated $4,795,000. No small sum even for Ford. But these financial losses were trifling compared with those of an intangible character which he sustained.[10]

Although Ford personally apologized to Aaron Shapiro, a Chicago Jew who sued him for one million dollars in 1927, and although he appeared to be contrite about the rantings of the *Dearborn Independent,* he did accept an Iron Cross from Adolf Hitler in 1938. The school-age population didn't know much about this. But it did grow up in a milieu in which Hastings Street was known as "Jewtown" and the inhabitants were known as "kikes" or "sheenies"; Hamtramck was where the "dumb Polacks" lived; the east side was where the "dagos" and "dirty wops" stuck together; Russell Street was "Hunkytown"; and farther south, near the downtown area, was "Niggertown."[11]

Most of this escaped the attention of Detroit's growing middle class, getting richer each year as the auto industry boomed. Grosse Pointe, Birmingham, and Bloomfield Hills developed into fine suburban areas, with no Negroes and very few Jews, thanks to an effective "point" system used by real estate interests as an exclusion device. As late as 1969, only one Jew was allowed to join the prestigious Detroit Athletic Club, so strong is the carry-over from the 1920's.[12]

As for Italians, Poles, and other nationality groups, their Ossian Sweets *did* make it. Sometimes they changed names and sometimes politics, but they were always able to move upward.

For the black man it was different. He had a handicap unlike that of any other minority group. He might change his name, might even have money, but he was black and identifiable as such, and therefore unwanted. He was permanently "ghettoized." In 1926 the report of the Detroit Mayor's Interracial Committee indicated what was happening.

"The Negro," the report stated, "is humiliated in so many public and privately owned institutions and amusement places that he has resorted to the church as a place in which he can be sure of spending his leisure time." [13]

But this description is incomplete, for the Negro community and the Negro churches were not totally insulated from the rest of society. They were largely subject to the domineering policies of Henry Ford. He exercised a controlling influence over the lives of Negroes through his hiring policies and his generous donations to Negro churches. Ford took Negro workers not from the open market, but on the recommendation of a favored individual or organization. Irving Howe and I pointed this out in our book, *The UAW and Walter Reuther:*

He had donated the Parish House of the St. Matthews Episcopal Church (colored) and befriended its Father Daniels; his Negro satrap, Donald Marshall, taught Sunday School classes at St. Matthews; and once a year Ford honored the church with a visit. He had also given substantial aid to the Second Baptist Church (colored), the minister of which, Rev. Bradby, was one of his personal favorites. When either Rev. Bradby or Father Daniels recommended a Negro for a job it was as good as had. Negro politicians, though seldom as successfully, also served as labor agents for Ford.

Ford went out of his way to win the support of the Negro community. He helped finance the all-Negro village of Inkster. He provided jobs at $1 a day to its unemployed residents. The Fords entertained committees from Negro women's clubs, invited George Washington Carver to their home, and paid Marian Anderson and Dorothy Maynor to sing on the "Ford Sunday Hour." These things made a deep impression on the Detroit Negro world, for no other wealthy white man was quite so bountiful.[14]

Ford's authority, in short, encompassed the Negro worker's private life as well as his labor. He was a latter-day plantation owner.

But the Negroes soon demonstrated that they did not care at all for this setup, rebelling against it when the opportunity arose. In the 1932 election, they voted Democratic overwhelmingly—in some neighborhoods 20 to 1 —although Ford had helped finance and organize the Republican party in the Negro districts and had placards favoring Hoover placed in the River Rouge plant.[15] Later Ford would suffer a much more serious reverse in the Negro community during his violent struggle against organized labor.

By 1930 the black ghetto had expanded to over 120,000 people, most of whom had migrated from the South. Their arrival added to the already crowded conditions; the newcomers felt strange because of the different laws and customs, and were neglected by their neighbors who themselves were hard pressed to exist. This created a setting which was ripe for prostitution, gambling, and assaults—a situation which heightened the wall between the Negroes and the contemptuous police force.

A Negro author wrote about the migrants of the 1920's:

The newcomers became victims of many money-baiting and "get-rich-quick" schemes in their struggle to make a living.

31

> The spiritualists, cult leaders and fortune tellers made large sums from releasing "tips" to those who played the "numbers" and policy game.[16]

Enlarging upon this, the same author, after reporting growth of a small business and professional class of Negroes in Detroit by 1940, made the following comment:

> No chapter on Negro business in Detroit is complete unless the largest business is included. This is the numbers and policy game which is illegal in the state. Because of the economic influence it has had over the Negro community, it merits attention since many legitimate firms were started with funds provided by the "numbers backers."
>
> This racket has all the earmarks of big business and grew from a penny game played chiefly by Negroes over twenty years ago to a ten million dollar a year racket, giving employment to hundreds of men and women in jobs such as clerks, writers, and pick-up men. This solely Negro game was invaded by White petty gamblers and racketeers in 1932 when White bootleggers were driven out of the liquor racket. Today, Negroes control less than fifty percent of this lottery. The growth of this numbers scheme can be attributed to the Negro's desire to take chances and to bet in hopes of getting enough money to help raise him from poverty.[17]

The white man's Detroit offered little inspiration to a viewer from the black ghetto. In the age of prohibition, under the Volstead Act, a whiskey-hungry generation created a new market and a new breed of entrepreneurs. What developed in the city was soberly portrayed in this fashion:

> Gangster activities, largely a product of prohibition in the lucrative rum-running from Canada, were at their height during these years. The city had a swarm of bootlegging kings, vice overlords, hijackers, blackmailers, and miscellaneous extortionists; it was popularly supposed to have Italian racketeers affiliated with the Mafia

or Camorra; it certainly had murder-men, and kidnap-
pers who terrified such magnates as Henry Ford. ("I can
replace factories but not grandchildren," he was reported
once to have said.) Lawlessness flourished. Nearly every
issue of the Detroit newspapers chronicled some horrify-
ing crime of violence. Inasmuch as any great factory was
pretty nearly a cross section of the male population, no
establishment so large as the Rouge could be without its
criminal element. Racial antagonism sometimes flared
high in this city of so many ill-digested national groups.
Gentiles who hated Jews, Poles who hated Germans, and
above all, whites from the Southern hill-regions, who
hated Negroes, were numerous. The Ku Klux Klan by
the late nineteen twenties had many fanatical adherents,
and not a few inside the Ford plants.[18]

But none of this checked the flow of humanity into
Detroit, for anything seemed better than the miseries of
life in the South, and there was the lure of jobs and the
promise of high wages. What the working man found
was something else—a dehumanized industrial machine
run by men with a total disregard for human feeling. The
dominant philosophy was "dog eat dog."

To begin with, there was the myth of the five-dollar
day announced in January 1914. As late as July 1916,
the Ford Motor Company's financial statement revealed
that despite the five-dollar day announcement, 14,000
Ford workers, or 30 per cent of the company's payroll,
were getting less than five dollars a day. Probationers got
only $2.72 per day, and thousands of workers, almost
7,500 in 1916, were hired, kept on for six months' pro-
bation, and then fired, to be replaced with other $2.72-a-
day workers. Most women workers were not eligible for
the five dollars a day pay. Nor were unmarried men under
twenty-two. Married men involved in divorces were not
eligible, nor was any worker who lived "unworthily." This
policy of hiring and firing and rehiring and refiring remained a practice of Ford Motor Company and other

33

auto manufacturers until the principle of seniority was established through union contracts.[19]

Work in the auto plants was dehumanizing. In Charlie Chaplin's brilliant satire, *Modern Times,* working on an assembly line does seem to have its humorous aspects. But for the men who worked on the line there was never anything funny about it. No matter what one did, there was simply no way to get ahead of the line—that is, to work a little faster and gain a moment or two of free time. If one fell behind in one's job, it disrupted the entire synchronized production process, and this was not permissible. The workers felt "chained" to the assembly line in the sense that the speed of the line determined their pace. The psychological impact of "fighting the line" was such that, as late as 1967, there were still dozens of wildcat strikes against speed-ups. The UAW and the "big three" auto companies found it much easier to negotiate over wages and other fringe benefits than to come to grips with the actual working conditions in the plants. The thousands of grievances still filed annually against these conditions, and primarily against speed-ups, testify to the fact that the basic problem has not yet been solved, although the UAW has made notable progress in this area.

Prior to the advent of unionism there was no concern—in fact only contempt—for the working man, reflected in such statements as "The average man won't really do a day's work unless he is caught and cannot get out of it"[20] and "The very poor are recruited almost solely from the people who refuse to think."[21] Although the work pace was such that it was almost impossible to get to know one's neighbor, standard operating practices forbade whistling, singing, smoking, talking, and conversing. There was no such thing as toilet time. Workers were given all of fifteen minutes for lunch, and that included wash-up time and going to and from the lunch wagon, in the event that they didn't bring their own. When the starting whistle or bell rang, men were expected to be standing at their machines, their time clocks punched, their working clothes on, and their tools in hand. They were supposed to remain on the job until after the quitting whistle blew. Another indignity that was a persistent source of trouble was management's habit of transferring workers from one shift to another without regard for personal inconvenience, time of service to the company, or any other humane consideration. Quite frequently shifts were changed every two weeks, so that a worker and his family barely got adjusted to one schedule of work and sleep before he was given another. And some people wondered why families tended to break up and family life disintegrated in the 1920's.[22]

Although both Upton Sinclair's description of the auto workers' lives in *The Flivver King* and Keith Sward's monumental book, *The Legend of Henry Ford,* were criticized for exaggeration, the best that the critics of the critics could say about Ford's policies was this:

> Contempt for seniority was especially resented. The laying off and rehiring of men was an unhappy process at best. In most factories, not merely in the Ford plant, veterans would see junior workers, the protégés of somebody with influence, taken back in their stead. As a consequence of all this the combination quit and turnover rate in many plants was as high as 40% annually.[23]

The men who quit in anger or in a moment of personal courage soon found that their new place of employment was simply another hellhole. There seemed to be no escaping the "butcher shops," as auto workers nicknamed the assembly plants. Life consisted of hard work, anxiety about layoffs, and a desperate desire to get out—with the knowledge that there was no place to go.

As if to emphasize the point of how little humans

35

counted, Ford Motor Company didn't hesitate to lay off 60,000 Detroit-area workers in one fell swoop when Ford decided to discontinue production of the Model T in 1927. The concept of long-range planning and a gradual model changeover was alien to Ford. Forty-five per cent of the relief roll in Detroit in 1927 resulted from the action of the company. As for the great entrepreneur himself, he was philosophic about the whole thing: "I know it's done them a lot of good—everybody gets extravagant —to let them know that things are not going along too even always." He added another gratuitous insult later with the statement: "If there is any unemployment, it is simply because the unemployed do not want to work."[24]

To keep control of his empire and, above all, to prevent the emergence of that dreadful idea—unionism— was a major Ford policy. Because working conditions in the plants were scarcely tolerable, they could be maintained only by a degree of physical terror alien to all concepts of a democratic society. For this the Ford Motor Company hired Harry Herbert Bennett, who was

> in charge of violence, underworld connections, gangster recruitment and personnel at the Ford Motor Company for some time in the early 30's up until he was fired by Henry Ford II after Henry Ford I died. Bennett rose eventually to a place as a sort of Arabian Nights prime minister who ruled the Ford empire in Henry Ford's name with a private army of 3,000 men. These 3,000 men were mostly ex-convicts, but also boxers, wrestlers, known gangsters, all-American football players, track stars, cops who had left their jobs under fire. At one time five convicts a week were paroled to the Ford Motor Company, according to testimony. One of them, Legs Laman, was the kidnapper of a child whose dead body was found in a gully shortly before the gangster himself was caught with $4,000 of the ransom money paid to redeem the child.[25]

The terror regime of the Ford Service Department

eventually broke down in 1941. Its history prior to that is a disgrace to modern America. The connections of the Ford Motor Company with Detroit gangsters are a sad commentary on Detroit in the twenties and thirties and the example of "progress" it gave to the Negro people.

Gangsters not only worked in the Ford Service Department. Through Bennett, the Ford Motor Company had a working agreement with Joe Adonis, key figure in Murder, Incorporated, who carried on his rackets at the same time he worked on an exclusive contract with the Ford Motor Company, by which he delivered cars from the Edgewater Assembly Plant to dealers along the eastern seaboard.

Another gangster who was in business with Ford while he carried on his underworld activities was Chester LaMare, the Al Capone of Detroit. He operated houses of prostitution, sold dope, hijacked trucks and freight cars, owned nightclubs and was also co-owner of a Ford agency and sole proprietor of a fruit company whose Ford concession gave it the exclusive privilege of supplying fruit for the lunches sold to Ford workers off plant lunch carts. LaMare was finally killed in a gang war.[26]

In this atmosphere it was not just the blue-collar workers who lived in fear. Recently, Henry Ford II—who fired Bennett—told how he and John Bugas, former Detroit FBI director and Ford official, armed themselves with guns before confronting Bennett in his office with a dismissal notice.[27]

One can glimpse the depth of Detroit's corruption in the murder of Jerry Buckley, a political commentator for a local radio station who had championed the recall of Mayor Charles Bowles in 1929—the same man who had barely lost in the election in 1925 with Klan support. Buckley was a foe of the underworld, and on July 22, 1930, after the mayor was recalled on charges of graft, Buckley was murdered in a downtown hotel lobby. It was the eleventh killing in two weeks.

37

Detroit: City of Race and Class Violence

The brutality, violence, and lawlessness of life strained but did not tear apart the social fabric. For even stronger than the tensions and hatred—in fact, inherent in them—was the common desire to get ahead, to get the almighty dollar. The American dream of personal riches permeated every segment of the population. It was a time when the mark of personal success depended on how much one made or how much he was worth.

This materialistic impetus was reflected in the voting patterns. In 1920 only 19 per cent of Detroit's workers voted Democratic; by 1928, a year when the ten largest cities in the country went Democratic for the first time, the figure was 37 per cent. Staunch Republicanism had a last stronghold in Detroit. In the 1928 presidential election, Democrat Alfred E. Smith received a bare majority of the urban vote, but industrial Detroit gave a whopping 63 per cent to Republican Herbert Hoover. Besides the vast appeal of laissez-faire Republicanism, the influence of the KKK's anti-Catholicism had added to the sweep.[28]

Although the harsh living and working conditions of the lower classes seemed to illustrate Karl Marx's criticisms of capitalism, the tiny radical movements which viewed Detroit from that perspective failed to make a dent among the workers and black people. This could be attributed in part to their preoccupation with "defending the Soviet Union" and to internal factional struggles (see the following section of this chapter). But more significantly, the Marxist appeal couldn't match the lure of the American dream and the economic prosperity which did trickle down. Compared to a peasant village in Europe, or a sharecropper's lot in the South, raw factory life wasn't worse; in many instances it was better.

It would take a cataclysmic economic event to shake the status quo and create a fertile soil for the seeds of radicalism. Then a new and young generation of radicals would change the course of American history—at least temporarily. And Detroit would appear to be a city of social innovation and progress.

Although in September 1919 the Communist party united various factions—including the foreign language federations, the Michigan group, and the other English-speaking Left Wing Council—its gains, notably in Michigan, were soon dissipated. The Michigan group was centered around a so-called Proletarian University in Detroit which held views that were considered heretical and which refused to accept the supervision of the Central Committee. Faced with expulsion, the prominent Michigan leaders organized in June 1920 a self-styled Proletarian party which remained an irritant to the Communist party for a number of years. As late as 1936 the Proletarian party was influential in turning many young auto worker militants against the Communist party. A notable example was Emil Mazey, whose training in the Proletarian party later made him one of the prominent anti-Communists within the Socialist party.[29]

Each attempt of the Communist party to acquire a monopoly of leadership on the Left created factions and splits which in the later years kept the party from achieving its long-range goal: control of an auto workers' industrial union movement. From the 1928 expulsion of James P. Cannon, Max Shachtman, and Martin Abern as Trotskyites, arose a splinter group called the Communist League of America, which late in 1934 merged with A. J. Muste's American Workers party to form the Workers party. This organization was a source of constant opposition to the Communist party in subsequent years. Its press was notable for exposing every tactic and maneuver of the Communists, who were to become an important political force in the 1930's in Detroit.

The 1929 split and the expulsion of J. Lovestone created another group of opponents to the Communist party. They played a very important role in the 1936–1939 factional dispute in the UAW centering around Homer Martin, the first UAW president, whose personal brain truster was J. Lovestone. Last, and by no means least, the residual elements of the Socialist party remained alive during the 1920's and became the base for the resurgence of a lively political faction in the 1930's and 1940's. While the Socialist party at times cooperated with the Communist party in the auto union, ultimately this strange misalliance was broken, giving rise to political forces that destroyed the Communist party's major influence among the auto workers. From that milieu, among others, came the Reuther brothers Walter, Victor, and Roy, along with Leonard Woodcock and other current UAW leaders.

The auto industry was relatively quiet in 1919 in contrast to the steel, textile, and coal industries which had major strikes supported by the communist movement. There were small, sporadic, and largely ineffective walkouts, usually under the auspices of the Machinists Union or the now extinct United Automobile, Aircraft, and Vehicle Workers of America (UAAV). Given the limited scope of agitation in the auto industry, it is understandable that little attention was paid to the activity of the communist movement, which, despite a few minor successes, was relatively inconsequential. In the Communist press of the time, only Local 127 of the UAAV merited any mention or praise. It was described in 1919 as the "largest and strongest single labor union in Detroit and for that matter, of any place west of New York City." Its nucleus was formed by workers from the old Fisher Body Corporation plants, and it did have members in many auto and auto parts plants in Michigan, but the 1921 depression wiped it out almost completely.[30]

When William Z. Foster, the steel-strike leader who had been converted to communism, founded the Trade Union Educational League, its operation became a focal point of activity for all Communists in the trade union movement. At a national conference held in 1922, a three-point program was adopted which called for: (1) amalgamation, (2) formation of a Labor party, and (3) recognition of Soviet Russia. It had less relation to the life of auto workers than to that of almost any other industrial workers, for at that time the auto unions were only paper unions, in no way ready to be "amalgamated" —except perhaps on paper. Fewer than 25,000 auto workers out of 400,000 were organized.[31]

When in 1928 the Communist party decided to transform the Trade Union Educational League into a Trade Union Unity League and build industrial unions, it simply meant that the handful of Communists now called themselves an auto workers' union, with no more strength or influence than the Trade Union Educational League had commanded. At the 1929 convention of the TUUL the delegates from the auto industry were scarcely noticeable among the 690 persons present, most of whom were from the coal, steel, and textile fields—the party's major centers of concentration.

The sum total of the Communist party's activities in the auto industry during the 1920's, in contrast to its considerable activity in other industrial areas, can be thumbnailed in this fashion:

> As in other American industries, this part forms its own nuclei also in the various auto plants. They are chiefly engaged in preliminary educational work and elementary political propaganda. The party has published the first agitation papers ever issued in the industry for workers of particular companies or plants. Some of those published in Michigan are *The Ford Worker, The Fisher Body Worker, The Dodge Worker, The Packard Worker, The Hudson Worker, The Chrysler Worker* and *The Buick Worker.* Those little four page papers which range in circulation from 1,000 to 20,000 (Ford has the largest) carry about two pages of general news and editorials and two pages of shop reports, notes and letters with the purpose of relating the daily grievances of the

workers to the broader issues of their life and status under capitalism.[32]

In this imitation of "going to the masses," which was the alpha and omega of the Russian Bolshevik tactic, the auto cadres of the Communist party found themselves stymied by a lack of any rapport with the heterogeneous auto workers, and by the criticism of the Political Committee in New York, which complained, "Our papers can be criticized as being too little international; in fact, they do not even deal sufficiently with the problems of the Soviet Union."[33]

The Communist party claimed a total of 407 members in the auto industry in 1929, with party factions of 175 members in Detroit and 100 in Cleveland. Its limited following among the vast majority of American-born native workers was shown by a special analysis of its membership in the Cleveland area. The party claimed 103 South Slavs, 56 Hungarians, 13 Russians, and 180 others, but only 70 Americans.[34]

How the Communists sought to organize the auto workers, again in imitation of the Russian methods, was described in a convention report in 1929.

> We have an auto workers union there. You can talk to the workers for years to join the union; they are afraid to join the union. Because, if it is organized, as it was up to recently, every worker that comes to an open meeting knows that his job is endangered, and because they know that, they do not come. The factory committee, organizing the workers in each department, through a delegate system; the captains in all the departments into a central bureau or committee of the factory; this is the basic unit of the auto workers union. On such a basis can we build the Autoworkers union.[35]

At the same Sixth Convention of the Communist party in which its work in the auto industry was reviewed, there was some embarrassment over the fact that the Detroit delegation did not include a single Negro.[36]

The Depression and the Growth of Radicalism

3

T HE GREAT DEPRESSION was an experience most Detroiters could never forget. The devastation of human lives and hopes left a permanent scar on the people. The Wall Street panic in October 1929 crushed the dreams of the middle class, who had believed that the way to get rich was on the stock market, and that they could all do it. After that blow, the middle class simply drifted with the times, its aspirations gone, its will paralyzed.

Blue-collar workers were hit harder. In 1929 there were 475,000 workers in the Detroit area auto plants. In 1930 over 125,000 lost their jobs and had no regular source of income. In those times even the American Federation of Labor was officially against unemployment insurance. In 1931 almost 100,000 more were laid off, and most of the 275,000 remaining workers had only part-time employment in the plants.[1]

The number of small business failures soared; hundreds of small shops just closed their doors. There weren't enough paying customers, and who could afford to give credit?

Hardest hit, as is usual in any economic reverse, were the Negroes. No other minority was ever subjected to the job discrimination which was standard toward blacks, always last to be hired and first to be fired. Unemployment among Detroit Negroes reached 80 per cent in the depths of the Depression.

Detroit gradually sank into a wasteland of idle men and idle factories. By 1931 the sole source of income for about 48,000 families, or approximately 210,000 people, was city relief. This was after an estimated 150,000 persons had left the city for the small towns or rural life they had once abandoned. Over half the families on relief were Negro. The industrial stagnation also affected white-collar jobs — layoffs were numerous. Sober estimates were that 66 per cent of the working population was either entirely or partly out of work.[2]

The sense of despair was heightened by fifteen bank failures which wiped out life savings; it was before the creation of the Federal Insurance Deposit Corporation. "Soup kitchens" where unemployed received pitiful handouts were commonplace and crowded.

Those who did manage to hold a job had little to cheer about.

The mayor's committee for investigating unrest offered a glimpse of the situation in the automobile industry. Workers were paid ten cents an hour for a fourteen-hour day. Many workers were kept on their jobs five or six hours but were paid only for one or two hours of actual working time. Women were required to conceal their time cards to evade the consequences of violating the state's ten-hours-a-day limitation. Even *Business Week,* a management publication, warned that the conditions at Ford exceeded the absolute limit of human endurance.[3]

Perhaps the most demoralizing of all was the practice of plant foremen to walk up and down the lines of the unemployed at factory gates and pick young, husky men for jobs while ignoring oldsters who had spent many years at the company. For a while both black and white workers were too numb to feel the kind of anger which leads to protest. However, the social dynamite was accumulating; class hatred was building up with a far greater intensity than was generally realized. Sooner or later violent strikes would explode and new ideas capture the minds of the people, notably the young unemployed.

The time was ripe for radical agitation, and the Communists, Socialists, Trotskyites, and followers of Lovestone competed in denouncing the "wicked capitalists" and the American social system. Each political sect had a program envisioning the day when they would lead a social revolution in America; but blueprints for a way out of the Depression were not an exclusive prerogative of the Left. Members of the middle class and business leaders had programs which turned out to be even more irrelevant. The press and many businessmen took technocracy seriously. One prominent Detroit businessman solemnly declared that the Depression could be solved if everyone stopped spending money. Michigan's most powerful public utilities spokesman urged "an unconstitutional dictator" to clean up America.[4] Henry Ford stated that the Depression was good for the nation.

What distinguished the young radicals from other panacea-advocates was their passionate idealism, their revulsion against human suffering, and a determination to act.

In every respect the Detroit they viewed was a mess. Its nonpartisan government was torn apart by the half-hidden issues of religion and race and class. The election of Frank Murphy as mayor in 1930 seemed to offer some hope, but Murphy was under two handicaps. The city was in a state of financial chaos, and the conservative business and banking interests viewed him as a dangerous person because of his avowed liberalism. As the Depression deepened, City Hall became a target for the anger and frustration fermenting in the community. Murphy extended relief payments to the poor, but these were inadequate. Nevertheless, they were criticized by the business community. Murphy's dilemma as a liberal in power was portrayed perceptively by Edmund Wilson in his book *The American Jitters:*

> A more attractive figure is Frank Murphy, the young Irish Mayor of Detroit. Murphy took the unemployment crisis seriously and was elected on the strength of his promise to deal with it. When a certain point had been reached, however, he found himself empty handed and helpless. He has, it is true, guaranteed free speech: the Communists meet, display their *placards* and make their speeches unmolested in Grand Circus Park in the heart of the business district, as they would never be allowed to do in New York. And the Mayor has given as much money as he could get for free lodging, clothing and food. But lately the City Welfare Department has been spending $2,000,000 a month, and has even at that rate not been able to allow more than $5 a week for a family of four. At last the Mayor has been forced to announce that the city can supply no more relief. The nearby town of Royal Oak has gone bankrupt, and Detroit itself is now in a position in which it can borrow from the New York bankers only on condition of agreeing not to undertake the public works which the Mayor, at the time he was elected, was promising as a means of providing jobs.[5]

The time was ripe for radical action, and it was soon in coming.

The Communist party in Detroit called for a demonstration by the unemployed on March 6, 1930, and was as surprised as anyone at the massive response. Thousands demonstrated, uncowed by the aggressive and heavy-handed tactics of the police. Soon Communist

46

workers set up 26 Unemployed Councils whose chief activity was moving evicted families back into their homes. Demonstrations at relief offices for more relief increased. Conservatives and police officials were very much bothered by "communist-inspired" activities, but the unemployed couldn't care less. They would be the beneficiaries of such action, and no one else cared or had a program of immediate consequence. However, neither the protest of the unemployed nor the liberal policy of Mayor Murphy prevailed against the increasing hardships of the Depression. In January 1932, Mayor Murphy reported that there were 4,000 children standing daily in the long bread lines—a permanent sight on Detroit's landscape.

The Board of Health reported that 18 per cent of the schoolchildren were suffering from serious undernourishment. The city Welfare Department reported it was getting calls for assistance in eviction proceedings at the rate of 7,000 a month.

This was the time of payless pay days for city employees as Detroit went deeper into debt, even after cutting thousands off the relief rolls. The indebtedness of Detroit had risen tenfold to about 278 million dollars for June 1932. It took $43 million to pay the interest on the city debt, but the revenue from taxes had dropped from $71 million in 1931 to $51 million in 1932. Much of this debt was due to the expansion of public services in the late 1920's—new streets, sewers, waterworks, and transportation facilities.[6]

Detroit banks which had criticized the city for irresponsibility soon found themselves in a similar predicament. Fifteen Detroit banks had failed earlier in the Depression with 35,000 depositors losing their money. The capital stock of the city's banks dropped from $114 million in 1929 to $77 million in 1933.[7]

The impact of the Depression was visible everywhere. In the region around Highland Park which Ford had abandoned when he moved his production to Dearborn, the sign "For Rent" could be seen on many stores and hundreds of empty homes.

The employers were gloomy, too, for their world had also fallen apart. There was no longer an unprecedented demand for American cars and car parts. Dynamic Detroit suddenly seemed old and deserted.

In the top power structure of the city there was, however, a contemptuous attitude. America's richest man, Henry Ford, kept pouring salt in the wounds of the unemployed. Among his pronouncements on the Depression were the following:

> The very poor are recruited almost solely from the people who refuse to think and therefore refuse to work diligently. (1930)

> It's a good thing the recovery is prolonged. Otherwise the people wouldn't profit by the illness. (Statement on leaving for a vacation abroad on September 7, 1930)

> The average man won't really do a day's work unless he is caught and cannot get out of it. *(Detroit News,* March 16, 1931)

> If we could only realize it, these are the best times we ever had. *(Pictorial Review,* October 1932)

Ford's views were in tune with the thinking of Detroit's business community. When Mayor Murphy enlisted the city's industrialists to serve on a committee on unemployment, they withdrew after the committee recommended federal aid for the unemployed, arguing that this was a "Moscow-inspired idea." There was a social myopia in the attitude of the power structure in those days. Business and conservative political circles thought that new ideas, social reforms, or manifestations of unrest could be dismissed by labeling them "communist or socialist-inspired." There was no understanding of the changing mood in the nation. Time was running out on policies designed to preserve the status quo or to bring back the good old days.

Liberal thinking was more sensitive to the problems of the Depression and the rise of radicalism, but as Louis Adamic, himself a liberal writer, pointed out, it was torn by an inherent dilemma: until there was violence, social redress always seemed inadequate. Only after the violent and bloody reaction to the demonstrations of the unemployed in the early 1930's did the Communists (and others) achieve a true mass following and the poor get some measure of relief.[8] And this violence could not be successfully attributed to "outside agitators or radicals." The programs of the radicals were not more radical in the 1930's than they were in the 1920's. It was the shock of the Depression, with mass unemployment, which created despair and then violent reaction. The farmers in the Republican states of Iowa, Nebraska, and elsewhere reacted to low prices and farm foreclosures before the workers in the cities went on sitdown strikes. America's farmers in many areas had taken things into their own hands for self-preservation—preventing foreclosures of farms, releasing their pickets from jail, and burning crops in protest.[9] No radical plan of conspiracy, however brilliant it might be in conception, could bring 100,000 unemployed Detroiters to march in the demonstration. The breakdown in the social system was responsible for the discontent.

Police brutality and the stupidity of many public officers was another factor which contributed to violence and the growth of radicalism. This was more amply illustrated in Detroit than almost anywhere in the country.

The outcome of the "Ford Hunger March" on March

7, 1932, enabled the Communist party to portray itself as the champion of the underdog in American society. What occurred was a preview of coming labor and civil rights struggles in the decades ahead.

It was public knowledge in Detroit that the Unemployed Councils were planning a protest parade through the city to Ford's River Rouge plant in Dearborn, carrying the usual signs demanding food and jobs, and a petition to the Ford Motor Company. Nor was it a secret that the Communist party would be directing the affair. Mayor Murphy had given his permission for a peaceful demonstration, and he had ordered the Police Department to escort the parade. As a consequence it was a peaceful event in the city.[10]

The importance of the march against Ford was emphasized by the arrival of William Z. Foster, national chairman of the Trade Union Leadership League, a Communist organization, to address a membership meeting on the demonstration. Foster warned the audience against provocation and violence and pointed out the political value of a successful demonstration at the Ford plant, which was considered a world symbol of the American open-shop industrial system and of anti-Semitism. Foster's speech was duly reported by the press, and thus provided excellent publicity for the Communist party as he had intended.[11]

In their march toward the Rouge plant, the 3,000 unemployed carried mild slogans: "Feed the Poor," "We Want Bread, Not Crumbs," "Open Rooms in the Y for the Homeless Youth," "Fight Against Dumping Milk While Our Babies Starve," and "All War Funds for Unemployed Relief." Among the leaders of the procession were Albert Goetz, Communist party spokesman in Detroit, and Joe York, district organizer of the Young Communist League. Goetz again warned against violence

50

as he instructed the marchers to advance to the Ford employment office in Dearborn.[12]

The march continued toward the city line where about fifty Dearborn police were stationed. As they approached the police, Charles W. Slamer, the acting chief, called out for their leaders. Shouts of "We are all leaders" came from the crowd. Slamer ordered the unemployed to turn back, and the reply was that they would not. The police opened fire with tear-gas guns, even though the marchers had moved to the side and had begun to quietly bypass the uniformed men. The marchers, whom reporters had described as good-natured up to this point, exploded in fury. Hand-to-hand scuffles began with the police. The skirmishes got closer and closer to the Ford plant as neither the police nor the firemen, who were using water hoses, could contain the pent-up fury of the marchers. It was give and take, with both sides inflamed and out of control. The fighting intensified when Ford servicemen joined the city forces, using hoses to pour streams of water on the demonstrators as they neared the plant.[13]

At this touchy moment, Harry Bennett, director of the Ford Service Department, drove onto the field of battle in a closed car, apparently to take charge at first hand. No sooner did he step from his car than he was knocked out by a flying brick, and was sent to the Ford hospital. Panic enveloped the police and the Ford servicemen. A *Detroit News* photographer declared later that at that instant he heard a policeman remark, "Get your gats out and let them have it."

They fired on the demonstrators at point-blank range. As a Detroit journalist on the scene later reported, "Then two guns behind the gate flashed through its opening. Policemen and guards leveled their guns and pulled triggers. I would say hundreds of shots were fired into the mob."[14] The gunfire cleared the field of battle in a matter of minutes—except for the dead and wounded. Besides three unemployed workers, Joe York, the Young Communist leader, was dead.

The shocking end to this tragic event created a widespread reaction. There were many critical stories in the public press. A *Detroit Times* editorial, quoted in the conservative *Reader's Digest,* reflected the views of large sections of the press:

> Someone, it is now admitted, blundered in the handling of throngs of hungry marchers that sought to present petitions at the Ford plant.
>
> With hundreds of hungry people in line, little was required to kindle violence. The opposition offered by Dearborn police evidently changed an orderly demonstration into a riot, with death and bloodshed as its toll.
>
> Communist leaders have made impossible demands on industry and the city government. But, however visionary some of their claims and demands, it is a mistake to use violence against such people until they themselves resort to violence.
>
> When the Dearborn police, the representatives of the established order, precipitate violence, they inflict terrible damage on the entire community.
>
> The killing of obscure workingmen, innocent of crime, is a blow directed at the very heart of American institutions.[15]

At first the Ford Motor Company remained silent about the entire affair. However, Republican County Prosecutor Harry S. Toy sought to turn the tide of public opinion by supporting Harry Bennett's assertion that the demonstration was a revolutionary plot to seize Ford plants. Toy announced he was calling a special grand jury to investigate violation of Michigan's Criminal Syndication Act of 1931. He ordered mass raids and the arrest of unemployed Council leaders, and even went so far as to require that two seriously wounded demonstrators be handcuffed to their hospital carts. While this legal sideshow was going on, the grand jury returned no indictments against the Communist party leaders, but also absolved the Ford Motor Company.[16] The Communist party held a memorial rally on March 11 for its four dead. More than five thousand persons attended. It also informed Detroit officials that it was going to hold a funeral march through the city on March 12. Again more than five thousand persons marched while thousands of others on the sidelines gave ample demonstration of their sympathy. Out at the Ford plant, Dearborn police and the Ford Service Department mobilized five hundred heavily armed persons in case of an armed insurrection, a gesture which no one took seriously.

The Ford Hunger March, thanks to the overreaction of the Dearborn police and Harry Bennett's servicemen, made the Communist party a significant political force in the new wave of radicalism sweeping the auto industry.

As for the company charge that the hunger march was a Moscow-inspired conspiracy, it was pointed out that on the very day of the march a large delegation of Soviet technicians was in the Ford River Rouge plant receiving instructions in Ford methods of production. This was part of a highly lucrative contract Ford had signed with the Communist regime in Russia, thus becoming one of the companies which agreed to school Soviet engineers for $30 million of "Moscow gold."[17]

Agitation about red scares served more to frighten the proponents than to influence the general public, for a deeper mood of protest gripped Detroit and the nation. President Herbert Hoover's visit to Detroit in the summer of 1932 during his reelection campaign reflected the new social climate. Over 150,000 persons, mainly unemployed, stood on the streets to watch him motor by. There were no boos, no cheers, just an eerie silence—the most disturbing reaction of all.

In November Detroit went Democratic for the first

time, in both white and Negro districts. Franklin D. Roosevelt won 59.4 per cent of the vote. An immediate result was the collapse of the Ford-backed Republican party machine in the black ghetto.

The Democratic sweep in 1932 was viewed by most blue-collar workers as the beginning of a new day for them. Their man was in the White House; now the government was on their side. Fresh hope sparked the unprecedented social protest soon to shake Detroit from top to bottom.

Big business' resistance to Roosevelt was enough to cause blue-collar workers to lose faith in the once-admired industrialists and bankers. The 1933 collapse of the banks added to their disenchantment. When Governor William A. Comstock shut down Detroit's banks early in 1933, it precipitated the nationwide bank moratorium declared by President Roosevelt in March of that year. The quarrel within the city's power structure over keeping the banks solvent incensed most people. How much of the predicted bankruptcy of the big Union Guardian Trust Company was due to poor banking practices and speculation? Who could trust the bankers and businessmen involved? Did the Detroit banks fail because they were unable to get funds from the Reconstruction Finance Corporation, and was this due solely to the feud between Henry Ford and Senator James Couzens?[18] There were violent partisans for each point of view, but most Detroiters didn't care about the details of the controversy. To them it was the bankers and the banking system that were guilty.

A new and radical voice kept pounding home that viewpoint. During the banking crisis Mayor Frank Murphy had appointed a Depositors Committee to protect the people. Its eloquent spokesman was Rev. Charles E. Coughlin; his dramatic appearance, his silver-toned voice, and his unrestrained attacks on bankers and the banking system quickly skyrocketed him to national prominence.

The verbal assaults on capitalism, banks, the auto barons, and business in general reached new degrees of virulence, with the radicals on the Left competing with Father Coughlin and the Senator from Louisiana, Huey P. Long.

The unrest of the early thirties exploded in the strikes of 1933, with over one hundred walkouts among the auto workers alone. In this period, racial and ethnic differences would be submerged by the sharp class tensions and conflicts.

It had been standard practice for manufacturers and businessmen to cut wages during depressions. How else could a profit be made or a firm stay in business in a declining market? For auto workers this had meant continual wage cuts as well as unsteady work and disgraceful working conditions. The first strike in reaction to those policies began in Detroit on January 11, 1933, in the Waterloo plant of the Briggs Manufacturing Company, which built bodies for Ford. This strike assumed unusual importance in the history of Detroit because it indicated how strongly the auto manufacturers would resist unionism. Second, it was the first clear example of the fanatic militancy which would develop among the auto workers. Third, it showed that unless Detroit's radical groups put an end to their internecine fighting they would be unable to provide effective leadership in the struggle which clearly loomed ahead. The early events of 1933 astonished Detroit. When the Briggs Company rescinded the wage cut which had caused the strike in January, the men returned to their jobs. The next week a strike broke out at Motor Products and this, too, led to a revocation of wage cut.

The strike fever spread to other plants. Six thousand Briggs workers in four plants walked out. Similarly, 4,000 Murray Body workers shut down their plants. On February 7, 1933, over 3,000 Hudson workers "hit the bricks," thereby closing down other facilities of the company and bringing another 6,000 workers out onto the streets.

Minor alleviations in working conditions soon ended the Hudson and Murray Body strikes.[19] But the second Briggs strike collapsed. Adamant company opposition to any collective bargaining or recognition of the union, along with persistent police harassment of the picket lines, eventually broke the back of the strike—even though impartial fact-finders declared that the strikers' cause was good. A committee appointed by Mayor Frank Murphy concluded that the Briggs workers were justified in complaining about low wages, speed up, and dead time (no pay while waiting for work within the plant). State conciliators had stated that the greatest percentage of the strikers were decent, law-abiding citizens who had reason to rebel against the conditions imposed upon them. This didn't keep Highland Park and state police from arresting dozens of pickets and breaking up the picket lines.

Although the Briggs management announced that it would reinstate a minimum hourly rate and eliminate dead time, it was implacable in its refusal to bargain. The reason was known to everyone in Detroit. The auto industry was firmly committed to retaining the open shops; that is, to resist unionism. If Briggs had broken with that policy it would have risked losing all its vital business with Henry Ford, the number one anti-union employer in Michigan.

Employer resistance was not the only reason for the workers' failure. The Briggs walkout had become the focal point of political maneuvering on the radical Left in which the Communist party sought to expand the influence it had achieved in Detroit following the Ford Hunger March. Among the 6,000 strikers were small but articulate and influential members of various radical groups: the Socialist party, the Proletarian party, the Industrial Workers of the World, and the Communist party. The strikers had asked Phil Raymond, the National Secretary of the Communist-dominated Auto Workers Union to help lead the strike, but when the Communist party brought in Earl Browder, its National Secretary, they overplayed their hand. At a job rally Browder said, "I read that company officials charge that we Communists are responsible for the strike. This is true. This is one of the most glorious pages in the history of Communism in America."[20] It was *not* true, as Norman Thomas, spokesman for the Socialist party, pointed out.[21] Company opposition, political bickering, police brutality, and the bleak outlook for settlement combined to demoralize the strikers, who gradually drifted back to work.

The waves of strikes early in 1933 were not the only manifestations of unrest. In April 22, 1933, it took Detroit's entire riot squad to prevent the lynching of a white officer who sought to evict a Negro family. In the Negro community, resistance to eviction paralleled the reaction of white unemployed workers. The Negroes protested violently against police brutality with delegates and a demonstration when many witnesses testified that two policemen held a Negro boy while whites beat him. Following the killing of James Porter in his home by a white officer on August 9, 1933, a second delegation was sent to the mayor, and over 5,000 people attended Porter's funeral and protest meeting. When police killed a Negro and seriously wounded another during a small riot on Hastings Street, an officer was charged with manslaughter but was freed by a hung jury.[22]

Almost unnoticed in all the turmoil in Detroit and the ghetto was the first tangible evidence that Negroes were being attracted to the idea of unionism. In October 1933, a handful of Negro unionists organized the Federation of Negro Labor, and also created their own postal union.

An old radical idea, "Black and white, unite and fight," was about to come into its own.

CIO Sitdowns: The Birth of Industrial Unionism

4

THE HOPES of the nation and the new Roosevelt administration for a return of peace and prosperity rested on the enactment of the National Industrial Recovery Act in 1933. The President stated his own expectations in these words:

> The workers of this country have rights under this law which cannot be taken from them; nobody will be permitted to whittle them away; but on the other hand, no aggression is necessary to obtain these rights. The proposal that applies to the employers applies to the workers as well and I ask you workers to cooperate in the same spirit.[1]

Neither management nor labor shared the illusions contained in that policy statement, if indeed it expressed a policy and not merely a hope.

American industry hardened its anti-union philosophy in a reaction to what it considered inflammatory remarks by the President. The employers' views were strengthened by legal counselors who argued that the Supreme Court would declare the NIRA unconstitutional. Which it did, in a landmark decision in May 1935. The feeling among employers that eventually "the law" would be on their side partly accounted for the intense resistance to industrial unionism during the violent struggles ahead.

The experiences of labor in the last six months of 1933 confirmed workers' doubts about relying solely on legal procedures or protection to assist their unionizing campaigns.

In that six-month period more than fifteen strikers were killed, 200 injured, and countless arrested in various strikes. Although the Norris–La Guardia anti-injunction act had been passed by Congress in 1932, more than forty sweeping injunctions had been issued against strikers. The brief importance of the National Labor Board, set up under the NRA, diminished with the onslaught of the employers.[2]

In Detroit, auto manufacturers added to the repressive techniques by firing known union supporters and employing labor spies to help them keep tabs on the people in the shops. General Motors alone paid the Pinkerton Detective Agency $419,000 and Chrysler gave $210,000 to the Corporation's auxiliary company for providing spies and informers. A warning by a government commission on the reactions these practices would provoke was ignored both by the companies and the government. The commission report pointed out that "labor unrest existed to degrees higher than warranted by the depression. The unrest flows from insecurity, low annual earnings, inequitable hiring and rehiring methods, espionage, speed-up and replacement of workers at an extremely early age—unless something is done soon, the workers intend to take things in their own hands to get results."[3] Events soon confirmed these forebodings. In Detroit a new and very militant union, the Mechanical Educational Society of America, won two significant tool and die strikes under the leadership of an Independent Socialist, Matthew Smith.

Early in 1934 hundreds of thousands of workers in the automobile, rubber, and other industries flocked into the AFL, the only union they knew about. On March 20, 1934, over 100,000 auto workers were ready to go on strike in Detroit, Lansing, Pontiac, Flint, and Cleveland, when President Roosevelt sent a telegram urging that the strike be postponed. On March 25, 1934, the Roosevelt administration appointed a National Automotive Labor Board, with the hope that it would solve enough of the labor problems so that an auto strike would not be necessary.

This board soon gave the NRA a reputation among the auto workers as the "national run-around." A labor expert analyzed the work of the board in the following manner:

> Until December it was inactive, inefficient and useless. A study of 195 decisions issued by the board from its inception until January 17, 1935, reveals that in the overwhelming majority of alleged discrimination cases the board ruled either "no discrimination" or "the employer did not err." In those instances where discrimination was so obvious that it could not be ignored, the board did not admit that the employer had used "discrimination" against active unionists in so many words; it merely "recommended" that the employer rehire a discharged worker.[4]

The personnel of the board consisted of Nicholas Kelley, attorney for the Automobile Manufacturers Association, Dr. Leo Wolman, representative of the federal government, and Richard Byrd, an automotive worker from Pontiac, Michigan. Mr. Kelley represented the manufacturers. Dr. Wolman was considered the brains of the board, but his record had been consistent in the tacit and direct promotion of company unions against free trade unions. Byrd, supposedly representing labor, could only serve as Dr. Wolman's "office boy." Since his first act was to agree to unanimous decisions, he could not, even if he disagreed with any ruling, issue a minority report, and soon he was repudiated by every section of organized labor. Nevertheless, the AFL hierarchy tried unsuccessfully to work with the Automotive Board. This attempt, and its attempts to divide the auto workers into different craft unions rather than build industrial unions, soon turned most auto workers against the AFL.[5] So thoroughly was it discredited among the rank and file that when the National Automotive Labor Board held an election in the spring of 1935, over 88 per cent of those voting voted for no union. Only 8 per cent voted for the AFL. Employers generally tended to misinterpret the significance of this vote, as they would in the future. The workers' vote was not anti-union, it was an anti-AFL craft union protest.

The young radical movement in America analyzed the results differently. A former teacher at Brookwood Labor College, viewing the strife in Detroit, wrote his two brothers who were traveling around the world to hurry back because "big things are going to happen." Walter and Victor Reuther heeded Roy Reuther's advice, and came back to earn themselves a place in labor's history.

Events in three major cities in America proved this conclusion to be right. In nearby Toledo one of the most violent strikes of the 1930's took place. In the spring of 1934, Toledo Auto-Lite Workers, who had been organized into an AFL federal local, went on strike. What made their strike so unusual was the successful intervention of a group of young radicals who were followers of A. J. Muste, former director of Brookwood Labor College and a labor leader since World War I. The radicals had organized an unemployed league with thousands of members. They used mass picketing and volunteered to assist the Auto-Lite strikers after an injunction was issued

61

against picketing before the company gates. Since almost one-third of the work force in Toledo was unemployed, it wasn't very difficult to get 10,000 men on a picket line. The deliberate violation of the injunction had, in fact, been announced by the Lucas County Unemployed League's Anti-Injunction Committee, in a letter to the judge who issued the injunction.

Each day when the Detroit auto workers woke up, they heard the radio report and saw the blazing headlines in Detroit's dailies describing the events in Toledo. One of the participants, Art Preis, who became labor editor for the *Militant,* summarized the strike as follows: "By May 23, there were more than 10,000 on the picket line. County deputies with tear gas guns were lined up on the plant roof. A strike picket, Miss Alma Harm, had been struck on the head by a bone curl from a plant window, and had been taken to the hospital. By the time a hundred more cops had arrived, the workers were tremendously intense. The police began roughing up individual pickets in the line."[6]

What happened when the police tried to escort workers through the picket line was described by the Associated Press:

> Piles of bricks and stones were assembled at strategic places and a wagon load of bricks was funneled to a point near the factory to provide further ammunition for the strikers. Suddenly a barrage of tear gas bombs were hurled from upper factory windows. At the same time company employees armed with iron bars and crops dragged a fire hose into the street and sprayed water onto the crowd. The strike sympathizers replied with piles of bricks.
>
> The police charged and swung their clubs trying to clear a path for the strike breakers. The workers held their ground and fought back. Choked by the tear gas fired from inside the plant, it was the police who finally

gave up the battle. Then the thousands of pickets laid siege to the plant, determined to maintain their picket line. The workers then propelled giant bricks through the plant windows. The plant soon was without lights. It was not until the arrival of 900 National Guardsmen some fifteen hours later that the strike breakers were finally released, but the situation was now well in hand. With their bare fists and rocks, the workers fought a six-day pitched battle with the National Guard. They fought from roof tops, from behind billboards and came through alleys to fight the Guardsmen.[7]

On May 24, the guardsmen fired point blank at the Auto-Lite strikers, killing two and wounding twenty-five. At night, 6,000 workers returned to renew the battle. In the dark they closed in on groups of guardsmen in the six-block martial law zone. Twice they drove the troops back into the plant. At one stage a group of troops threw their last tear-gas bombs, then quickly picked up rocks to throw at the strikers. The strikers recovered the last gas bomb thrown before it exploded and flung it back at the troops. On Friday, May 31, the troops were speedily ordered withdrawn from the strike area when the employer agreed to keep the plant closed.

This had not been the usual battle, with the workers getting shot. The Toledo experience showed the radicals that the once successful technique of red-baiting was no longer effective in scaring workers and breaking strikes. On the West Coast young Harry Bridges, always denounced as a Communist, led a strike of longshoremen which became a general strike. It was the beginning of the success of unionism in San Francisco, and made Bridges a leading spokesman for the pro-communist forces in American labor.

In Minneapolis, two hard-fought teamsters' strikes were organized and won by the Dunne brothers and Farrell Dobbs, acknowledged leaders of the Trotskyist radical movement. Vincent R. Dunne, the soft-spoken but avowed revolutionary, soon became the most important man in the Minnesota labor movement; his talent for union organizing was admired and copied even by hostile teamster leaders like Dave Beck in Seattle.[8]

At this point two conditions necessary for the success of industrial unionism existed. First, the willingness of blue-collar workers throughout America to man picket lines—by the thousands if necessary—to get unions of their own choosing. Second, the existence of a large cadre of young and talented radicals eager to participate as leaders in the spreading struggle.

What was still lacking was a national leader of unusual talents and a national organization to direct a growing social movement for industrial unionism.

The most unlikely candidate, based on his past performance and opposition to radicalism, was John L. Lewis — a Republican in politics, a follower of Adam Smith in economics, and an autocrat in his union. Yet Lewis more than filled the need for a national leader. He became the symbol and guiding force of the labor crusade known as the CIO. In 1934 Lewis revitalized the United Mineworkers into a union of 400,000 men. He argued with his closest colleagues on the AFL council over the need for an industrial form of organization for mass-production workers. A split between the craft-oriented hierarchy and the spokesman for industrial unionism was inevitable. In November 1935, Lewis and ten other top union leaders formed the Committee for Industrial Organization (CIO).

His first act was to hire the most talented, aggressive, and passionate radicals of every kind to supplement his organizers for the mineworkers. Management in Detroit and other industrial centers never quite really knew what hit them during the next two years; the combination of

64

Lewis, the radicals, and the restless workers completely overwhelmed them. A change in the Communist party line removed another obstacle for the organizers. The party dropped its self-defeating line of independent "red trade unions," and decided to work within the framework of the American labor movement. It was part of the policy of a popular front, dictated by Stalin.

In January 1935, a conference of auto delegates from throughout the country was held in Detroit. As the result of an agreement between various radical political tendencies, a four-point program of action was adopted. The points were (1) industrial unionism in the auto industry, (2) initiation of a large organizing drive, (3) democratization of the unions, and (4) independent labor activity and politics. The broad coalition of radicals kept pressuring John L. Lewis to intervene and assist auto workers' organizing efforts. They forced William Green, the president of the AFL, to call a convention of AFL auto delegates in Detroit in August 1935. At that convention the structure of a national union was created and a young baptist preacher from Kansas, Homer Martin, was elected vice-president.

This skeleton of an auto workers' union faced many obstacles. Besides the economic power and influence of the auto industry, there was the problem of Father Coughlin's influence over the Detroit auto workers. Coughlin had been denounced as anti-labor by Frank Martel, president of the Detroit AFL. Nevertheless, Coughlin was popular in the auto shops, which had many Catholic workers, and he was influential in creating independent automotive industrial unions — mainly in the Dodge, Chrysler, and Plymouth plants. Even President Roosevelt was concerned about his influence; he asked former mayor of Detroit Frank Murphy, a one-time friend of Father Coughlin, to return from the Philippines, where he was governor general, and try to work out a deal with him.[9] Although this failed and Father Coughlin went his own way, he was influential enough to be invited to the May 1936 convention of the auto workers in South Bend, Indiana. His dramatic statement on that occasion, "I believe in industrial unionism," assisted the new auto workers' organization in convincing Plymouth, Dodge, and Chrysler independent divisions to join the main union.

Another problem that deeply concerned the young auto workers' union was that of winning over the vast number of Southern workers who either belonged to or had been influenced by the Ku Klux Klan. There were at least 200,000 members of the Klan in Michigan, and an even more dangerous offshoot of the Klan, known as the Black Legion, was spreading throughout the state and was held responsible for many murders, including those of union organizers. Forrest Davis, in describing the activity of the Klan and Black Legion elements, wrote: "The night rider, 1936 style, in Ford's Detroit is likely to be a labor spy as well as a Catholic baiter. The lash that speaks his dark will may as well be hatred of communists, i.e., union organizers, as distrust of Jews." Davis pointed out that George Marchuk, treasurer of the communist auto workers' union, was found murdered in a ditch in Lincoln Park on December 22, 1933. Lincoln Park, a suburb adjoining Dearborn, is populated predominantly by Ford workers and was once a Ku Klux Klan stronghold. In March 1934, the body of John Bielak, a member of the Hudson Company local of the AFL, was discovered by a roadside near Monroe, Michigan. He had been beaten to death. Under Bielak's head his murderer had placed a stack of applications from other workers for union membership. It was estimated that during the 1933–1936 period over fifty murders in Michigan could be attributed to the Black Legion.[10]

Given the heterogeneous social composition of Detroit's work force, the young radical unionists wondered just how effective an appeal to industrial unionism would be against racial, religious, and ethnic prejudices among the auto workers. Could the hatred of the workers for the employers be molded into a class solidarity strong enough to overcome their prejudices? An answer came from Akron, Ohio, which was a small edition of Detroit in terms of the problems involved. Akron was a one-industry rubber city, with an open shop tradition and a mixed working population. It was known as the "capital of West Virginia" because so many West Virginians had moved there, and was also a stronghold of the Ku Klux Klan, whose members and chief supporters were rubber workers. The Goodyear strike in early 1936 provided a satisfactory answer to the disturbing question. John L. Lewis and the CIO appealed to the Goodyear strikers to build an industrial union, and succeeded in unifying Akron's rubber workers. The eleven-week Goodyear strike ended in victory. Now the auto workers and the entire nation knew that Lewis was truly determined to build industrial unionism. Furthermore, the so-called hillbillies had transferred their fanatic allegiance from the Ku Klux Klan to the CIO and the idea of industrial unionism. Among the most effective Akron unionists were former members of the KKK. Earlier prejudices were erased by class solidarity—in fact, an important contribution of the CIO was its role in weakening the influence of the KKK on blue-collar workers.

The Akron rubber workers made another contribution to the young auto workers' union by developing a new strike technique called the sitdown. In 1936–1937 a series of sitdown strikes swept the auto and other industries. They were highly controversial, contagious, and generally successful—a boon to John L. Lewis, who didn't expect

67

them any more than did the Roosevelt administration or the nation's business community. Implicit in the sitdown strikes was the moral belief that human lives are more important than property rights, and this philosophy was the rationale for seizing plants and business concerns. The legal issue involved was finally settled in 1939, when the U.S. Supreme Court declared sitdown strikes illegal, but by then the decision did not matter, for the sitdowns were over and the CIO was organized.

The sitdowns that began in Akron quickly spread, for a sitdown strike had many advantages over a regular strike with picket lines. Within a plant strikers were far less vulnerable to police attack than they were on a picket line, and only a minority of workers was needed to keep the plants shut down.

As the nation learned anew in 1968–1969 in the student sit-ins, this technique dramatized issues more effectively because of the great publicity attending it. The panic of the university administrators in the late 1960's had its counterpart among employers in the 1930's.

For the business and industrial circles the sitdown strike wave seemed to be the beginning of a revolution. *Business Week* magazine spoke for the business community when it said:

> By means of sitdown strikes, the country has been put at the mercy of thoroughly irresponsible groups which in effect have no leadership, no control, no authority that can restrain them. Great industries, whose operations affect the daily welfare of millions, are confronted with demands to sign contracts with groups which, day by day and hour by hour, demonstrate that they have almost no control over their own people, no conception of the validity or the sanctity of a contract, no respect for property rights or for rights of any sort except their own.[11]

Neither the sitdowners, the radical organizers, nor the

CIO paid much attention to the conservative views, although the AFL did proclaim its opposition to sitdown strike tactics.

The sweeping reelection of President Roosevelt in November 1936 added to the confidence of blue-collar workers, who saw it as their victory and a repudiation of the anti-unionism of big business. As a consequence, the Akron sitdown strikes spread like wildfire, beginning with a seven-day sitdown in the Bendix plant in South Bend, Indiana. Next there was a two-week sitdown in the Midland Steel Plant in Detroit, where black and white workers joined together and won. Then there was a five-day sitdown at the Kelsey-Hayes plant in Detroit, followed by sitdown strikes at Chrysler, Briggs, and some Fisher Body plants. In each instance, the sitdowns won quick concessions for the workers and the plants were organized. Labor was on the march.

The small auto workers' union, which had 7,000 members at the time of its May 1936 convention, had recruited thousands of workers. Young Walter Reuther and an able staff were transforming a small west side local into a vast union of 30,000 members. On the east side of Detroit, Emil Mazey, the tough independent radical, led the drive which quickly organized the Briggs Manufacturing Company, for the 1933 strike had been broken. The former Communist candidate for governor, John Anderson, who had become the outstanding leader of the skilled tool and die workers, took his union from the Mechanical Educational Society of America into the new UAW, and Detroit skilled workers in the jobbing plants were largely organized. These tumultuous events had not yet affected the big three auto manufacturers: General Motors, Ford, and Chrysler. Then, in January 1937, the greatest sitdown strike of all shut down the General Motors empire.

Ironically, the first General Motors plant to be closed

by a sitdown was the white racist assembly plant in Atlanta, Georgia. Late in December 1936, the sitdowns spread from there to Cleveland and Detroit and then to Flint, Michigan. Since Flint was the heart of the General Motors empire (its transmission and engine plants were located there) and General Motors was the largest auto manufacturer, the time of decision had arrived for the CIO and the auto industry.

As was the custom, the first response of the company was to use police in an attempt to isolate the strikers in Flint and starve them out. Next, an injunction was obtained against the seizure of the plants by the strikers. Both policies failed. The sitdown strikers of the Fisher Plant #2 in Flint not only held their own in a five-hour battle with the police but for good measure later seized a transmission plant to bolster the strike.

In these circumstances Governor Murphy called up the National Guard, but this only accentuated the tension. For it was clear that only the bloodiest and most violent of all labor battles could dislodge the sitdowners.

Contrary to public opinion at the time, the General Motors sitdown strike was not part of the CIO strategy. John L. Lewis had sought privately to discourage the sitdowns. He had planned to organize the steel industry first, but the mass uprising of the auto workers could not be contained and Lewis was forced to change his strategy. The aggressive but inexperienced auto union leaders convinced Lewis he should come to Detroit and take charge of negotiations with General Motors. The auto workers knew that Lewis' negotiating ability and national stature as a labor leader were necessary for the success of the General Motors strike. Lewis accepted the challenge, knowing that his personal prestige and the fate of the CIO were at stake.

When he arrived in Detroit he informed the nation

that "I did not ask these men to sit down. I did not ask General Motors to turn off the heat. I did not have any part in either the sitdown strikes or the attempt to freeze them in. Let General Motors talk to them."[12]

When Governor Murphy hinted that he might use national guards to oust the sitdowners, Lewis declared: "I shall personally enter General Motors plant, Chevrolet #4. I shall order the men to disregard your order and to stand fast. I shall then walk up to the largest window in the plant, open it, and divest myself of my outer raiment —remove my shirt and bear my bosom. Then, when you order your troops to fire, mine will be the first breast that its bullets will strike."[13] It was, from a union standpoint, John L. Lewis' most dramatic and finest hour, and it worked. On February 11, 1937, General Motors signed a six-month agreement reassigning the UAW in the plants closed by the union and agreeing to rehire all union strikers. It soon committed itself to negotiate wages, hours, working conditions, and other issues. This victory caused the sitdown strike fever to spread even more rapidly.

In March all of Chrysler's Detroit plants were shut down by sitdowns. The greatest difficulty of the UAW leaders was having to ask thousands of workers to leave the plants, since so many wanted to remain. In each plant cadres of active unionists were chosen for the honor of occupying Chrysler's factories. The new mood of Detroit in those days was revealed when city police and county deputies indicated they might expel the sitdowners forcibly. A massive auto worker demonstration of about 150,000 packed downtown Detroit—an act which gave police authorities some second thoughts about such a policy. John L. Lewis returned and personally negotiated a settlement with Walter P. Chrysler.[14]

The sitdown wave continued in 1937 as dime-store

clerks, Western Union employees, restaurant and hotel workers, garbage workers, steel workers, and garment workers went on strike in many sections of the country.

A unique sight in the Detroit area in that turbulent time was the UAW "flying squadrons," colorfully garbed union militants chosen for their aggressiveness in defending picket lines. Walter Reuther personally led 500 members of Local 174 to Flint to boost the strikers' morale at a critical moment. On Detroit's east side Emil Mazey, later secretary-treasurer of the UAW, directed the most popular of all flying squadrons, the young militants from Briggs Local 212. Their appearance on any picket line usually signified two things: first, that the police would have more than they could handle if they used force, and second, that the union was going to win.

Almost unnoticed in the excitement was the emergence of a new color on the picket lines, in the flying squadrons, and in the unions. It was black, and it suggested that something new was happening among the Negroes in Detroit.

Labor's Triumph: The Fall of Ford

5

T HE INVOLVEMENT of black workers in the growing union movement in Detroit was due primarily
to the deliberate efforts of the radical unionists. While
political differences grew into outright hostility and a
deadly struggle began for domination of the UAW, on
one point there was still agreement: All radicals felt that
Negroes were entitled to full social, economic, and political equality. The 1919 strikes had been broken partly by
the use of Negro strikebreakers, and this had not been
forgotten; it had been one cause of the disastrous race
riots in the post–World War I period.

Thus the cardinal point of faith in the new CIO movement was to organize all workers regardless of race,
creed, or color. Such a policy had long been part of the
coal miners' tradition, even in the South.

In suburban Pontiac, Oscar Noble became the first
Negro elected to the shop committee in a major auto
plant, though most of the workers were white. In the
Chrysler sitdown strike, one of the leaders was Sam Fan-
roy, who was popular with his white as well as his black
co-workers in the paint shop. Perhaps the most dynamic
black leader of the time was Hodges Mason, who shared
the leadership of Bohn Aluminum Local 208 with Fred

Williams, a well-known Communist. Neither whites nor blacks concerned themselves much with the political beliefs of the strike leaders in those days. Results counted more, and the antagonism of the employers was a much greater worry.

Mason was largely instrumental in winning over many young potential leaders and giving them an active role in the auto workers' union. The flying squadron of Local 208, with its sizable Negro contingent, was very prominent on many picket lines.[1]

In its formative years the CIO was the only large-scale organization on the American scene which offered talented young blacks opportunity, dignity, and a sense of genuine participation. This was in marked contrast to the AFL's long tradition of discrimination against minorities.

For Negro workers the success of the CIO meant the creation of a social institution devoted to civil rights and which provided blacks with a job safeguard never before known. Seniority clauses which said that employment depended on length of service made illegal the standard policy of hiring Negroes last and firing them first. In spite of all the obstacles to achieving equal employment opportunities, Negroes sensed the value of the unions, and, generally speaking, the black ghettos tended to be pro-union then.

How much unity between black and white workers had been realized was tested in Detroit in November 1939, when Chrysler Corporation hired sixty Negro strikebreakers to walk through UAW picket lines at the Dodge plant in Hamtramck. (Chrysler knew that there were still strong prejudices among many Polish workers against Negroes.) Dozens of Negro unionists from other plants and a few Negro community leaders urged the sixty blacks not to break the picket lines. A leaflet was distributed among Negroes signed by Rev. Horace A. White of the Plymouth Congregational Church; Rev. Charles A. Hill of the Hartford Avenue Baptist Church; State Senator Charles Diggs, the father of the current Congressman; and Editor Louis Martin of the *Michigan Chronicle,* the Negro newspaper. It said:

> It has come to the attention of some leaders of the Negro community of Detroit that there is an effort to get Negro workers interested in a back-to-work movement in the Dodge and Chrysler plants.
>
> Such a movement can have no benefit for Negro workers. Such a back-to-work movement contains possibilities of race riots and race conflicts.
>
> Race relations in Detroit have been making definite progress. We do not want to spoil what progress has been made in this direction by having Negroes used as dupes in a back-to-work movement.
>
> If Negroes are to have jobs they must have them in cooperation with all workers.
>
> Any efforts to put Negroes back to work in the factories, over the majority of all workers, will spell doom for Negro workers in the factories.
>
> Negro workers must not allow themselves to be used by irresponsible leaders.[2]

A new idea was gaining hold in Detroit. Nevertheless, a few days later the company enlisted 187 Negroes to march into the plants under police protection. But the UAW pickets refused to be provoked, for the union leaders realized these potential strikebreakers were not ordinary scabs, and knew that in time they could be won over by black unionists who were on the picket line.[3] Race tensions were exacerbated in parts of Hamtramck, but the company failed in its objectives and the strike was won.

Many employers did not give up their hope that Negroes could be used against the UAW, even though General Motors and Chrysler were organized. After all, Ford was still untouched by unionism, and there were about 10,000 blacks working in the River Rouge plants whom the Ford Motor Company expected to remain loyal to it.

Before the decisive confrontation at Ford in 1941, the auto industry tried once more to make Detroit an open shop town again. It attempted to eliminate the UAW by taking advantage of a split between the pro-AFL Homer Martin group and the pro-CIO unionists. Martin, the president of the UAW, had been expelled and had formed a new union chartered by the AFL. Briggs Manufacturing rejected the demand for recognition of the UAW-CIO headed by Mazey, but was unable to dent the solidarity of the workers, and the UAW-CIO eventually won, after a lengthy strike. In the spring of 1939, General Motors announced it was suspending collective bargaining with the UAW, since the AFL union was also demanding recognition. GM then learned its first lesson about the talents of a brilliant strategist named Walter Reuther. He pulled a unique strike, calling out only the tool and die workers at the peak of the summer change-over season. The response was total. Meanwhile, unskilled workers were drawing unemployment insurance because they were not on strike. GM retreated and resumed a more normal bargaining relationship with the UAW and Walter Reuther, who was director of the UAW's GM section. The open shop drive failed. Then came the acid test for industrial unionism: the drive to unionize Ford.

The following account of that drive and of the 1941 strike is given by Irving Howe and myself in *The UAW and Walter Reuther:*

> The Ford workers had plenty of reason to feel discontented, and when the UAW began organizing them in 1937 they responded favorably. But most union leaders underestimated the difficulties of the job.
>
> After having organized General Motors and Chrysler

in 1937, the UAW began to move against Ford. Hundreds of workers signed up during that year. But when Ford said in April, 1937, that he would never recognize the UAW or any other union, he meant it, and he used weapons that neither GM or Chrysler had had. The two bitter corporations had been caught unaware by the union drive, for sitdowns were new and difficult to handle. But Ford could learn from his competitors' misfortunes. He also had a hard-boiled plant leadership and an efficient espionage service that the two other corporations had not had. When isolated strikes broke out in the Ford plants in the late thirties, he broke them without difficulty.

Ford was encouraged in his opposition to the UAW by some temporary defeats that the CIO met shortly before the drive to organize his plants. Little Steel had won at least a partial victory over the CIO's organization drive. The Memorial Day Massacre in Chicago had led President Roosevelt to denounce both the CIO and the independent steel corporations, and the CIO had called off its strikes at Republic, Bethlehem and other companies. If getting tough worked, well . . . wasn't Henry Ford the man to get tough? And weren't Harry Bennett and his gentlemen ready for action?

On May 26, 1937, they went into action. The UAW had previously announced that, for the first time, it was going to distribute leaflets at the Rouge; Dearborn's municipal administration had granted it a permit. When the sixty union distributors, two-thirds of them women, came to the Rouge, they were set upon and severely beaten by Ford Servicemen, whose ranks had been augmented by recently employed Detroit thugs. Two of the union's officials, Walter Reuther and Richard Frankensteen, singled out for especially rough treatment, were knocked down, lifted up and knocked down again. One unionist had his skull fractured, another was sent to the hospital for two weeks. The Dearborn police stood by but did not intervene in "the battle of the overpass."

Photographers from the Detroit papers, the *New York Times* and the Associated Press had their cameras snatched away from them. When *Time* published a devastating account of the beating, the Ford Company withdrew its advertising for a year and a half. One Detroit paper, the *Daily News,* did manage to salvage some pictures and these later appeared in papers throughout the country. On May 27, 1937, the *News* published two pictures. One carried the caption "The Start" and showed Servicemen approaching Reuther, Frankensteen and other union officials. The union men are smiling and the burly Servicemen walking grimly toward them. The second picture, captioned "Action," showed Frankensteen's coat and vest pulled over his head and his body being beaten by the attackers. In subsequent government hearings some of the assailants were identified as professional boxers and thugs. Among them was the president of the fascistic Knights of Dearborn, Sam Taylor, also a Ford foreman, and Charles Goodman, a thug with a record of twenty-one arrests.

Three months later the UAW tried again, this time with 1,000 husky workers ready to match blow for blow. The Servicemen stood by and watched but did nothing; they did not relish combat under such conditions. Soon Ford developed a new technique. The Dearborn City Council passed an ordinance which prohibited distribution of literature at congested areas—namely, the approaches to the Rouge at the times when shifts changed. In the following months nearly 1,000 unionists were arrested for giving out leaflets. To avoid court tests of the ordinance, those who were arrested were jailed and then released without charges. Thus no trials were held while distribution was effectively curtailed.

The next three years, 1937 to 1940, were full of terror and violence in all the Ford plants. By 1940 the National Labor Relations Board had judged the Ford management guilty of unfair labor practices in nine plants. The story of the Service Department's activities in Dallas is almost unbelievable, but it is all there, black on white, in an NLRB report. The report describes how toughs were armed with blackjacks, rubber hose and pistols to intimidate union men. A liberal lawyer not

connected with the UAW, W. J. Houston, was beaten
so hard he required hospitalization. An organizer for an
AFL union, George Baer, was beaten into insensibility.
A. J. Lewis, a twin brother of a Dallas businessman who
had expressed himself in favor of unions, was beaten by
mistake and, on his deathbed a few months later,
charged that the beating had led to his death. Described
as "organized gangsterism" by the NLRB, these methods
proved successful for a few years in keeping the union
out of the Ford plant.

By 1940, the tide began to turn. The factional struggle
within the UAW, which had hampered the Ford drive,
was temporarily at an end. A large fund, half provided
by the national CIO and half by the UAW, was set aside
for cracking Ford. John L. Lewis, then CIO president,
sent some of his toughest organizers, led by Michael
Widman, to Detroit. The UAW assigned a group of able
unionists to Ford, including Richard Leonard, former
DeSoto worker and vice-president of the UAW, and
Emil Mazey, former president of Briggs Local 212.

What probably helped most, however, was that the
entire union movement of Detroit pitched in. Local
unions formed volunteer organizing committees which
canvassed neighborhoods and talked to Ford workers.
A CIO dairy workers' union supplied the names of Ford
workers living on the routes of its members. Special
groups were set up to contact foreign-language workers.
All the while the union kept harping on the fact that,
despite decades of Ford publicity about a living wage,
the average wage at Ford was five cents less than for
the entire industry and more than ten cents less than at
Chrysler and General Motors.

In the Ford plant itself the UAW supporters gradually became bolder. A rudimentary organization was
created on a department and building level and each
unit elected a chairman—usually a courageous man
ready to risk his job. These were trying days for the
rank-and-file unionists who were doing the job at Ford.
One day a worker might agree to sign up, and then the
next day back down unaccountably, the victim of pressures from management or from a wife afraid he might

lose his job by "getting mixed up with the union." The men were extraordinarily sensitive to the slightest pressures from either side, and the UAW had to calculate each step with the greatest care. A small minority was bold, a small minority contemptuous, but the bulk of the workers fluctuated, hopeful and fearful, many eager to join the union even as they wondered if this time it would be strong enough to do the job.

When the U.S. Circuit Court of Appeals upheld an NLRB decision which had attacked Ford for unfair labor practices and had ordered the company to rehire twenty-two discharged union men in the Rouge plant, hundreds of Ford workers were encouraged to join the union. When Justice of the Peace Lila Neuenfelt of Dearborn declared in October, 1940, that the town's ordinance prohibiting literature distribution was unconstitutional, and her ruling was reinforced by a circuit judge who issued an order prohibiting further interference with union distributions, UAW victory at Ford was closer. By January, 1941, the UAW was strong enough to sign men up openly in the Ford plants.

Ford fought back. In December, 1940, the company had fired between 300 and 400 union supporters from the Lincoln plant alone, but such methods no longer worked. Spontaneous walkouts and sitdowns took place in many of the plants. On December 30, 1940, some 1,000 men in the Rouge tool-and-die department struck over a dispute involving rest periods. For the first time, in many of the plants the men felt free to act as an organized body. The Service Department could intimidate individuals, but was helpless against organized thousands.

Early in February, 1941, when the U.S. Supreme Court refused to review the Rouge case, the company lost its last hope of legal delay in its struggle against the NLRB decisions. Ford had to rehire the twenty-two discharged workers as the NLRB had ordered, and the UAW seized the opportunity for all it was worth. Triumphantly, the men marched into the plant, wearing CIO buttons—and in a few days thousands of such buttons appeared.

By February, 1941, both sides were jockeying des-

perately, with the UAW determined to push ahead to
victory, and the Ford Company often unable to decide
whether to meet the UAW drive head-on or try to de-
flect it by gentle tactics. A major crisis developed when
the union served notice tò the Michigan State Mediation
Board on February 26, 1941, that a strike was imminent
in the Rouge, Highland Park and Lincoln plants. The
atmosphere among the workers was by now simply
feverish; the tension and resentment accumulated over
years was about to explode.

But the company pulled back a bit and began rehiring hundreds of the men it had fired during the organization drive. It seemed that a strike would be
avoided, as both James F. Dewey, the federal labor
conciliator, and the union leadership wished. Hoping to
win by an NLRB election, the UAW heads failed to see
how unavoidable and necessary a strike was as a means
of self-assertion for the workers.

Shut-down after shut-down took place in the plants
during March. Most were settled on the union's terms,
and each time more workers joined. The company tacitly
recognized the union by agreeing to meet with its plant-
wide committees, though it still refused to talk to the
UAW national leaders. But in April company policy
took another sharp turn. On April 1 Ford refused to
meet with any union committees, and in the rolling mill,
pressed steel, tire plant and B buildings UAW committeemen were discharged. What was the company's strategy? To provoke a hasty, poorly organized strike? To
wear down the union? Or was it just tacking and veering
without any overall purpose, in the hope of hitting on
some improvised way of defeating the union.

No one gave any orders; no directives came from the
union. On April 1 the men just quit working and waited
for the company to rehire the committeemen it had discharged. In the rolling-mill plant, where 6,000 had
stopped working, tempers flared after 110 Dearborn
police were rushed in. But when thousands of Ford men
from other buildings moved toward the rolling-mill plant
the police prudently withdrew.

The strike spread from building to building, until the

huge Rouge plant was uncannily still. Begun late in the afternoon, the shut-down was completed in the evening. UAW officials didn't know what had happened, for the strike had not been planned and they had no way of communicating with the plant. But the report, which Detroit still thought was unbelievable and impossible, spread through the city like a licking flame: Ford is shut down.

Union officials quickly held a conference, and even though some had been against a strike they endorsed the one that had developed spontaneously. In a strike-conscious union it is always possible to move quickly into an unexpected strike action, and that is what happened in the UAW. Inside the plants the men waited for word from the union. Sharp discussion flared, tempers were short. Local leaders worried about the 17,000 Negroes employed by Ford: would they follow Don Marshall, Ford's negro agent, or would they come along with the union? At 12:15 a.m. on April 2nd the union officially called a strike at Ford. In the dead of night a parade of shouting men formed at the plant and marched to the union hall a mile away.

What took place that night near the union hall is surely one of the most extraordinary events in American labor history. All night long men talked—loudly and plainly, with hardly a trace of fear or anxiety. The union kept an all-night meeting going at which leaders spoke, but simultaneously and probably more important, groups of men milled around talking the whole thing over, estimating their chances, enjoying the sheer sensation of expressing themselves freely. A soup kitchen was organized, a union hospital set up, flying squadrons instructed. The union had learned a lot in the General Motors and Chrysler strikes and now it worked with skill and dispatch. The men watched and were impressed. They had found themselves and the union; they had begun to respect both.

Most of those who stayed in the hall through that night had been up since the morning, but no one thought of sleep. They enjoyed watching their spontaneous action transformed into the detailed organization of an expertly run strike. In the corners, in the back of the hall, outside of the hall men just milled around, talking, laughing, worrying. For years they had accumulated the steam of repression, and now they were ready to let it loose. They were finally on their own.

Emil Mazey, who chaired the all-night session at which spoke every important union leader (Widman, Reuther, Addes, Thomas, Leonard and many others), remembers that night as "among the most exciting in our whole experience in the labor movement. It was like seeing men who had been half dead come to life. And did they come to life! It was hard to keep things going, hard to organize, so eager were they just to mill around and talk and let some steam go. That night you really understood what the union could mean to men."

The first big test came early the next morning. Harry Bennett had inserted ads in the Detroit papers urging workers to report at the plant "as usual." There were still many hundreds of Negro workers left in the plant who were terrified of both the union and the company, uncertain which way to turn and fearing punishment no matter which way they went.

The Ford plant is like an island surrounded by an ocean of roads. Inside this island Ford Servicemen were concentrated at the gates, ready for action and bristling with arms. For pickets to have approached the gates or to have tried to penetrate beyond the huge walls that surround the plants would have meant exposing themselves to attack by the Servicemen. Instead, the union chose a clever strategy. Barricades of automobiles were set up at all the incoming roads: at Eagle Pass and Wyoming Avenue, at Miller Road and Airport Drive, at Schaefer Road and Dix Road. These barricades prevented anyone from getting in or out of the plant without the pickets' approval. Later they even took control of the Dearborn drawbridge and prevented delivery of supplies by water on the River Rouge. As 6:00 A.M. approached the Servicemen were waiting at the gates of the plant; they waited and waited but nobody came.

An hour later the first fighting broke out. "Iron bolts and nuts flew through the air in a wholesale barrage from the factory roof, while several hundred Negroes with steel bars and knives charged out of the main gate, No. 4, of the Rouge plant in two assaults on the UAW-CIO picket lines there." Thirty-six unionists were hurt and treated at the union's hospital. The pickets had not expected this attack and their lines were broken.

Picket lines were soon re-formed and at 9:00 A.M. another assault took place from within the factory. This time the pickets were ready and slugged it out with baseball bats, fists and sticks. The battle was brief, bloody and decisive for the lines held and, casualties aside, the union had shown it could close the plant. Thousands of automobile workers and curious spectators who drove out to the Ford plant helped choke up the roads. The Servicemen did not move for there were just too many unionists, many of them ex-Ford workers, ready to give as well as take. By now the mood of the strikers had changed from gaiety to grimness. They had watched the Dearborn police stand idly by while their lines were attacked. At a mass meeting on April 2nd, Emil Mazey said that, "If we need a labor holiday to win this strike, we'll have one," which, as everyone understood, meant a general strike in Detroit.

The Ford Company fought hard. It issued statements denouncing the strike as a communist conspiracy. It obtained an injunction ordering the pickets to clear the roads leading to the Rouge plant. It began to organize a back-to-work movement and on the second night of the strike arranged a meeting in Detroit's Negro neighborhood at which Homer Martin, now representing himself as an AFL organizer, urged 3,000 Negroes to "march back in a body." This was more than a "back-to-work" move—it could very likely mean a race riot. And finally, the company demanded that the federal and state governments send troops to Dearborn.

Of all these counter-moves, only the one concerning the Negroes represented an immediately serious threat to the union. A group of Negro leaders mobilized public sentiment in the Negro neighborhoods for the UAW and caused the "back-to-work" movement to collapse. Detroit's AFL unions repudiated Homer Martin as a strikebreaker.

But at the plant the problem of the Negroes remained acute. There were some 800 inside it, some of them Ford workers, and others newly hired Southern Negroes brought up by Harry Bennett. Using loudspeakers, Walter White and other Negro leaders urged the Negroes in the plant to leave, and about a third did. But most stayed in, cowed by the Servicemen. Though their ranks had been augmented by 250 special deputies, most of them Ford Servicemen and gate guards, the Dearborn police did nothing. Finally, with a promise of safe conduct from the UAW in his pocket, federal conciliator James Dewey persuaded the remaining Negroes to leave.

When Michigan Governor Van Wagner proposed a compromise settlement, the UAW quickly accepted, even though the terms were not wholly satisfactory to it. Reluctantly and "with reservations," Ford accepted too. On April 10th the strike ended. The union was still wary since Ford had sent an extraordinary mission to the first peace conference: a group of plant detectives and prize-fighters employed by the Service Department.

In late May an NLRB election was held and the UAW received 58,000 out of 80,000 votes cast. The AFL union, which had suddenly poked its nose in, received about a quarter of the votes and "no union" received less than three percent. Harry Bennett, who felt that he had been betrayed, said the election was "a great victory for the Communist Party, Governor Van Wagner and the National Labor Relations Board."

At this point the Ford Company made the most complete about-face in labor relations in U.S. history. Negotiating with Philip Murray, Harry Bennett agreed to a union shop, dues checkoff, grievance machinery, seniority, time and a half for overtime, premium pay for night workers and two hours' pay for employees called in but not given work. After the agreement was signed, the UAW negotiated wage agreements which gave Ford employees an additional fifty-two million in wages within a year. Why did Ford suddenly shift policy? Was it, as some observers felt, a move dictated by the simple business consideration that it might be cheaper to work with the union than to fight it? Was it a maneuver to gain time for a later fight? Or was it, as Emil Mazey believes, based on the hope that "the company might be able to take over the Ford local from the inside"?

For the entire CIO and for the UAW in particular, the organization of Ford marked the end of a period. The "last citadel of open shopism" had been defeated. As long as Ford remained unorganized, the unions could never feel quite safe. With Ford signed up, the UAW was clearly here to stay.

Ford Local 600 soon became the largest local union in the world, the owner of a building valued at $200,000 and the scene of a turbulent intra-union fight. For a few years it was controlled by pro-Stalinist officials, but since the victory of the Reuther group in the union that is no longer the case.

The decisive footnote to the story of the campaign to organize Ford was provided by an NLRB election in 1948 in which the Ford workers, under the provisions of the Taft-Hartley Act, voted on whether they wanted the union shop to continue. Although the election was held outside the plant and was inconvenient for most Ford workers, their participation was remarkable. Of 98,989 eligible workers, 90,157 cast ballots; 88,943 voted to continue the UAW shop.[4]

Union solidarity did prevail over race prejudice when effective union leadership was available. This was perhaps the most important lesson of events at Ford.

Obscured in the astonishing union triumph over Ford was an important by-product, and a tragic social fact.

Ford Local 600 was a highly valuable training school for Negro militants, who would play an important role in the destiny of the UAW and the political direction of Detroit. Shelton Tappes, the first Negro secretary of the local; Horace Sheffield, the foundry leader; Robert Battle III; Marcellius Ivory; William Oliver; William Hood; James Watts; Frank Edwards; and Tom Wilson—to mention a few names—became important influences in the UAW and Detroit politics. A new kind of Negro leader had emerged, one whose success was due to the success of the union movement.

The sad fact is that union solidarity never went beyond the plant in Dearborn. In 1970 it was still an all-white community and Orville Hubbard, its mayor for twenty years, was still quoted as calling blacks "niggers."[5] Racism proved an insurmountable obstacle for both Henry Ford II—the largest taxpayer in Dearborn—and Walter Reuther, the powerful leader of the UAW, although they were the most enlightened and socially conscious members of "the Establishment" in the Detroit area.

Unionism– A New Foothold for Negroes   6

WITH THE ADVENT of World War II, Adolf Hitler's racist views found an echo in Detroit. Time and again mob attacks were made on black people in an effort "to keep the niggers in their place," that is, out of decent housing and jobs. While public relations campaigns succeeded in portraying Detroit as "the arsenal of democracy" and its output of war goods was huge, the city was also a hotbed of race prejudice and social violence. The power of the Black Legion had collapsed when its leaders were convicted of murder, but its ideology persisted among poor whites and many newcomers to the city. The membership of the Klan had diminished, but its ideas were revived with the influx of whites from the South. Henry Ford's active anti-Semitism was silenced, but its legacy remained.

Economic and social dislocations created by the war were fertile soil for demagogues. It was a time of discontent and anxiety. The most influential exploiter of these sentiments became Father Coughlin, whose earlier manifestations of anti-Semitism had turned into an open defense of Hitler and Hitlerism. Only when he appeared to violate the espionage law about wartime publication was his popular magazine, *Social Justice,* suppressed and his voice silenced by the Catholic hierarchy. However, his views remained influential in many parts of Detroit and its suburbs.

Another demagogue who discovered that Detroit was suitable ground for his right-wing views and avowed racial prejudices was Rev. Gerald L. K. Smith, a Southern Democrat. He became the spokesman for the vast number of young, uprooted, and frustrated Southern workers who had migrated to the auto center. Reverend Smith's views and his formula for handling Negroes were quite popular among Detroit's residents. In his publication, *Cross and Flag,* he wrote:

> I know of no self-respecting person in the city of Detroit who is opposed to Negroes having every modern facility necessary to make them comfortable and to assist them in a desire to be progressive. But most white people will not agree to any of the following suggestions: (1) Intermarriage of blacks and whites; (2) Mixture of blacks and whites in hotels; (3) Mixture of blacks and whites in a restaurant; (4) Inter-relationships between blacks and whites in a school system; (5) Wholesale mixtures of blacks and whites on streetcars and on trains, especially where black men are permitted to sit down and crowd close to white women and vice versa. I have every reason to believe black women resent being crowded by white men on streetcars and elsewhere; (6) Permitting mixtures of blacks and whites in factories, especially where black men are mixed with white women closely and in daily work.[1]

Reverend Smith's objectives clashed basically with the inexorable pressures of a war economy. With car production stopped and gas rationed, it was inevitable that all workers — male and female, white and black — be crowded together in buses. In some cases it was even necessary to allow Negroes to eat in white restaurants. Eventually the companies were forced to hire blacks in large numbers—due to sheer manpower shortages, the pressure of the UAW, and the threat of a black March on Washington. Reverend Smith's activities added havoc to this painful transformation.

Naturally, the anti-black propaganda and discrimination on all economic levels fostered resentment in the Negro community. And the attitude and behavior of Detroit's police did not help matters. Nothing had changed from the 1920's and 1930's. In the ghettos the police were "white cops," and for most Detroit policemen Negroes were still "niggers." One police officer, Lieut. Fred Provinger, expressed without serious rebuke what was a common opinion among his men: "If you lock them up, they just eat free. If you shoot them, they don't have to worry any more."[2]

By June 1941 there had been an immigration of over 350,000 war workers into Detroit, of whom about 50,000 were Negroes. As a consequence, the acute housing shortage became intolerable. The black ghetto was a hellhole of filth, overcrowding, and misery; its inhabitants sarcastically called it "Paradise Valley."

The social dynamite inherent in these crowded conditions seemed obvious to everyone except the city managers. Official city policy was to keep Detroit's population segregated, and the Detroit Housing Commission had declared this publicly. In the minutes of one Housing Commission meeting it was stated that:

> The Detroit Housing Commission will in no way change the racial characteristics of any neighborhood in Detroit through occupancy standards of housing projects under the jurisdiction. The importance of housing war workers is recognized by the Detroit Housing Commission, and every effort will be made to accomplish this task. It is the opinion of the Commission that any attempt to change the racial pattern of any area in Detroit will result in violent opposition to the Housing Program. This could

very easily reach a point where war production efforts of this entire community could be endangered. The Commission therefore reaffirms its policy of respecting neighborhood racial characteristics and will not sanction any deviations from this position that could lead to internal conflict during this war period.[3]

Only one member of the commission rejected this policy —he was Rev. Horace White, a Negro member.

Nor was this policy statement an isolated opinion. Although the Ford Motor Company had announced it would hire 50,000 workers for the new bomber plant at Willow Run, on the outskirts of Detroit, no provision was made for housing the expected flood of workers.

As a matter of fact, seven months after Pearl Harbor, the Ford Motor Company, the Washtenaw County Board of Supervisors, and the real estate interests of Ypsilanti presented testimony opposing government housing for bomber workers before the Truman committee in Washington.[4]

It was as if pressure was deliberately being allowed to build up in Detroit over housing shortages. How much of the opposition to government housing was due to fear of "socialism," how much to fear of blacks, fear of changing neighborhoods and areas, or a desire to prolong the boom in available real estate never was fully assessed, but these elements—plus a lack of concern for social problems—were the determining factors.

Early signs of renewed race troubles were largely ignored in the city, state, and federal governments. On July 5, 1940, the *Detroit Free Press* headlined a story "Police Hurt as Mobs Stone Belle Isle Station." Below, the story read as follows:

A dozen patrolmen and a number of civilians were injured when up to 3,000 Negroes stormed the Belle Isle police station at 7:00 P.M. Thursday and attempted

91

to liberate a youth who had been suspected of stealing a canoe. Rioting continued for more than half an hour, and ten scout cars, four patrol wagons, several cruiser crews were dispatched to the island to augment special holiday forces on duty there.[5]

Ironically, the riot took place on July 4, a date when all Americans ostensibly were celebrating the proclamation of the equality of all men.

Almost every policy on both the local and national levels fueled the anger of the Negro community. The Red Cross called for blood donors and then segregated "black blood" from "white blood." Negro volunteers and enlistees in the armed forces found themselves discriminated against. Conditions were so bad that William H. Hastie, the civilian aid to Secretary of War Henry Stimson, resigned with the charge that the War Department had an anti-Negro bias and that his work there was a travesty.[6]

The four freedoms proclaimed by President Franklin D. Roosevelt were clearly not within the reach of *all* Americans. Although there was a great need for more workers, Negroes still were denied the right to work. The employment record of the auto manufacturers showed how discriminatory their policy had been. In 1941 there were 11,000 Negro workers in the Ford Motor Company, but most of them were restricted to dirty foundry work, general labor, and janitorial assignments. In the spring of 1941, Chrysler hired about 1,850 Negroes, which amounted to 2.5 per cent of its work force in the Detroit area. About 1,400 of these were in the Dodge Motor Division, again mainly in the foundries. A large Packard plant had about 400 Negro workers, while at the Hudson factories there were 225 Negroes out of a total of 12,000 employees. Murray Body Corporation had about 315 Negro workers—about 5 per cent of its total work force. Out of 22,000 employees at Briggs Manufacturing Company, about 7 per cent were Negroes. They were mainly used in the paint shops or as handlers of labor materials.[7]

It took the combined effect of two social movements to change this pattern.

Negro labor leader A. Philip Randolph led a movement for a black march on Washington to force the federal government to act more vigorously; for its policies until then, outlined in Executive Order 8802, had been limited to the establishment of a fair employment practices committee and the prohibition of discrimination in war industries. After a successful conference in Detroit in 1942, Randolph proceeded with his plans, which caused President Roosevelt to issue Executive Order 1098 — a far stronger directive.[8] As a result, over 75,000 Negro men and women were hired in Detroit war plants, as the UAW, the NAACP, and other local groups kept up the pressure on the employers. But integration of black and white in war work didn't come easily.

Typical of the difficulties facing Negroes was the situation in Chrysler's Dodge plant. In August 1941 management decided to transfer workers to the tank arsenal as auto production was phased out. But they would only transfer whites. Indignant workers held a short work stoppage in protest of the company policy—that management and only management would decide who was to be transferred. At the urging of UAW representatives, the blacks returned to work until the matter could be settled in Washington. In the interim, Dodge management continued to transfer whites who had less seniority than Negroes who also wanted the jobs.

When R. J. Thomas, UAW president, and Washington officials met, the company admitted that Negroes had not been transferred, but they placed the blame on local union officials, which was partly true. Finally, over a period of time, blacks obtained work at the Chrysler

93

tank arsenal, but opposition to an integrated work force did not end. On the contrary, it spread to many other plants.[9]

In September 1941, 250 white workers staged a forty-minute sitdown strike at the Packard Motor Company. Afterward two Negroes were transferred to defense work in an all-white department. A similar wildcat strike took place at the Hudson Motor Car Company in January 1942 for roughly the same reasons. In each case the UAW's top leaders did an outstanding job of seeking justice for the Negroes in the face of pressure from anti-Negro elements within the union.

Many white workers made no bones about their antagonism to the Negroes. In a typical interview one of them said:

> About forty percent of the workers here are Polish—there are also a lot of southern whites. Both of them are very prejudiced. The rumor got out not long ago that Negroes were going to start to work in the trim department where I work. Most of the men there are southern whites. They said, "I'll be goddamned if I am going to work with a goddamned black Nigger."[10]

In August 1942, *Life* magazine published an article warning of the dangerous situation in Detroit. The article pointed out:

> Detroit workers seem to hate and suspect their bosses more than ever. Detroit manufacturers have made a failure of labor relations. Too many of the people in Detroit are confused and embittered and distracted by Hitler.[11]

Life declared that the morale in Detroit was the worst in the country and suggested that the city could blow up Hitler or blow up the United States. The response in Detroit was anger at the magazine and approval of Mayor Edward Jeffries, who ridiculed the analysis. The power structure of Detroit preferred to live in its own dream world—not the least of the reasons why it was so stunned by the devastating riot in 1943.

Life's conclusions had been drawn, in part, from the Sojourner Truth riots, which occurred early in, 1942. They were in many respects a preview of events to come.

In September 1941, a housing project intended for Negro occupancy, which had been financed by the federal government under contract to the Detroit Housing Commission, was named Sojourner Truth, in memory of the poet and writer of pre–Civil War days. The whole concept of the project so aroused the passions of white people living on Detroit's east side that Michigan Congressman Rudolph G. Tenerowicz, a Democrat from the first congressional district, began a campaign for a change from black to white occupancy. The buildings for 200 families were completed on December 15, 1941, but remained unoccupied while conflicting political interests pressured Washington for a firm decision. On January 20, 1942, the Detroit Housing Commission was told by federal officials that Sojourner Truth had been designated for white workers.[12]

This reversal of the original decision led to an aggressive campaign by the so-called "Black Cabineteers," who joined forces with the UAW, the Detroit NAACP, and the national Urban League to get the latest decision rescinded. Washington reversed itself again, this time in favor of Negro occupancy.[13]

Meanwhile, in Detroit white racists were picketing City Hall daily, protesting the decision. On the night of February 27, 1942, the evening before the first Negro families were to move in, a KKK cross was burned near Sojourner Truth to the cheers of 150 whites who were picketing the site. By dawn the mob had swelled to 1,200, many of whom were openly armed. On the morning of February 28, the mob intimidated the first Negro tenants, who fled, but shortly thereafter two Negroes tried to go through the picket lines by car.

Soon bricks were flying back and forth as white and black groups lined up on opposite sides of Ryan Road, a street near the project. This skirmish was stopped by sixteen mounted police, but fighting resumed shortly after noon when a truckload of Negro men carrying pipes crossed Ryan Road from the west into Nevada Avenue. Whites bombarded the truck with bricks, and the flare-up ended with the Negroes being placed "under protective custody." At this point authorities decided to postpone moving anyone into the project, whereupon the white mob cheered and attacked the Negroes, who were greatly outnumbered. Mayor Jeffries had stationed 200 police-men in the area, but even with the use of tear gas they were unable to control the situation.[14]

The police bias showed itself in the record of arrests. Out of 104 persons arrested for rioting only two were whites, which caused a group of religious and union leaders to charge the police, in particular the bluecoats from Davidson station, with inciting the fighting in con-spiracy with the KKK.[15]

For three weeks the project remained closed while city officials debated among themselves what they ought to do. Meanwhile, the anti-Negro forces reorganized under the direct leadership of Joseph Buffa, president of the Seven Mile Improvement Association, who on March 10 headed a march of 500 whites on the project until tear gas dispersed his followers. Buffa was taken to jail but released on grounds of insufficient evidence, and the whites renewed their picketing. By refusing to obey any police commands about picketing, the Buffa followers overplayed their hand, and Buffa was arrested again. Sub-sequently he was acquitted.[16]

National indignation at this disgraceful situation

mounted, and Attorney General Francis Biddle announced a federal grand jury investigation. Prominent Catholic and Protestant clergymen, the UAW leadership, the Negro press, and the exigencies of war finally prevailed, and black families occupied the project.

On June 19, 1942, Detroit had another preview of the riot to come. In the suburb of Inkster, which was heavily populated by Negro war workers, an argument between some Negroes and whites turned into a free-for-all. It continued for a few hours, climaxed by the entry of 200 soldiers stationed nearby to aid the white civilians. A heavy force of military police and state troopers finally brought the riot under control.

Two days later, 200 white high school students and some soldiers tried to run 100 Negroes out of the Eastwood Amusement Park, which led to a brawl between Negroes and whites in that area.

Neither the military authorities nor the law enforcement agencies appeared overly concerned about the white mobs. No evidence exists that legal punishment was given the violators of "law and order."

The frustrations in Detroit seemed to increase faster than any measures to alleviate them. On April 11, 1943, over 10,000 unionists and blacks held a protest rally sponsored by the UAW and the NAACP to demand firmer government action and to protest police conduct. Speaking for the UAW, Walter Reuther said that the union would tell any worker who refused to work with another that he could leave the plant, for he didn't belong there.[17]

Regrettably, the UAW policy did not prevent a strike of 25,000 white workers at the Packard plant a few days later. The walkout was in retaliation to a brief shutdown by Negroes over their failure to be promoted. R. J. Thomas, the union president, tried vainly to convince the Packard workers to return to their jobs. He was booed down. Thomas charged that the Klan was behind the strike, for there were many Klan elements in the plant. The UAW and the NAACP specifically charged three management personnel with provoking the strike by urging white workers to hold out in their insistence that blacks not be hired or promoted.[18]

Eventually, the pressure of UAW leadership, the policy of the federal government, and the acquiescence of management overcame the forces opposing an integrated wartime work force in Packard and other plants. Social coercion kept relative peace—or at least a state of truce —in the plants, but also resulted in a transfer of the clashes to a more dangerous and uncontrollable milieu: the city itself.

The police commission noted a big increase in the number of mixed fights; bus drivers and streetcar conductors were reporting an increased number of racial incidents; Detroit was filled with ugly rumors and stories calculated to inflame racial hatred.

The storm signals were either ignored or underestimated.

Then social dynamite exploded.

Wartime Detroit: Racial Tension Explodes

7

NO ONE BLAMED the war for the savage race riot of June 1943, which left thirty-four dead, hundreds injured, millions lost in property damage and man-hours of work, and a city torn apart by ugly conflict. Wasn't the war being fought to eradicate the racist ideology of Hitler and his allies? Yet it was one of the underlying causes.

War provided a climate of violence. It increased the rising expectations of the blacks seeking entry into the mainstream of American life as economic and social equals. And for the more privileged whites, war created new fears of being uprooted, which were aggravated by the demands of the Negroes.

The New Deal had become the war deal. Domestic needs were given less priority than urgent war requirements. The risks inherent in this policy were not unknown to the Roosevelt administration.

Fifteen months before the 1943 riot, the Office of Facts and Figures had submitted a confidential report on Detroit. It warned, "Unless some socially constructive steps are taken shortly, the tension that is developing is very likely to burst into active conflict." The report was suppressed until a day after the riot began, when the *Detroit Free Press* obtained a copy.[1]

Detroit: City of Race and Class Violence

The Wage Earner, the highly respected Detroit newspaper of the Association of Catholic Trade Unionists, said in its June issue, "To tell the truth, there is a growing subterranean race war going on in the city of Detroit which can have no other ultimate result than an explosion of violence, unless something is done to stop it."[2]

Walter White, national director of the NAACP, told a Detroit audience on June 3, "Let us drag out into the open what has been whispered throughout Detroit for months — that a race riot may break out here at any time."[3]

City officials also expected a riot. There had been meetings between police officials and the military to determine what procedures to follow in the event of a serious outbreak requiring federal forces. No thought was given to the genuine alleviation of the causes of social unrest. Even the discussion about procedures was inconclusive and proved to be costly during the riot because of bureaucratic fumbling and time delays in calling out the federal troops.

The only real question facing Detroit, then, was what incident would be the spark to ignite the explosion. It occurred sometime on the afternoon of Sunday, June 20, in Belle Isle. The setting was made to order for trouble.

The day was hot and humid. About 100,000 people, mainly blacks, had crossed the one bridge to the island, or taken the small ferries, to escape the heat in the city. With too many people, slow bus service, not enough picnic tables or recreational facilities, and nerves on edge because of the war, friction was inevitable.

What occurred that day on Belle Isle has never been fully reconstructed, but the main incidents were reported. In that kind of situation, what actually happened was not as significant in exciting people as what they heard or thought happened. The power of rumor is great; people

100

wanted to believe the worst, many did, and they acted accordingly.

There were many complaints that day pouring into the police station on Belle Isle. A Negro boy and a white boy had a fight. Two Negro women charged that they had been molested by a white man and a woman. Two white men and five Negroes had fought over the possession of a picnic oven. There was a fight at the skating pavilion, involving Negroes and whites. A 16-year-old white boy was beaten up. There was friction between whites and Negroes at a bus stop. Negroes claimed they were called "goddam niggers" by police and whites. Whites claimed they were threatened by Negroes. And then there was a fight between a white and a Negro on the Belle Isle bridge leading to the mainland. All these incidents were occurring while hot, tired, and irritable picnickers were trying to leave the island on the narrow bridge in the usual Sunday night traffic jam. The friction soon created a brawl between Negroes and whites, and this turned into a general riot when over 200 sailors from the nearby armory rushed out and joined the whites. For the sailors, this was a culmination of a whole series of brawls with Negroes in recent months.[4]

The action of uniformed men from a branch of the military service notorious for its anti-Negro policies emboldened the whites, whose number grew rapidly. Soon about 5,000 were milling around the Belle Isle bridge area seeking to pick off isolated Negroes. From midnight until 2 A.M. the mob violence continued until an augmented police force arrested some blacks and whites.

By then police seemed to have the situation in the Belle Isle area under control. However, this was just the beginning. For the reports and rumors about the fighting had spread throughout the city. One particularly inflammatory rumor mobilized the Negro community. Shortly

101

after midnight, a Negro jumped on the stage at the Forest Club, a popular Negro hangout about three miles from the Belle Isle bridge, and, passing himself off as a Negro police officer, told the audience of about 700, "There's a riot at Belle Isle—the whites have killed a colored lady and her baby, thrown them over the bridge. Everybody come on, there's free transportation outside." When most of the crowd rushed outside and found that there wasn't any transportation, they took their frustrations out on white motorists driving along Forest Avenue, one of the main crosstown arteries of Detroit.[5]

Later, Police Commissioner John H. Witherspoon would put the blame for the riot on Negroes, ignoring the conduct of the police, the rioting of the white sailors, and the failure of Navy officers to exert any military discipline.

During the night the disorders spread into two other areas. In a sense two different riots developed, each handled somewhat differently by the police. Hastings Street, in the middle of Paradise Valley, contained a number of small businesses operated by whites, mainly Jewish merchants. Negroes stoned, burned, and destroyed these shops; soon all white businesses in the ghetto were gutted. To control the riot police poured in heavy reinforcements, among them a lieutenant whose inflammatory remarks had earlier incensed the Negro community. The hatred between the police and the blacks was visible everywhere. Seventeen blacks were killed by police during the riots but not a single white man, although the black rioters numbered in the hundreds, while the whites were in the thousands. Dozens of Negroes were beaten up for no reason whatsoever, and hundreds were injured.

The ferocity of the police in the ghetto was not evident in their handling of the white mobs, which were increasing in size through the night and milling around Woodward Avenue—a main street on the edge of the ghetto. The first black victims were moviegoers coming out of a late show. They claimed that the police gave them little protection while the whites worked them over. The lust for victims grew with success and was inflamed, as usual, by rumors, particularly the one that Negroes had killed 17 whites overnight in Paradise Valley.

On Monday morning downtown Detroit was out of control—or at least the police weren't trying to control it —as thousands of whites roamed the streets looking for victims. The country got some idea of how Detroit was behaving when newspapers printed a photograph of a Negro World War I veteran being held by police while a white man hit him. City officials and military liaison men saw a white mob chasing a Negro down the street, while a discussion was taking place on how and when to bring in the military.

Mayor Jeffries deluded himself for a while that the situation might be brought under control. Early that morning he refused a request from Negro leaders that federal troops be called in. But when the number of whites increased by thousands—at one point the mayor estimated 100,000 were on the streets—he reversed himself and called Governor Harry F. Kelly to urge army help.

It was a day of infamy for the city, with lynch spirit running high. Malcolm Bingay, the popular conservative writer for the *Detroit Free Press,* compared the horror to that of a near-riot he had once seen in Atlanta, Georgia. "I thought that I had witnessed an experience peculiar to the Deep South. But many years later I was to learn differently. On the streets of Detroit I saw again the same horrible exhibition of uninhibited hate as they fought and killed one another—white against black—in a frenzy of homicidal mania, without rhyme or reason. Their faces were all the same, their lips drawn back, their teeth bared like fangs, their eyes glazed—bestial faces bereft of all human expression."[6]

What thousands of whites had talked about or muttered in the shops and in their neighborhoods, "We got to put the niggers in their place," they now attempted. City officials and Mayor Jeffries, who had believed that it was simply a matter of restoring law and order in the black community, looked on helplessly as the mobs raged up and down the streets seeking their prey.

Could the riot have been prevented? The Detroit chapter of the NAACP said yes. "There is overwhelming evidence that the riot could have been stopped at its inception Sunday night had the police wanted to stop it. So inefficient is the police force, so many of its members are from the deep south, with all their anti-Negro prejudices and Klan sympathies, that trouble may break out again as soon as the troops leave."[7]

Why, one might ask, should the police want to stop it? Even the police commissioner said the Negro had an antagonistic attitude toward the police officer. Perhaps this way the blacks would learn the need for police. And with a police officer who believed the Old South's philosophy that "the only good nigger is a dead one," directing some of the forces in the ghetto, why should the police not use the opportunity to put "them" in their place?[8] How many blacks were beaten up that day, not only by whites but by the police, before and after arrest, was never estimated. But the emergency wards of the hospitals told the story.

For the Negro people, two incidents relating to police conduct were seared in their minds. As the white mobs roamed through downtown Detroit all day Monday, growing larger in the evening, some of the Negro residents of the nearby Fraser Hotel armed themselves. The following is a cautious account of the affair by the *Detroit News:*

> One of the most serious of the shootings was at the Fraser Hotel, Vernor Highway and Brush Street. Patrolman Lawrence Adams of the Accident Prevention Bureau was shot in the back and wounded seriously when he and Patrolman Howard Wixcom's squad car answered a riot call. A Negro fired on him as he was getting out of the APB car. This was shortly after darkness. Adams' assailant was shot and killed. A dozen more patrolmen arrived. Shots rang out from a dozen windows of the hotel, and the bullets began peppering the streets where the officer stood. The police returned the fire, blazing away at windows in which partly concealed figures could be discerned. Tear gas bombs were hurled. A block away, at Vernor Highway and John R. Street, sniping began, with bullets coming from a three story multiple dwelling. Officers poured round after round of bullets into the building. They fired more tear gas projectiles. Screams, smoke and occasional rifle fire presented a scene of din and confusion. Nearly 1,000 spectators gathered and were dispersed with difficulty. When firing from the building ceased, officers wearing white outfits and Civilian Defense helmets entered with drawn pistols. The lights of the bordering structures began to be extinguished, and finally they were in total darkness. Dozens of Negroes were hustled off to jails and hospitals.[9]

It was later revealed that the residents had been pistol-whipped and clubbed without mercy.

The other unforgettable incident occurred at the St. Antoine YMCA. There are two versions of this affair. One is called the white version, and the other the Negro version. Each really speaks for itself. The white version *(Detroit News)* is as follows:

> Julian Witherspoon, Negro, was wounded in the back by Theodore Anderson, of the State Troops, in the St. Antoine YMCA. Anderson and three policemen stopped

3 Negroes in an automobile at 11:00 P.M. to question them about the curfew violation. Anderson said that Witherspoon watching from the sidewalk began yelling "Heil Hitler." Anderson walked over and questioned Witherspoon. Witherspoon made a move toward his pocket, Anderson said. Anderson fired as Witherspoon reached the door of the YMCA.[10]

The Negro version *(Racial Digest)* reads:

At 8:00 P.M. several men were playing softball on the sidewalk in front of the St. Antoine YMCA. As the police passed, one of the boys was told to get his goddamned ass off the streets. "We don't give a goddamn who we shoot tonight," the policeman said. An attendant saw Julian Witherspoon enter the YMCA door. An officer jumped out of a State car, ran toward the YMCA door, raised his gun, and shot through the glass in the door, hitting Witherspoon. He is reported by the police as having said, "Heil Hitler," to them. Witherspoon staggered up the steps and fell in the lobby. The officers lined up the other men including the desk clerk, with their faces toward the wall, after clubbing and beating them. The police searched desk drawers, and locker doors. They threw out NAACP literature saying, "Here's something to read," as if in fun. David Morgan, one of the men, looked around; an officer walked over and asked him, "What in the goddam hell are you looking at?", and slapped him. The officers called the men "black bastards, apes, sons of bitches." George Reams (?) who had come from downstairs from his room upon hearing the commotion was also lined up against the wall. He remarked, "Shame we law-abiding citizens have to be treated like Fascists." The officer struck him with his club. A Sheaffer fountain pen was taken from one of them. Before searching the men, an officer said, "Shoot any of them that moves, because we have plenty of bullets left, and you'll get the same thing as your buddy." The officers did not find as much as a pen knife, or anything else on the men. One trooper asked: "Is he (Witherspoon) dead yet?" The reply was no. One officer walked over toward him and said to his companion, "Don't forget to say he pulled a gun." There was no attempt made to get medical aid to Witherspoon, until five minutes before the officers left. He was on the floor for 40 minutes.[11]

Thurgood Marshall, then chief NAACP counsel, collected many affidavits concerning police brutality. Church and civic groups also protested police conduct during the riot. But such groups would be accused of being biased.

However, one witness to the events was an unimpeachable source of information. He was Brigadier General William E. Guthner, a former police chief of Denver, and, during the Detroit riots, the army officer in charge of the federal troops. He was so disturbed by the behavior of the Detroit police that he complained.

> They've been very handy with their guns and clubs and have been very harsh and brutal. I asked both State Police Commissioner Olander and Police Commissioner Witherspoon if they didn't think it was time to admonish their men to ease off and make their job better. They have treated the Negroes terrible up here, and I think they have gone altogether too far. That kind of treatment will keep this thing going longer than if they get back to normal. If they want everybody else to get back to normal, the police will have to get back to normal themselves.[12]

The violence at the St. Antoine YMCA occurred after federal troops had taken over the city and Detroit's police were able to concentrate on "curfew violators," especially in the ghetto. Backed by federal troops the police could afford to be less restrained and responsible, and this apparently was witnessed by General Guthner.

Nor were those higher up free from blame. By dillydallying for fifteen hours before formally requesting the army, Mayor Jeffries and Governor Harry Kelly shared some of the responsibility for the situation first getting out of hand. When the troops arrived late Monday night it took them only one half hour to clear the streets without firing a shot. And this was against rioters armed with clubs, bricks, stones, and other missiles, who were intent on a pogrom of the black ghetto. The military police battalion used tear gas and rifle butts against the stone-throwing rioters, who gave way completely.

Bloody Monday was a day of hysteria even for whites and blacks not involved in the actual events. Harold True, a popular radio newscaster, frightened Detroit with the report that state police had been warned to watch out for carloads of armed Negroes coming to Detroit from Chicago. This inflammatory newscast was completely false. Stores, factories, and businesses were closed. In the ghetto there was heightened fear of the police, running amuck in the guise of law and order. The Tuesday night shooting at St. Antoine's YMCA was an example to the Negroes of what to expect.

By Wednesday, army intervention had reduced the violence to a simmering point, with only minor skirmishes by young gangs. "There is a bitter feeling between Negroes and the young hoodlum element of the Polish population in Detroit," General Guthner reported. "This element on several occasions razzed federal troops on patrol for intervening in the riot, and have called the patroling troops 'nigger-lovers.' "[13]

Within a week, the city was back to its wartime pattern of life, but the racial wounds were open and raw.

Aside from the handful of Negro leaders, the only social authority or institution in the Detroit area that offered a sensible program to stop the bloodshed and create some measure of social stability was the United Autoworkers Union. At a Monday noon meeting of the Detroit Citizens Committee, headed by Mayor Jeffries, the union's president, R. J. Thomas made a blistering attack on the failures of the city and police officials, and the UAW supported the demand of some Negro leaders for the declaration of martial law. The union also called a citywide meeting of all its plant leaders to coordinate efforts to quiet the situation down and keep peace in the factories. It became a matter of record that no brawls occurred in any auto plant during that turbulent week, a situation assisted, no doubt, by the absence of between 50 and 80 per cent of all Negro workers, and half the whites.

On Wednesday, on behalf of the union Thomas issued an eight-point program to forestall future riots. He called for:

(1) a special grand jury to investigate causes, (2) adequate park and recreational facilities, (3) new housing plans for Negro slums, (4) effective curbs on racial intolerance and discrimination in industrial relations, (5) investigation of why more drastic action to subdue the mobs had not been taken earlier, (6) impartial justice to the rioters, regardless of color, (7) restitution of losses to innocent sufferers from the reign of terror and (8) creation by the mayor of a special bi-racial committee of ten to make further recommendations looking towards elimination of racial differences and friction.

Thomas made a special point of the need for a concentrated campaign on the high school level, since Detroit's schools had permitted racial hatred "to grow and thrive" in recent years."[14]

The *Detroit Free Press* endorsed the proposals, but they died an early death. The last thing in the world city or state officials or the police wanted was a grand jury investigation. Imagine the impact of the testimony of General Guthner, to name only one.

Perhaps some valuable lessons might have been learned from Detroit's race riot if the UAW's demand for a grand jury investigation had been accepted. Instead, subsequent reports—all of them crudely biased—served only to confirm the worst fears and prejudices of Detroit's vast white majority. The conclusion, stated politely, was that the riot was the Negroes' fault. Or, as many whites would have put it, "The niggers caused the trouble, and deserved what they got."

Even before a self-serving fact-finding committee was appointed by Governor Kelly to analyze the riot, one of the committee members, County Prosecutor William E. Dowling, blamed the Negro press and the NAACP as the principal instigators. Dowling said, "I do charge, and so I told the committee, that the Negro Press and Martin of the *Detroit Tribune,* Louis E. Martin, Editor of the *Michigan Chronicle* and J. Edward McCall, Editor of the *Detroit Tribune* have fomented dissension. I do charge Martin of the *Tribune* with being the principal instigator of dissension in this area." As for the NAACP, the prosecutor said, "They have been fomenting trouble with their crusades in the Negro neighborhoods from the start. If they want to do something constructive they might try to control the Negro Press."[15] Police Commissioner Witherspoon supported the prosecutor's statement. And yet these two individuals were placed on a fact-finding committee by Governor Kelly. The governor's committee, which also included State Attorney General Herbert J. Thrushton and State Police Commissioner Oscar Olander continued to put the blame on the Negroes. It attributed race tensions particularly to "the positive exhortation of many Negro leaders to be militant in the struggle for racial equality." The report added:

> Such appeals have been unfortunately made commonplace in the Negro newspapers. Can it be doubted that they played an important part in exciting the Negro people to the violence which resulted in Detroit on June 21? A theme repeatedly emphasized by these Negro newspapers is that the struggle for Negro equality at home is an integral part of the present world-wide struggle for Democracy. These papers loudly proclaimed that a victory over the axis will be meaningless unless there is a

corresponding overthrow in the country of the forces which these papers charge prevent true racial equality.[16]

For good measure, Mayor Jeffries added, "I would say that the Fact Finding Committee's Report is a good report."[17] In an effort to offset these biased findings, City Councilman George Edwards, who later became Police Commissioner and now serves as a Federal Court of Appeals Judge, again demanded a grand jury investigation, especially since there were still twelve unsolved murders—but to no avail.

The *Detroit Free Press* branded the Governor's Committee Report a "whitewash," and noted that "it was largely drawn up by Police Commissioner Witherspoon, the apple-cheeked boy scout Mayor Jeffries placed in charge of the police department. . . . With Commissioner Witherspoon furnishing most of the evidence it is hardly conceivable that he would suggest an investigation of himself and his department."[18]

The tragedy for Detroit was that most whites were more than willing to believe the report. The police remained immune to any probe of their harsh tactics, while the white mobs, with minor exceptions, had done their damage to people and property with virtual impunity.

The Negro reaction to the riot was bitter. "We better be frank about this," declared Martin, the editor of the *Michigan Chronicle*. "The race riot and all that has gone before have made my people more nationalistic and more chauvinistic and anti-white than ever before. Even those of us who were half liberal and were willing to believe in the possibilities of improving race relations have begun to have doubts—and worse, they have given up hope."[19]

However, that viewpoint neglected another development which had taken place in the struggle for equality. If the war could be blamed as the catalyst of the riots, it had also made possible the first significant economic breakthrough for 75,000 blacks who, due to urgent manpower needs, did get war jobs. Because of the protection of union seniority clauses they kept most of those jobs after reconversion to a peacetime economy, and integration at the work place began. The economic, political, and social power of the growing black minority in Detroit was not to be denied, and it was backed by a union movement and its own organizations. In that sense, the anti-Negro elements had won only a Pyrrhic victory in the riot.

Detroit underestimated the strength of the Negro's drive to achieve a decent life as an equal human being. Outside of a brilliant short study by two Wayne State University sociologists, no serious effort was made to understand the total nature of the riot. The politicized UAW leaders, some Negro spokesmen, and a few churchmen were the only people who grasped the full impact of that disastrous week in Detroit. It did seem to indicate, however, that, except in times of deep economic crisis, race differences influenced men's actions far more than class attitudes.

McCarthyism and   8
Vigilante Democracy,
Detroit Style

THE END OF World War II did not bring social stability to Detroit any more than it brought peace to
the world. Racial friction persisted, although it was submerged during the wave of postwar strikes which kept the
city in a state of turmoil until the Korean war.

For Negroes the postwar period was a decade of resistance; a continual struggle against discrimination in
employment, in housing, in the use of public facilities, in
treatment by the police.

And for all workers it was a period of economic uncertainty. Many suffered from a "depression psychosis," as
each postwar recession (there were four up to 1960) reminded them of the Great Depression of the 1930's.
Chronic unemployment plagued the unskilled, the dis-
carded, and the black workers.

In the early postwar period, Detroit became a battleground on which the big three auto companies—General
Motors, Ford, and Chrysler—encountered the auto workers' union. The 113-day General Motors strike in the winter of 1945–1946 aggravated the many reconversion
problems. The verbal cross fire suggested a reversion to
the class conflicts of the 1930's. The frustrations of wage
and price controls, and of abiding by an unpopular no-

strike pledge, had raised auto workers' tempers to a boiling point. In many cases, a healthy accumulation of reserve funds, due to wartime overtime, restricted buying, and the growth of two-income families, provided a financial backstop for any strike action.

The auto workers were fed up with the status quo, and no man understood this better than Walter Reuther, director of the UAW's General Motors department. He had solid backing in his campaign for higher wages without price increases through strike action.

Even though a Truman fact-finding board agreed with Reuther's contention, General Motors remained unconvinced, and Reuther had to settle for an 18½-cent hourly pay increase, along with other concessions. General Motors raised its prices. Ford and Chrysler had already signed similar contracts. The strike propelled Reuther to national prominence and was a major factor in winning him the presidency of the union.[1]

His opposition caucus, in which Communist party stalwarts had played an influential role as "braintrusters" and "vote getters," collapsed after an intense factional struggle within the union. Reuther's aggressive tactics and his flair for leadership were unbeatable, and the Communist influence was reduced to almost zero with changes in party policy and the ousting of Earl Browder as its leader.[2] The Reuther forces assumed complete control of the Wayne County CIO organization, which became an important base for political activities in the city and state.

In the excitement generated by Reuther's triumphs, a profoundly significant change in the labor climate of Detroit—and in the labor-management relations of the auto industry — was largely overlooked. The 113-day auto strike was entirely peaceful, in marked contrast to those of the 1930's or the post–World War I strikes. The UAW had a basic strength which the industry recognized and which led the big three finally to accept the idea of union-ism—thus setting a pattern that was followed by other mass-production industries like steel, rubber, and mining.

The UAW as an American institution was here to stay; its finances were collected by the auto industry through check-off arrangements and its security assured by the gradual inclusion of union shop clauses. (General Motors alone collected over $203 million for the UAW from 1948 through 1964.) The influence of the union soon extended to all spheres of activity in both the city and the state.

The three-week Chrysler strike in 1948 and the one at Ford in 1949 reflected management's new philosophy. The acrimony at the bargaining table occurred within the framework of a belief in mutual accommodation. Even the prolonged Chrysler pension strike in 1950, which lasted 103 days, did not change the pattern. Picket lines were small—really symbolic—during this peaceful strike. Class war had been turned into a truce through negotiation. This general understanding was formalized in 1950 when General Motors proposed, and the UAW accepted, a five-year contract. Two innovations introduced by General Motors added a new dimension to collective bargaining. First, under an "annual improvement factor clause," it was stipulated that labor would get annual wage increases with higher productivity, and this idea was adopted in other industries. Second, to counteract labor's dissatisfaction at rising prices, GM gave its employees protection against inflation through the so-called escalator clause, which automatically gave pay increases as the cost of living went up.[3]

The national impact of these innovations, the postwar strikes, and Reuther's political triumphs in the union obscured the limitations of unionism in a city wrestling with racial problems and other social ills. Yet Detroit had constant reminders that life was still in many respects a jungle existence. On April 20, 1948, a would-be assassin shot and almost killed Walter Reuther at his home. A year later Victor Reuther was the victim of a second unsuccessful murder attempt.

From this violent environment another labor leader emerged to become a powerful influence in Detroit and the nation. He was James H. Hoffa of the teamsters, who not only survived in the jungle of Detroit, but with his enormous talents and keen mind seemed to thrive on it. Hoffa's eventual tragedy was his inability to adapt to a changing society, and to develop a more sophisticated manner of operations acceptable to that society. But until his imprisonment at the pinnacle of power, Hoffa had enormous economic and political influence in Detroit.

Hoffa's recollections about Detroit's police in the 1930's remained pertinent in the postwar decade, for their methods of conduct against underdogs had not really changed. "The police were of no help. The police would beat your brains in for even talking union. The cops harassed us every day. If you went on strike, you got your head broken. The whole thing didn't take months. It took years," he commented, in explaining how in one strike in 1939 he was jailed 18 times in a 24-hour period.[4]

Detroit was given an embarrassing reminder of how extensive and brutal the jungle warfare against unionism had been when the Kefauver hearings took place in 1951. This is how it was described in *Labor Action*.

DETROIT, Feb. 11—For two days last week, thousands of people here sat glued before their TV sets at home or jammed the saloons and bars in what was described as "world series crowds" to watch a sensational drama of real life that surpassed the imagination of any Hollywood racket story.

How could the show miss? Its cast included top auto industry executives and their silent partners, the racket bosses of Detroit. Its director was the Kefauver Senate Crime Investigating Committee. Scheduled for three days, the public hearing was called off after two days. But the damage was done, and the subsequent developments have left many embarrassing questions unanswered.

What began as an investigation of "rackets" in Detroit touched the most sensitive spot in the sanctimonious air of respectability of business and industry here: the not-so-strange alliance of the underworld czars and major segments of the auto and business world, with the union movement as the victim.

For a long time, the smug apology in Detroit over the well-known links between the mobsters and the Ford Motor Company of the days of Henry Ford and Harry Bennett consisted of saying, "Well, the new Ford regime eliminated Bennett, and it's all past history."

But the public hearing showed that the big-time racketeers, like Joe Adonis and the man described by the Senate committee as the head of the Mafia gang in Detroit, D'Anna, still hold lucrative contracts with Ford!

Harry Bennett's performance before the committee, with excellent closeups over TV, simply served to increase suspicions, for his blank unwillingness to testify on important questions confirmed every question asked him.

He had no recollection of how these racketeers received their very profitable contracts—Adonis for his exclusive conveying business in the East and D'Anna for his Ford agency. Bennett denied it had anything to do with "labor troubles," and as for the gangsters on the payroll, it was just a "rehabilitation" program.

When asked to name some of the key figures in Detroit's gangland, Bennett declared heatedly, "What do you want me to do? Get my head blown off?" The amazing thing is that the committee did not see fit to take up this remarkable statement. Is Bennett on the spot if he tells what he knows? Whose power is so great that Bennett fears it?

Who Paid for the Briggs Job?

The Kefauver committee did not go as deeply into the Ford setup as does Keith Sward in his brilliant and monumental work, *The Legend of Henry Ford,* for Sward adds more names, from major political figures in Michigan to the top racketeers, in developing the theme that the connection was based on the idea that Ford would get protection against unionism in return for major concessions to and protection for the racketeers.

Nor did the Kefauver committee dig into the interesting question of how the former FBI chief in Detroit, whose knowledge of gangsterism would naturally be pretty complete, has become a major figure at Ford, replacing none other than Harry Bennett. We refer, of course, to John Bugas.

But the Ford story is not a new cue. What is "new" is that the story remains the same today. And the Ford Motor Company is not the only concern embarrassed by its close links—on a business basis, to be sure—with top racketeer elements.

For the truly sensational story of the Briggs Manufacturing Company's "business deals" with strikebreaking racketeers—deals that are still going on—was the highlight of the hearings.

And the mystery of who beat up six prominent Briggs Local 212 leaders since 1945 doesn't seem like much of a mystery any more. What is curious is why there have been no arrests of company officials and racketeers. More exactly, why a special so-called "labor rackets" grand jury failed to return indictments in 1947.

Ken Morris, president of Briggs 212, was nearly killed in 1945. Genora and Sol Dollinger were brutally assaulted. Art Vega was nearly killed. So were others. Who was behind these murderous assaults? Who paid for the jobs?

To understand the whole picture it is necessary to go back to 1934, when a strike at the Michigan Stove Company on East Jefferson Avenue was broken. It employs around 1,000 persons. As the Kefauver committee pierced the fog of ambiguous answers from reluctant witnesses, a 16-year record of violent anti-unionism revealed the following:

Sicilians were illegally smuggled from Canada and hired by the company as virtual slaves of one Sam Perone, a man with a criminal record. The whole plant consisted of relatives or people from the same community in Sicily. This element acted as strikebreakers in 1934 and established its power.

When Perone was convicted of a federal offense, the CIO got a foothold. Then in 1943 Perone busted up another strike. CIO organizers always got the rough treatment there, and even today the place is not organized!

Perone's connection with the company was established when he applied for a trucking license. His application had the following endorsement from John A. Frey, president of the Michigan Stove Company and prominent Detroit business leader:

"Mr. Frey endorses this application because he is indebted to Ispano Perone for helping the company break the strike in 1943, in April."

Perone was one of the characters who fascinated TV audiences. He disclaimed any ability to read or write. He simply couldn't remember answers to anything. He was just a poor honest man, with a magnificent home in Grosse Pointe, and a salary of $50,000 from a concession on scrap metal he had with the Michigan Stove Company.

John Frey, president of the company, suffered from memory lapses too, and his evasions and squirmings made juicy drama over TV. The sarcastic committee lawyers had a field day with him.

"How did you happen to give a day laborer, who could neither read nor write, a business contract that furnishes him $50,000 a year salary?" a committee lawyer asked. "Just a business deal that looked good at the time," Frey replied.

Is it a wonder that Detroit was agog at these hearings?

But this turned out to be just small stuff, somewhat bizarre but only a prelude to the next aspect of the hearings. This concerned the Briggs Manufacturing Company, one of Detroit's major supply companies. It was a follow-up to the Perone story.

For it seems that Perone's son-in-law obtained an exclusive contract with Briggs to handle its $1,000,000-a-year scrap-metal business! How did this happen? What did it mean?

W. Dean Robinson, president of Briggs, explained it merely as a business deal about which he knew very few details.

To refresh Robinson's memory, the Kefauver committee read him excerpts from his testimony before a secret one-man Grand Jury hearing, headed by Judge George T. Murphy. It seems that Robinson at that time knew some of the details.

But what exploded the hearing was the action of Judge Murphy, who decided to make public the 28 bound volumes of testimony around the very delicate subject of Briggs contracts and Briggs beatings.

Here is what it said, in summary form:

(1) Top Briggs management forced through the contract, over the objections of subordinates who were suspicious of the beneficiary, Renda, and his hoodlum father-in-law.

(2) By simply asking for it, Renda got the contract— though he was only about 26, a $1.50-an-hour factory worker, without capital, equipment, trucks, experience, or even a telephone— "a man who didn't have one thing to recommend him except he is the son-in-law of Sam Perone."

(3) In return, Renda offered the Briggs Company protection against strikes which had plagued its plants—and these strikes dropped sharply after the Renda association began in April 1945.

(Emil Mazey, UAW-CIO secretary-treasurer, testified that the contract was a payoff for the murderous beatings.)

"MY STORY MAY SOUND FISHY . . ."

(4) The company lost more than $14,000 a month on the contract for many months.

(5) Henry J. Roesch, former industrial relations director for Briggs, called the contract a company attempt to buy industrial peace.

(6) Walter Briggs, Jr., executive vice-president, said there was no connection between the contract and the terrorizing of unionists.

(7) W. Dean Robinson, Briggs president, said that though the Briggs-Renda relationship "does seem strange," the company made no effort to sever it.

(8) A Briggs official who opposed the contract and went to the FBI about the "Renda plot" was fired by the company!

In these days when Senator McCarthy can ruin people by mere accusations, without any proof whatsoever, it is something more than insidious that no indictments were returned in the Briggs beatings, after all this testimony!

Why didn't the Kefauver committee call the victims of the beatings to give their views? Genora Dollinger could certainly tell the committee an earful.

W. Dean Robinson, son-in-law of Walter Briggs Sr., was allowed to testify. His answers convicted him, for he used the evasive tactics employed by the racketeers in reply to questions.

And for sheer understatement that brought howls and jeers from TV audiences, Robinson's remark "My story may sound fishy but it's true" took the prize. As president of a major company he couldn't remember how or why the company gave a contract that cost them so much money to a man who knew nothing about the business and couldn't handle it. Actually, it turned out that a regular scrap iron company did the work, but nonetheless, Briggs paid Renda, as though he were in charge. Thus the $14,000-a-month loss!

"WHO, ME? I DON'T REMEMBER . . ."

Between these major hearings, the committee paraded before it all of Detroit's top racket bosses, Pete Licavoli, Mike Rubino, William Tocco, Louis Riccardi, Angelo Meli, and others. In each case, a neat bit of irony was furnished by the revelation that these men, as well as Perone, own palatial residences in the snooty Grosse Pointe area, where the auto tycoons and Detroit business executives live.

How these men obtained control of major laundry companies and other service businesses was not completely brought out. But that they did control them was indisputable. How one racketeer loaned a steel company $100,000 cash was told on the stand.

121

For sheer entertainment it would be difficult to compete with the picture of these men seeking to cover themselves and the men behind them, during these hearings.

Riccardi, for example, was a typical witness: "I'm just an ordinary man, making a living. I have no record." He couldn't recall five arrests on murder charges. "Who, me? I don't remember, but if you say so, maybe I was."

"What do you do at the Kleen Linen Company?"

"Oh, I just work there."

"You make a living?"

"Just a living."

"Do you call $60,000-a-year salary just a living?"

And later: "How is business?"

"Just fair."

"Do you call $500,000-a-year business just fair?"

Of course, everyone in Detroit laughed. It was a funny show. But it took on a different character when John Frey and Dean Robinson, two of Detroit's important industrial figures, looked just as ridiculous with their evasive testimony.

The whole story of the tie-up between industry and racketeers as an alliance against the union movement hasn't been told. It should include a far more thorough investigation of the Reuther brothers' shooting. For no longer is Detroit a city of incredulous people, who think that Hollywood exaggerates its plots in gangster stories. The two-day TV view of the real Detroit which its residents saw has shaken much of the smugness.

The Kefauver hearings just touched on the delicate and acute problem of organized rackets in the shops. A Ford official testified that the company was helpless against them. He said the UAW top officials were strongly against rackets, but that some men in the union worked with bookies and numbers men.

Almost buried during the hearings was the testimony of a jukebox operator who described how the business agent of an AFL union, affiliated to the Teamsters Joint Council, quit as president of a million-dollar-a-year jukebox company to take a job as business agent because there wasn't enough money in his job as president.

Surely, a joint AFL and CIO investigating committee

should take up where the Kefauver committee left off. For the story of the dialogue between business and the racketeers has just begun. Its effect on the union movement and its anti-union significance requires far more attention to this problem than the union movement has given it.[5]

In the 1950's labor had become too strong for that kind of intimidation by industry. The brutal side of life in the city was in the black ghetto—continuously harassed by the police.

When a fifteen-year-old high school student, Leon Mosely, was shot and killed by police in June 1948, over 3,000 Negroes rallied at his funeral and then marched downtown in protest. It was the fourth such death in a year. The police were operating under a "shoot to kill" policy handed down by Police Commissioner Harry S. Toy.

In the Mosely death, the evidence was too strong for a cover-up about "resisting arrest" or "trying to escape." Witnesses told a special investigative panel that Mosely was beaten up, and then killed as he staggered down the street. An autopsy showed a skull fracture and other injuries. Two policemen were suspended, and one was charged with manslaughter, but a jury found him not guilty.[6]

Early in August, James Chichocki, a UAW local union president, stopped his car and implored police not to beat up a Negro youth they had handcuffed and bound. They were using clubs and a flashlight on the youth. Chichocki was arrested for "resisting an officer."[7]

Negroes were fair game for white mobs too. On September 13, 1948, hundreds of white racists milled around two homes on Harrison Avenue purchased by Negroes. In spite of the property damage there were only three arrests, and the prosecutors' office changed the charge from "inciting to riot" to a misdemeanor, "disturbing the peace." Only after the Negro press broke the story did Detroit's papers inform their readers what was going on in the city, and this was a commonplace occurrence.

In spite of all these obstacles, the Negroes of Detroit persisted in their struggle to achieve some degree of equality. As a result of campaigns by the NAACP under the direction of Herbert Hill, and the efforts of UAW local union leaders, restaurants and hotels were increasingly forced to serve black people.

By 1950 Detroit again faced a potential racial crisis. In this instance the tension was created by the housing shortage and the persistent attempts of blacks to break out of the Paradise Valley ghetto. A proposal for a cooperative housing project to be occupied by 54 families, three of whom would be black, precipitated the crisis. The public hearing by Common Council to reconsider the issue drew a violently partisan audience of 500 persons, most of them opposed to integrated housing, especially since the site was northwest Detroit—a white stronghold. Neither Victor Reuther of the UAW, Frank X. Martel of the AFL, nor church leaders could get a decent hearing at the scene.

The black community was outraged by the failure of the Detroit Housing Commission to act decisively in these matters. Nor was its anger diminished when Mayor Albert Cobo fired Rev. Robert L. Bradley, Jr., a prominent black minister, for stating this publicly.

The background of the crisis was outlined by W. George Schermer, director of the city's Interracial Committee. (He resigned his post soon afterward.)

(1) The Negro population is now near 300,000, having doubled in the past ten years.

(2) This population was terribly crowded into existing Negro communities during the war years, with only

small expansion at the edges and with a small fraction accommodated in temporary war housing.

(3) During and since the war Negro buying power has been increased, even though the patterns of racial discrimination in employment change very slowly.

(4) The increased purchasing power has made itself felt on the housing market.

(5) Most of this is being expressed in older sections of Detroit where population shifts are becoming very noticeable. However, a considerable number of Negroes are trying to get newer, better-quality homes in outlying areas.

(6) The trend of the federal courts and agencies to limit racial discrimination has intensified the drive of Negroes for decent homes.[8]

Adding to the tension in the community was the whites' frustration over the headway being made by Negroes in the auto plants—an area over which racists had little control. The hope of many white workers that after the war "we'll get rid of the niggers" proved illusory, thanks to the functioning of the UAW.

On V-E day in 1945, the main plants of the auto industry had about 75,000 black workers including a large number of women. The number of black women employed by Chrysler, for example, went from zero at the beginning of the war to about 5,000 in April 1945. However, during the transition from war- to peacetime production, the women were largely ignored. In a most flagrant case at Dodge Truck, 31 Negro women were just laid off, without regard to contract rights.

When Art Hughes, president of Dodge Truck Local 140, insisted on their being retired, company officials used trumped-up excuses to eliminate the women: difficult jobs, no breaking-in period, etc. They were finally sent home under a "no work available" argument.

However, the union had an important asset in the bargaining over this issue. The UAW's standard contract clause banning discrimination read, "The Company agrees that it will not discriminate against any applicant for employment, promotion, transfer, lay-off, discipline, discharge or otherwise because of race, creed, color, national origin, political affiliation, sex or marital status." When the union's grievance was heard by David Wolff, the permanent arbitrator for Chrysler and the UAW, he ruled in favor of the women and ordered Chrysler to provide $55,000 in back wages. The UAW had also established a Fair Employment Practices Department to keep an eye on such shenanigans on the part of management.

Nor did numerous wildcat strikes succeed in stopping the promotion or introduction of black workers into all jobs and areas within the plants—the exception being the skilled trades, where no real progress in breaking down discrimination was made for twenty years. Once again the white racists tended to take out their frustrations on the Negro community.

Under UAW pressure, the auto companies finally began to penalize wildcatters who refused to work with Negroes, but in some cases it wasn't easy, as lower echelon management often shared the workers' anti-black feelings.

A typical situation occurred in a metal shop employing 2,000 men, half of whom were Southern workers, the rest Polish or Italian. Under the union contract, the expansion of seniority rights gave Negroes a chance to apply for metal finishing work, attractive because it paid 15 cents an hour more than assembly jobs. The whites refused to break in the Negroes, and walked out. In a raucous union meeting the issue was resolved when the wildcatters were threatened with discharge unless they returned to work.[9]

In another instance, union officials insisted on a firm commitment from the company that it would fire the ringleaders of any anti-Negro walkout. This prevented a work stoppage since the potential wildcatters knew they would lose their jobs permanently. It didn't lessen their prejudice but it did establish job rights for many Negroes.[10]

The outbreak of the Korean war caused employers to seek all available manpower, and a full-employment economy once more meant jobs for Negroes. In addition, Detroit's largest department stores, like J. L. Hudson and Federal's, accelerated their hiring of blacks very visibly. City and federal government jobs in lower categories also opened up. War needs overcame some prejudicial practices.

But the bigots in the plants and the city had their moment of revenge—futile as it turned out to be—early in 1951, when Detroit responded to the rise of McCarthyism with an outburst of mass hysteria and mob violence directed against "reds" and "nigger lovers."

This occurred, ironically enough, at a time when there no longer existed any live radicalism in Detroit — after Reuther had totally purged the UAW of any serious "left-wing" influence, and only a token handful of Communists still clung to a once lively and influential party. The spark that ignited the outburst was the decision of the House Committee on Un-American Activities to expose the "communist menace" in Detroit. This is how the events were recorded in *Labor Action:*

> DETROIT, March 2—For any social historian anxious to get the "feel" of dark epochs like the Salem witch-hunt or the Stalin purges in Russia, there is fertile soil in this tense, febrile city since the opening of the hearings by the congressional Committee on Un-American Activities last week.
>
> Nor is there any consolation, except to blind men, in the fact that the treatment Stalinists received here is simply a taste of the brutality that Stalinism employs wherever it takes over.
>
> The real victim in Detroit last week was civil liberties,

127

the idea of a fair hearing and a trial by jury, the right of dissent, and the basic legal concept "innocent until proven guilty."

It was a fantastic week. Guilt-by-accusation was the method employed. Friendly witnesses, hostile witnesses, Stalinists or ex-Stalinists; it didn't matter. They all felt the wave of hysteria that the committee, aided by the three daily papers, whipped up in Detroit.

It Is Happening Here

Only one social force sought to stem the tide, and without much result. That was the UAW-CIO, which publicly proclaimed that its membership must not take matters into its own hands; that even Stalinists had the right to live and work; that vigilante methods were not in the way to combat Stalinism. Nevertheless—

In one auto plant, the wife of a man named as a Stalinist was tormented and driven from the plant. The newspapermen were there with photographers, egging on the workers for "some action shots."

Employers issued public statements [that] they couldn't fire suspected Stalinists because of the contracts with the UAW-CIO.

A school teacher, Mrs. Maki, was fired by the superintendent of schools when she was named as a Stalinist. Everyone at her school, from children to fellow teachers, said she was an excellent teacher. Detroit newspapers demanded an investigation of all school teachers.

A violin player in the Detroit orchestra was suspended by the union. "We don't have any Communist rats in our union," the musicians' union business agent said. The violinist had been named as a Stalinist.

A prominent radio commentator issued a public statement. He was *not* the man with a similar name who had been named by an FBI agent as a Stalinist. Ditto a prominent businessman who said he had received threats over the phone.

A sheriff's deputy, once upon a time a Stalinist, was a friendly witness. No one would talk to him the next day. He was forced to resign his job! A hotel porter was named, cleared, but still fired. "We hope they rehire him," a congressional committee spokesman said.

Sensational stories, filling four and five full pages of the daily press, kept pounding away at Detroit readers about the "menace of Communism."

NEGROES HIT BACK

In another section of the daily press was a story headlined, "Moody Puppet of the CIO." W. H. Hall, secretary of the Board of Commerce, who had said that 105,000 unemployed in Detroit was "normal," denounced Senator Blair Moody as "the Socialistic CIO junior senator from Michigan," and his bill to increase unemployment payments as "another step toward the socialistic state with Walter Reuther, his sponsor and director."

The congressional committee didn't do so well with the prominent pro-Stalinist Negro leaders in Detroit. William Hood, recording secretary of Ford Local 600, refused to answer questions except to say that it was a damned lie that he was a Communist Party member. He got in a few digs at Congressman Wood from Georgia. The Rev. Charles Hill stood on his rights and dignity, and proclaimed himself a fighter for complete equality for the Negroes no matter what any committee said or did.

Coleman Young, former Wayne County CIO Council secretary-treasurer, kept chiding the committee spokesmen for their Southern pronunciation of the word Negro. He stood up boldly, spoke against Jim Crow, and otherwise had a good propaganda field day at the expense of the committee. Interestingly enough, the Negro press here gave the Negro leaders a good press. Stalinism didn't lose that battle. This was evident from the remarks here and there of Negro workers.

Pat Rice, vice-president of Ford Local 600, was charged with making a misstatement in a passport application. Criminal action against him is pending.

The biggest sensation came on Friday. Mrs. Baldwin returned from Washington and testified. She named, club by club, name for name, every Stalinist on the party books in 1947. That some persons broke from the CP after

129

that, and are fighting them within the labor movement, was of no importance. This coming week dozens of auto workers face the crisis of their lives. Can the UAW-CIO keep them from being run out of the plants, suspected Stalinists and ex-Stalinists?

On Sunday, Congressman Potter announced that Ford Local 600 would be the target when the committee returns in the middle of March. He also charged that Governor Williams and Senator Moody might try to prevent the committee from returning to Detroit. [On an inside page another newspaper story said that Potter was testing his voting strength and popularity by the hearings and would run against Moody.]

Governor Williams replied that "Potter's statement is an example of guttersnipe politics based on falsehood and innuendo. It's McCarthyism at its worst." Then Governor Williams endorsed the work of the congressional committee!

The *Detroit News* began a campaign to assure that future hearings are on TV. Speaker Rayburn's order to keep it off TV has caused Potter and other Republicans to charge that the Democratic Party is covering up for "the reds."

Note : One ex-Stalinist testified that he was a member of the state central committee of the Democratic Party in 1946. Imagine what McCarthyism will do with that!

ACUTE DANGERS

It doesn't take a political genius to see that the main attempt of the congressional committee hearings here is directed at the UAW-CIO–Williams-Moody alliance in the Democratic Party. And the more the Democrats retreat, the greater will be the fury of the attack, the mudslinging, and the hysteria.

Within the UAW, where factional opponents already are trying to embarrass each other by red-baiting, the approach of local union elections hastens the process and makes more difficult the task of the leadership to maintain the democratic traditions of the union.

The purely factional character of the congressional hearings here is illustrated by the methods employed. The mere calling of an individual before the committee is considered guilt. It is considered by the committee a crime for a man to refuse to incriminate himself. Like the Moscow trials: If a man doesn't confess, he's guilty of hiding his crime; if he confesses, he's guilty. Detroit's papers keep suggesting that guilt-by-accusation process.

Names of suspected "reds" are being bandied around and called into the committee. A chance for grudges to be paid off, a chance to embarrass political opponents; in the case of embittered and uprooted workers, a chance to get their pictures in the papers, driving out the "reds."

Given the social tensions of Detroit, its mixed and restless population, the kind of hearings conducted, the newspapers' lurid coverage, and the ignoble silence of the city's liberal and labor elements—except the one UAW-CIO policy statement—all this feeds the passions and inflames the professional witchhunters.

Nor is this the end—merely the beginning. For the national elections are not until next November.

In an epoch where General Marshall is called the top fellow traveler of Stalinism, where General Eisenhower is branded by a wing of the Republican Party as "pro-Russian," it was perhaps inevitable that the crudest form of McCarthyism would find its most vehement and dangerous expression in this industrial melting pot.[11]

DETROIT, March 11—This has been a tragic week in Detroit.

The aftermath of the first week of hearings by the House Committee on Un-American Activities was a violent flurry of un-American activities typical of a vigilante-democracy.

All week long, the hatreds, prejudices, and passions inflamed by the sensational anti-Communist stories in Detroit's daily papers exploded into mob rule in many auto shops.

Not since the disgraceful race riots of 1943 has Detroit seen such an eruption of lynch spirit and venomous race hatred. In those days, it was the streets that were the scene of clashes, while the plants were quiet. Last week, the trouble occurred in the auto shops. And it all made meaty grist for Stalin's propaganda mills.

Detroit: City of Race and Class Violence

It is such an unpleasant story that its details were reported neither in Detroit's papers, nor in the *New York Times*.

The cold facts say little, impressive as they are: Seven persons named as Communists were fired, one was forced to quit, and ten were marched or ordered out of plants, in spite of efforts of United Auto Workers secondary leaders to keep things under control.

For once, the uprooted, frustrated and bigoted new milieu of workers, drawn from the deep South, had a chance to blow up, and they did. Against them stood only desperate union officials, inside and outside the plants, a minority of oldtimers whose years of fighting for unionism and fighting against Stalinism give them a sound approach to defeating Stalinism . . . and many Negro workers who were determined to prevent any Negroes from being the victims of mob action.

Among the plants where trouble took place were Midland Steel, Hudson, DeSoto, Metal Products, Dodge, Cadillac, Briggs, and Chrysler.

The kind of tension and trouble that marked Detroit this past week was illustrated best perhaps by the case of Leon Englund, a former Stalinist, who is an active member of Local 7. He is a Negro.

Since 1947, when Englund publicly broke with the Communist party, he has been a staunch right-winger. This meant nothing to the vast majority of workers in his division, for on Monday morning, the fact that he had been named as a Communist in 1947 was enough. All day Monday, shop leaders argued; they were abused and cursed, and called "Communists" and "N . . . . r lovers," as they tried to keep the predominantly Southern workers from running Englund from the plant.

On Tuesday morning, his co-workers, around 100 Negroes in that division, were determined to keep him working. A larger number of whites were determined to run him out. To prevent a riot, union leaders asked him to leave the plant, and he did.

RACE HATE BOILS UP

A meeting of the entire local union leadership was

called, and a strong stand was taken to uphold the official
UAW position, which says:

"The UAW-CIO is opposed to violence in any form
that attempts to substitute for democratic processes. Violent action that deprives individuals of their democratic
rights is the weapon of totalitarians themselves. It is not
a weapon of democracy.

"We cannot defeat the Communists or the adherents
of other forms of totalitarianism by falling into the trap
of using their own tactics.

"The democracy of our union and of our nation is
strong enough to bring to justice any person who gives
reason to believe that he is engaging in subversive activities or is otherwise engaging in conduct detrimental to
the best interests of our union."

Many local unions did as Chrysler 7. They issued the
UAW statement as a leaflet, and called on the workers
to stick to their union and its constitution. For this attempt, these leaders were abused, red-baited, and finally
found themselves lost in the tide of passion. By the end of
the week, every suspected Stalinist was out of work. In
the case of Englund, his public denials, the firm stand of
the union, and a feature story in the *Detroit News* enabled
him to come back to work and remain. In another part of
the Chrysler plant, this was not the case for another Negro
named as a Communist. He also denied it, but at present
to no avail.

What was especially tragic about the Chrysler situation was the vicious anti-Negro sentiments, the obscene
anti-Negro comments, that spread throughout the plants.
An effigy of one Negro was hung up. In other plants,
workers came in with ropes, just as in the deep South.

In another plant, where the local union president is
Jewish, vulgar anti-Semitic signs were posted or scrawled
on bulletin boards. It was a week of hate and fear and
violent anger. Many a committeeman or steward was
threatened for defending the union position.

The auto corporations, usually so quick to discipline
or fire workers for engaging in "wildcats," tolerated the
lawlessness. They used it to further divide the workers in
the shops. Outside of the policy statement, the top UAW-

CIO officials were silent. They didn't display the vigor shown at times against unauthorized strikes.

Today the UAW stands torn by bitter internal dissensions, a seething cauldron of emotional reactions. The whole week was a body blow to the UAW's democratic traditions.

WILL REUTHER GIVE THE CUE?

Nor is the end in sight. This week the congressional committee returns. Its announced target is Ford Local 600. Subpoenas have been issued to many officials, including Dave Averill, editor of *Ford Facts,* Shelton Tappes, now on the international union staff, and Jimmy Watts, who brought five minor officials at Ford 600 up on charges as Communists.

What the exact course of developments shall be, no one knows. What effect further hearings will have in inflaming the city is a matter of conjecture. The outlook is dark.

This past week the Detroit edition of the *Pittsburgh Courier* carried a strong defense of Rev. Charles Hill, signed by most prominent Negro ministers. No Detroit newspaper carried the blast at the congressional committee by the Americans for Democratic Action.

Walter P. Reuther, UAW president, has wired the committee for the right to testify in the hearings. In his message Reuther said, "In nearly all local unions, Communist influence has been eliminated. It has been generally recognized that we have successfully eliminated Communist influence at the top level of our international union."

Congressman Potter replied, "As far as I'm concerned, he can testify. I don't know how much he knows about Communist organizations but he has been fighting them, so I'd be very happy to have him appear." No formal decision of the committee on Reuther's demand has been made yet.

This situation places a grave responsibility on Reuther. As yet the UAW leadership has not directly criticized the conduct or results of the hearings. Will Reuther roll with the punch? Will he try to take the play away from the committee as being more "anti-Communist" than it?

Will he vigorously defend the present UAW stand on democratic rights for Stalinists? Speculation, opinions in advance or faith in Reuther are beside the point. The events of the week will speak for themselves.

This much is certain. The entire UAW secondary leadership will take its future cue from Reuther and his stand. Unless he strongly defends the traditional views of the UAW, the secondary leaders will retreat, and a debacle for democratic rights is inevitable.

Perhaps the fate of the UAW is at stake here.[12]

The fate of the UAW did not, of course, depend on these events. It was a viable organization. The fate of many individuals did, and the human cost of the hearings can never be measured. Walter Reuther easily eliminated the small influence of the remnants of a Communist cadre in Ford Local 600. In Detroit, as in many large cities, there now existed dozens upon dozens of depression radicals, who had been destroyed by the nightmare of McCarthyism.

As for the independent radicals who prided themselves on being "anti-communist," their fate was similar to that of the American Legion president who attended a Communist rally in New York City "to see for himself," so the story goes. When the police started clubbing the demonstrators, they whacked him too. He protested, "But I'm an anti-communist." The police didn't stop, but merely replied, "We don't care what kind of a communist you are."

The hysteria spread into the state political arena, and the Michigan state legislature passed a sweeping "anti-Communist" act known as the Trucks Law. Although its broad provisions were clearly unconstitutional, as the American Civil Liberties Union pointed out, Governor Williams succumbed to the hysteria and signed it. After all, CIO members who were state legislators had voted for it. Shortly thereafter the Michigan CIO denounced the law,

135

and it was eventually declared unconstitutional by the Michigan Supreme Court. Only one labor leader in Michigan had assailed it: Gus Scholle, the militant and independent president of the Michigan CIO.

Detroit's weeks of war madness had other effects. Congressman Potter *did* defeat Senator Blair Moody in his bid for reelection, and General Eisenhower easily took Michigan against Adlai Stevenson. Governor Williams, his liberal reputation somewhat tarnished, survived.

Postwar Reconstruction in Reutherland 9

N o other American city in the 1950's suffered the severe dislocations which were the lot of Detroit—changes which were often underestimated, since most government and private reports or analyses were based on the statistical concept of metropolitan Detroit, not the city itself. The image of Detroit as the "automotive center of the world" was also misleading because it created the impression that whatever happened in the auto industry was automatically reflected in the city.

Actually, while the auto industry survived its "feast or famine" production schedules and sales to reach new and unpredicted success in the 1950's, the city of Detroit steadily deteriorated.

Chronic unemployment plagued many auto workers, particularly in Detroit, due to: (1) the effects of the four postwar recessions, (2) the elimination of small manufacturers and the loss of defense jobs, (3) the impact of automation and technological changes, (4) the decentralization of the auto industry, and (5) the disastrous years at Chrysler, whose plants were concentrated mostly in the city.

Over 77,000 jobs were lost when Hudson, Kaiser-Frazer, Packard, and Midland Steel, unable to compete with the big three, closed their plants. Among those affected were about 50,000 older workers, who had no hope of finding new jobs once they exhausted their unemployment compensation benefits.

In the winter of 1949–1950 sudden layoffs in the auto industry gave Detroit 127,000 unemployed. Then the Korean war altered the picture overnight. Spurred by memories of World War II shortages, the American public bought an astonishing 8,000,000 vehicles, and for a brief period unemployment disappeared. In the winter of 1951 more drastic cutbacks occurred, and unemployment was back to the 127,000 figure. Defense orders filled the production gap in 1952, and wartime production created 221,000 additional jobs in Michigan's defense industries including the auto industry, whose blue-collar workers rose to 930,000 nationally. (By the end of 1958 only 30,000 defense-related jobs were left in the state.)[1]

The 1953–1954 recession hit the auto industry very hard. According to government statistics, in metropolitan Detroit there were 107,000 unemployed. "Unemployment in Detroit," said Henry Ford II, "does not amount to a hill of beans." Under pressure from the UAW, the Department of Labor did a resurvey of unemployment and reported 121,000 out of work in the Detroit area. For Michigan the total was over 200,000.

The economic outlook did not disturb C. E. Wilson, Secretary of Defense and former General Motors president, who declared: "Detroit is able to look after itself. I wouldn't worry about it. Come spring and it's going to be all right." Nevertheless with over 6 per cent unemployment, Detroit was reclassified as a "distressed labor area."[2]

It wasn't until 1960 that government officials realized the limitations of their unemployment analysis. If a metropolitan area included a city like Detroit and its wealthier suburbs, an unemployment rate of 6 per cent signified at least double that percentage within the city, and half as much in the outlying areas. Moreover, thousands of blacks weren't included in the survey, since the "population basis" failed to take social changes into account soon enough. And a breakdown by race and age would indicate that Negro unemployment was double that of white unemployment, and the figure for Negro youth at least 35 per cent.

Scant attention was given to the human misery caused by this economic dislocation. Most of the time the majority of the unemployed were the same: the blacks, the newly hired, the unskilled. Layoffs were determined by seniority clauses in labor-management contracts. Total economic insecurity was the hard fact of life for thousands of blue-collar workers and their families.

When Chrysler lost its second place in sales to Ford and its share of the car market fell to about 10 per cent, the company almost collapsed, until L. L. "Tex" Colbert, its president, was replaced by Lynn Townsend. Chrysler employment in the 1950's fell from 100,000 to 35,000 blue-collar workers, most of the layoffs occurring in Detroit where its major plants were concentrated. Even 7,000 white-collar workers felt the ax.

1955 was a boom year for the auto industry, and the UAW won a modified form of a guaranteed annual wage, suggesting that prosperity had returned to the city. However, Chrysler had not yet recovered, nor were the unemployed rehired elsewhere, with auto production gradually shifting out of the city. New and prosperous suburbs were created in Trenton, Warren, and Utica, as auto plants—mainly automated—in the outlying districts replaced the old factories in Detroit itself.

Car and truck production would eventually soar to over 10,000,000 vehicles annually, but employment in the auto plants would fluctuate around 650,000 nationally, as machines replaced men to handle the extra output. During the 1956–1960 period 100,000 "hard core" unemployed persisted in Detroit, right through the auto boom. The retirement of over 150,000 auto workers over the next 15 years would ease the impact of automation, and the newly won modest pension plans negotiated by the UAW enabled the "too old to work, too young to die" workers to eke out an existence. Most lacked the money to leave Detroit and remained as a low-income group, becoming a source of "white backlash" as they were increasingly surrounded by the expanding black population.

The story of the pensioners was only part of the demographic change in the city. Between 1950 and 1960 more than 500,000 people left Detroit for life in the suburbs. In total population the city actually lost about 270,000 people, for migration was offset by immigration —mostly of blacks—and an increase in the birthrate among blacks and poor whites. By 1960 the number of blacks had risen from 303,000 to 487,000, while the total population had declined to 1,670,000—the old, the very young, the black, the unskilled, and the fearful.[3]

The flight to the suburbs alleviated some of the tension over housing. The many mob acts against Negroes moving into areas outside the ghetto were essentially rearguard actions.

The rise of new office buildings, the development of a large network of expressways which cut through the inner-city slums, and the growth of middle-income apartment projects provided Detroit with an aura of prosperity. Paradise Valley was almost obliterated, but the black ghetto simply moved to the Twelfth Street area, forgotten until it became the center of the 1967 riot. Twelfth Street had been the Jewish area; the Jews were now living in Huntington Woods, Southfield, and other suburbs, with less than 7,000 to 10,000 remaining in the city proper.

A close look at small businesses within the city would reveal block after block of empty stores, reminiscent of the Great Depression. Suburban shopping centers were taking their toll.

The exodus to the suburbs was, in fact, one of the major causes of Detroit's deterioration. East side auto workers who had missed the impact of the recessions and received good UAW-bargained wages moved to St. Clair Shores. Warren, Michigan, grew from a small suburb into a prosperous community of over 100,000 as new Chrysler, Ford, General Motors, and feeder plants were built there. GM's technical center expanded enormously. Until 1970 Warren also remained 100 per cent white, not even allowing a Negro army captain and his family to reside there.

Every period of prosperity enabled more whites to move to the suburbs, further isolating the Negroes within the city ghetto, and this was a conscious decision. The most overt scandal of the decade was exposed by Charles Abrams, the national housing expert, in his book *Forbidden Neighbors*. Abrams wrote as follows:

DEARBORN

The worst aspect of the Detroit situation today is found outside the city limits. It is a new and ominous phenomenon. Detroit, as the country's fifth biggest city, contains the mixed elements and varied interests which prevent democratic cities from sinking irretrievably into the quicksands of race prejudice. The situation is different in nearby Dearborn, a city of 94,994 (1950) and the site of the Ford Motor Company.

Dearborn is composed of thousands of little homes similar to suburban Detroit's. In fact, but for the legalized boundary, Dearborn would be just a borough of Detroit.

Dearborn elected Orville L. Hubbard, who campaigned for the mayoralty on the racial issue. Hubbard's big boast was that he had kept Negroes out of Dearborn. In 1948, the John Hancock Life Insurance Company decided to build a private rental housing project on land owned by the Ford Motor Company. The company had no intention of housing any Negroes. But Negroes were the problem in Detroit, and though there were almost no Negroes in Dearborn, the city was close enough to Detroit to give the issue political appeal. Hubbard found something to be against—Negroes. He also needed to show that it was he who was saving the day for Dearborn's white citizenry. The life insurance company provided him with the opportunity. He organized meetings and attacked the project as the opening wedge for a Negro inundation of Dearborn. Handbills and stickers were circulated and a "conspiracy" was laid to the Ford Motor Company and the insurance company, as unlikely a pair of racial conspirators as can be imagined.

One of the circulars read:

KEEP NEGROES OUT OF DEARBORN
X VOTE NO on (Advisory Vote)
(The John Hancock Rental Housing Project)

PROTECT YOUR HOME AND MINE!
X VOTE NO on (Advisory Vote)

Another circular, printed on official stationery and bearing the city seal, read:

WAKE UP, DEARBORN!
WAKE UP!
OPEN YOUR EYES WIDE!
JOHN HANCOCK GIVES HOUSING DOUBLE-TALK

"With none of the 15,000 Ford Rouge Negro workers living in Dearborn, don't be 'lulled into a false sense of security' that John Hancock—with 8,500,000 policyholders of every race, color and creed—can build in Dearborn a multimillion dollar terrace-type rental housing project from its huge insurance funds, including incomes from Negroes, and exclude Negro families from living in the Hancock row-housing project in Dearborn, 'if' you allow it to be built here. Keep Dearborn a homeowners city by voting NO on the (ADVISORY VOTE) which by 'stooping, squatting and squinting' you will find at the bottom of the right column on your voting machine."

The project was defeated and the citizens of Dearborn were happy. Orville L. Hubbard was reelected for his achievement in saving the city from the mythical corps of black invaders.

THE CLOSED CITY

The exclusion practices of Dearborn are practiced in Grosse Point, Bloomfield Hills, and Birmingham, which also adjoin Detroit.[4]

The contrast between the white suburbs and the city itself grew sharper with the shift in population and the restriction on Negroes' buying homes. The plight of the Negro and the causes of housing discrimination were described in 1960 by Robert M. Frehse, the chairman of the Detroit Council on Human Relations:

> The Negro is largely concentrated and segregated in the older, less desirable central area of the city. The practice of real estate brokers of not giving Negroes the opportunity to buy homes in certain areas of the city is generally defended by alluding to an inevitable decline of property values or of losing business of the larger white market. The generally lower incomes of Negro families automatically eliminate a large proportion from the housing market. The activities of white protective associations include harassment of Negro families which are able to purchase homes, pressures on white sellers, and even the removal of homes from the market through purchase. Perhaps organizations and activities which seek to deny the constitutional and legal rights of others should themselves be declared illegal. *Probably the most effective method of maintaining segregated housing patterns has been through financing agencies, including the Veterans Administration and the Federal Housing Administration.* One merely needs to determine how much new housing and financing has been made available to Negroes. Of the 87,000 new housing units built between 1940 and 1952, only 2 per cent were available to Negroes.[5]

The Council of Human Relations consisted of an im-

posing list of church, liberal, and labor organization leaders who worked hard to alleviate racial tension in Detroit.
Yet it was unable to make a serious dent in the problems
because it lacked real support from the auto industry or
the Chamber of Commerce, as it noted during its testimony before the United States Commission on Civil
Rights.

The council's advocacy of open housing was considered a "do-gooders" heresy. And the council never mobilized the support mustered by its main opponent, the
real estate interests, for most Detroiters were against open
housing. In an angry broadcast in 1957, Guy Nunn, the
UAW's TV and radio commentator, described the functioning of those interests:

> If you'd like to have a look at power—sheer authority,
> unchecked by law, unreachable by public opinion, capa-
> ble of setting aside the decisions of the Supreme Court
> itself—take a good close look at the Detroit Real Estate
> Board. Nobody elected the Board, nobody can depose the
> Board, nobody can, as yet, bring the Board to book in
> court—but there it is—and there it operates—a legisla-
> ture and court unto itself making law more effectively
> than the law itself.
>
> It would take a book, rather than a broadcast, to de-
> scribe how a private body can force upon us conditions
> which the law, the courts and public policy declare wrong,
> immoral or illegal, but perhaps this one example will at
> least suggest how the Detroit Real Estate Board does it.
>
> The Supreme Court long ago declared the restrictive
> covenant illegal—unenforceable. The decision said, in
> substance, that an agreement between sellers not to sell
> a home to persons of any particular race, creed or color
> was an illegal agreement.
>
> Now consider Detroit: The city has a Negro popula-
> tion amounting to about twenty percent of the total popu-
> lation, perhaps larger. The incomes of these Negro fam-
> ilies are adequate, at any rate, to permit many if not most
> of them to buy new homes. And large numbers of them,

compressed in the old slum ghetto sections of the city, desperately want and need new homes. And yet not one percent of all new residential construction in the city of Detroit is for Negro buyers. Not one percent. They make up better than twenty percent of the total population; they get less than one percent of the new homes.

Why? Ask the Detroit Real Estate Board. It isn't really neighborhood bigotry—it isn't really the Rose Petranskys of Cherrylawn—keeping the ghetto intact. It's the Detroit Real Estate Board. The Board's influence over real estate transactions stretches from the most elaborate expressway acquisition down to the sale of a two-bedroomer on a forty-foot lot. The Board pursues a fixed policy of condoning the expansion of the ghetto—inch by inch, house by house, block by block, but it will not tolerate the dilution of the ghetto. If a realtor dares sell a home to a Negro family even six blocks beyond the creeping ghetto's edge, the Board is ready to punish him with commercial reprisal or the threat of expulsion from the Board. Expulsion is not a trivial threat. For years the Real Estate Boards around the country have been working at creating a special aura of sanctity around the word "realtor." If you're not a member of the Board (it is claimed)—you can't use the designation "realtor." City and state agencies have been bulldozed, with time, into dealing only with "realtors." If a mere agent, a mere real estate "broker" wants "in" on a transaction of any size, he has to be a "realtor"—or use one as a front. The Board is an exclusive club—with exclusive extra-legal prerogatives. Two members of the Board, for example, sit normally on the City Planning Commission . . . become privy to the advance intentions of the city in the future . . . can pass the word along to fellow Board members where it would be well to buy—or sell—or "get aboard" when sizable land transactions are pending. If you're not a member of the Real Estate Board, try handling any appraisal involving more than 50 thousand dollars. The state Securities Commission doesn't have to confine such business to Board members: it simply has done so. Nonmembers who deal in real estate are excluded from vital information, vital financing, vital connections.

What does all this have to do with Negroes—with the persistent and flagrant violation of the Supreme Court's restrictive covenant decision? Surely there are Negro real estate agents willing to sell housing to Negro buyers? (There are.) Surely there are Negro builders willing to build for Negro buyers? (There are—mighty few, but there are.) So what stops them? The Detroit Real Estate Board. If the Real Estate Board says no, the Builders' Association says no, and if the Builders' Association says no, the Mortgage Bankers' Association says no. And twenty percent of the city's population gets less than one percent of the city's new housing. Senator Eastland doesn't have to proselytize up here; a stronger, a more effective, and more determined—and a more bigoted agent of segregation is already in control. It's the Detroit Real Estate Board.

We have reported now and again, over the years, the rejection by the Real Estate Board of Negro applicants for membership. The most recent is James Del Rio. Perhaps you saw his story in *Life* magazine. Del Rio is a real estate man—and builder—of impeccable reputation —a member of the Builder's Association—competent in the extreme (he's handled a gross of more than five million dollars a year, has over 30 employees)—intelligent —endorsed repeatedly for membership by the best known and most respectable realtors in the state—and unacceptable to the Real Estate Board's executive board. Each time he has applied for membership, some fresh and absurd and unmeetable stipulation has been laid down. And even as Del Rio, year after year, was being turned down for membership, the Detroit Real Estate Board has been beseeching its white members to go forth and recruit more members.

What happens to Del Rio may be of no great importance. It is an indignity, yes, an offense, a business liability, yes, but he is a tough young man. But what is the Detroit Real Estate Board imposing on this entire city? That is of importance—to our children no less than to us.

The policy of confinement of Negro home buyers— confinement not only in a geographical sense—but confinement to the purchase of older homes—means perpetuation of the ghetto and the gradual creation of new slums as the old slums crumble, are cleared, or house new arrivals. It means, further, the imposition of heavy economic penalties on Negro families who try to escape the slums. (Not that those who stay don't already pay the highest rents per square foot for the most miserable space in the city.) Excluded from new homes and the easier mortgage terms which accompany their purchase, Negro buyers are forced into buying on land contract—with its higher interest and nearly total absence of protection against repossession in the event of non-payment of an installment because of illness or temporary unemployment. Maintenance costs, moreover, run substantially higher on old homes than on new.

But this is only the beginning of the cycle which bigotry sets in motion. Without residential dispersion, there can be no real hope of school desegregation. There is some reason to believe that Detroit's schools are more sharply segregated in their pupil distribution today than they were before the restrictive covenant was outlawed. And the prospect is that without some dramatic effort at housing dispersion—the breaking open of outer areas to Negro residents—the segregation will grow more intense with the years.

The Real Estate Board pursues—and enforces—a policy which will in time spread the ghetto, block by block, until it becomes the entire heart of the city. You can watch it happening almost day by day. As a Negro family moves a block away from the ghetto's former boundary, real estate agents go to work on the fears of the white residents in that block. The prospect of a double sale is created; a new home to the panicked white seller, an old one to another Negro. Block by block it works. No "jumps." Keep it tight, keep it in turmoil and turnover, keep it profitable, and keep it tightly in the hands of the Detroit Real Estate Board.

There are no apparent legal weapons against a group of men who practice the most vulgar racism in their internal membership policy—whose external policy results in what we could only describe (should it happen in any other country) as a form of Fascist race segregation and economic discrimination based on race—but we can at least make known the identities of the group's guiding

147

officers. These men might be embarrassed at being seen in public with an organizer for the Ku Klux Klan—but their organization has done the Klan's work with an arrogance and precision which even the Grand Dragon himself would dare admire only at humble distance. What first-grader presumes to instruct the principal?

The present officers of the Detroit Real Estate Board, the most effective instrument of bigotry in our community, are: George C. Ewals, president; Hans Gehrke, first vice-president; Carl H. Plumhoff, treasurer; Rolland E. Fisher, executive vice-president—and Harry Mark, Norman C. Scudder and Kenneth W. Carter, vice-presidents.[6]

The economic restrictions on Negroes were illustrated by the testimony of Horace Sheffield and Robert Battle III, militant black trade unionists, before the Civil Rights Commission. They told of the enormous gap between the proportion of Negro and white skilled workers—a sore point in current times. The 1960 figures for skilled Negro workers were: tool and die makers, 159, or .7 of 1 per cent; structural steelworkers, 26, or .5 of 1 per cent; printing craftsmen, 15, or .9 of 1 per cent; carpenters, 360, or .2 of 1 per cent; electricians, 163, or 2.1 per cent; and machinists or job setters, 900, or 5.2 per cent.[7] This was five years after the AFL-CIO had united into one organization and pledged to eliminate job and hiring discrimination.

The UAW was embarrassed by the statistics for the auto industry, for the skilled trades there looked just like the building trades of the AFL. Chrysler admitted that out of 7,425 skilled workers only 24 were Negroes, and there was only one black youth among the 350 participants in the apprentice program. General Motors listed 67 skilled black workers in the Detroit area out of a total of 11,125, and Ford figures for the River Rouge plants were 250 Negro skilled workers out of 7,000.[8]

No one even bothered to ask if there were any Negroes in management positions.

Even these minuscule gains had not come easily. During World War II there had been much "upgrading" into skilled jobs, but afterward the restrictive policy of "journeymen only" was adopted by unions, including the UAW, and the black workers went back to their assembly line and other menial jobs. Out of resentment over this policy, and a keen desire to make the UAW and other unions live up to their repeated professions of equality for all members, a number of prominent black unionists in auto, steel, and other unions formed the Trade Union Leadership Council in Detroit. It was a forerunner of the National American Labor Council, which was organized by A. Philip Randolph in 1960 over the objections of George Meany, president of the AFL-CIO. The Detroit organizers were Horace Sheffield, a talented UAW staff man and long-time personal friend and political supporter of Walter P. Reuther, and Robert "Buddy" Battle III, the rugged and undisputed leader of the foundry workers in Ford Local 600.

Unlike many "black caucuses" in the union movement, TULC adopted an integrationist policy and invited white unionists to join. A few, including Brendan Sexton, educational director of the UAW, Guy Nunn, Bart Young, Leonard Woodcock, and myself, did. The essentially paternalistic attitude toward Negroes of the white leadership of most American trade unions and their inability to foresee the ground swell of the civil rights movement were reflected in their hostile reaction to TULC in Detroit, and to the NALC. Even the Jewish Labor Committee—itself an ethnic organization within the union movement—frowned on the formation of the Negro groups.

Sheffield became a controversial figure in the UAW and in Detroit politics, since his independent stance on issues jeopardized the trade unions' traditional modes of operation. In 1959 Sheffield had the temerity at the UAW convention to nominate Willoughby Abner—a Chicago black unionist of outstanding ability—for a post on the international executive board of the union. By publicly raising the question of Negro participation at policy-making levels, Sheffield earned many enemies. Emil Mazey, secretary-treasurer of the UAW, demanded that Reuther fire him. Mazey's own record as a protagonist for civil rights was far superior to that of most union leaders, but this long-time socialist simply couldn't tolerate the independent activity of Sheffield.

In 1965 Mazey reexamined his position on TULC and told its April membership meeting: "In all honesty and candor, I must confess that I had some misgivings about the formation of your organization. I believed that it would divide workers, and consequently, hurt the cause of labor and the cause of civil rights. I am glad to have this opportunity to congratulate you for dispelling my fears by your constructive actions and programs."[9]

Incidentally, in 1961 the UAW leadership did accept the Negro unionists' demand for participation at higher levels, and Nelson "Jack" Edwards, another member of TULC, was chosen for the post of UAW executive board member-at-large.

The unpopularity of TULC within the union movement increased its prestige in the Negro community, and soon white politicians hoping to win the support of black voters would eagerly seek its endorsement.

Mayor Cavanagh and the Limits of Reform

10

A T THE BEGINNING of the 1960's, "public opinion" in Detroit was excited by newspaper headlines about a "crime wave." According to newspaper accounts, the number one problem was crime on the streets. A City Planning Commission study of the socioeconomic crisis was quietly suppressed, and when some of its contents appeared in a *Time* magazine article, Mayor Louis C. Miriani denounced the article as a "smear." What Detroit needed, he insisted, was more vigorous law enforcement to curb the criminal elements roaming the streets, and he ordered a police crackdown. The police responded zealously.

Frisks and searches, mass arrests, and "holding on suspicion" became the standard pattern of police operations, which were concentrated in the black community. Soon feelings of fear, humiliation, and then anger developed among the Negro people—feelings to which the white community was largely insensitive. Only the traditional guardians of civil liberties, like the American Civil Liberties Union, and the NAACP protested the wholesale arrests and the practice of holding hundreds of persons in jail "for investigation" and then releasing them, when the only suspicious thing about them was the color of their skin.

No serious restraint was placed on police conduct, although the 1960 Civil Rights Commission hearings had uncovered much new evidence of police prejudice and mistreatment of blacks. One of the more vivid testimonies was that of a retired black policeman who had twice been assaulted by police: once while on the force and working in plain clothes, the other time just prior to the hearings.

Mayor Miriani (who was later convicted on criminal charges of income tax evasion) disregarded the protests and maintained his assertion of police "impartiality." Yet City Hall received reports of incidents involving prominent black leaders, among them the director of the NAACP who was frisked and searched. Many white policemen had learned not to call blacks "niggers," for there were now influential black municipal judges, a federal judge, and some business and union leaders. Instead, they would be called "boy," a derogatory term. A typical incident involved a $12,000-a-year union official. As he was driving into his bank's parking lot a police cruiser made him pull over to the curb and a white policeman called out, "Boy, where are you going?" When the unionist replied that he was going to bank his check he was asked, "Boy, where did you get that check, boy?" The provocation didn't work, and the police couldn't haul him in for "resisting arrest," the explanation given when Negroes somehow seemed to get injured on the way to the police station.

Between the high unemployment and the state of indignation over Miriani's mass arrest program, a race riot seemed inevitable. An upheaval did in fact occur, but it was different in character than anyone had imagined. Its first casualty was the incumbent mayor.

Miriani was the last of a series of mediocrities who had governed the city since World War II. His political victory—and that of his predecessors—reflected the very different nature of city and of state politics in Michigan.

152

On a state level, the all-out participation of the UAW in the Democratic party from 1948 on helped G. Mennen Williams to win the gubernatorial race six times and made the Democratic party a viable and influential political force in a once solid Republican state. This gave Negroes access to state government positions, concentrated mainly in Detroit. And within the city government a Harvard-educated Negro, William T. Patrick, did win election to the Common Council. However, the UAW had a record of unmitigated failure in mayoralty campaigns.

In theory Detroit's municipal elections were non-partisan. In practice the contests were generally between "labor-endorsed" and "business-backed" candidates. The usual "throw the rascals out" flavor of city elections was absent after the conviction of Mayor Reading, the county prosecutor, and 137 policemen on various charges of bribery and corruption in 1939. The city was relatively "clean" after those scandals, and the new role played by the CIO in Detroit politics gave them the coloring of a class contest. A closer examination would reveal, however, that Detroit's politics were a struggle between old prejudices and newer union consciousness. Or, to paraphrase Samuel Lubell's perceptive analysis of union politics, between class feeling and racial or religious feeling. The first evidence of this conflict was the abortive campaign of Richard T. Frankensteen, a UAW official, to unseat Mayor Jeffries in 1945. According to an oversimplified analysis of that campaign, Frankensteen was "labor's candidate," although he lacked the support of the AFL building trades and the Teamsters union. A more proper designation would have been "CIO candidate," yet even that is inexact, since part of the UAW failed to support him. The split in the "labor vote" partially accounted for his defeat. Perhaps more important, he was the victim of an effective race-baiting campaign. Thousands of leaflets had been distributed in the city declaring that if Frankensteen were elected, "you couldn't keep the niggers out of City Hall."[1]

The persistence with which the racial issue permeated local politics, long before the concept of "white backlash" became widespread, was reflected in every mayoral campaign. In 1947 the CIO endorsed incumbent Mayor Jeffries against Eugene Van Antwerp, a conservative councilman. Van Antwerp won. In 1949 the racial issue caused the UAW to suffer its most important defeat, when George Edwards was beaten by Albert Cobo, the city treasurer, in the contest for mayor. Edwards was the most attractive candidate to appear on the Detroit scene since Mayor Frank Murphy in the 1930's. A former UAW organizer and close friend of Walter Reuther, he had returned from army service to win the presidency of the Common Council by the highest vote of any candidate. He was a law school graduate, articulate, and capable. Cobo swamped him primarily because he had stood for open housing. At dozens of property owners' meetings Edwards was denounced as pro-Negro. The AFL endorsed Cobo. To the astonishment of secondary UAW leaders, the new homeowners in Detroit among the auto workers spoke openly in the shops against "labor's man."

After that debacle Cobo had little difficulty in repeating his triumphs against inconsequential candidates backed by the CIO. And Cobo ran as an avowed conservative. His only defeat came on a state level when he ran for governor as a Republican candidate. When Cobo died in office, Councilman Miriani succeeded him as mayor. In 1957 the influence of labor in Detroit elections was so weak that almost all unions joined with business and the press to endorse Miriani. He won easily.[2]

When the time came to face reelection in 1961, Mayor Miriani was the picture of self-confidence, if not smugness. He was the unanimous choice of the entire power structure in Detroit: the UAW, the Teamsters, the AFL-CIO council, the Chamber of Commerce, the auto companies, the newspapers. Moreover, his opponent was a comparatively unknown young lawyer, a newcomer in city politics. No one in the Establishment took Jerome P. Cavanagh seriously.

Perhaps the most significant aspect of the 1961 mayoralty campaign was not the fact that the 33-year-old Cavanagh beat Miriani by over 40,000 votes, or that it was the biggest political upset in Michigan politics in 32 years, but rather its disclosure of a growing gap in attitudes between institutions, such as unions, and the people they ostensibly represent—in particular the split between white liberals and the black community.

Considerable credit for Cavanagh's victory went to TULC, which mobilized the black community against Miriani, protesting his support of discriminatory police practices. The long-neglected city employees, notably the firemen, worked hard for Cavanagh. In a postmortem, the *Detroit Free Press,* which opposed Cavanagh, stated that he "owes his victory to Detroit's Negroes, blue-collar workers and the unemployed." Five liberal councilmen also won in this tide of protest.[3] The growing division between labor leaders and the ranks was indicated by the campaign to fire Horace Sheffield, the head of TULC. The victory of Cavanagh gave TULC too much prestige for that kind of bureaucratic stupidity.

Suddenly it appeared as if a new day had dawned for Detroit. Almost overnight the city gained a new image under the direction of the talented, articulate, and personable mayor, who soon became a favorite of the nation's press and television. It seemed that Detroit had also found the road to racial peace in the programs and policies instituted by Cavanagh, with assistance from the Democratic administrations in Washington.

As a first act in office Cavanagh persuaded Alfred

Pelham, an acknowledged and successful Negro expert on municipal finance, to leave Wayne State University and the county auditor's office and direct city finances. Cavanagh made another shrewd political move in persuading George Edwards, the one-time mayoral candidate who had become a justice of the Michigan Supreme Court, to accept the tough post of police commissioner. Both the police and the black community knew that this meant the end of overt police harassment of blacks. As Edwards told a TULC audience one night, "My first job was to teach the police they didn't have a constitutional right to automatically beat up Negroes on arrest."[4]

Soon Henry Ford, Walter Reuther, and the press were praising Cavanagh's administration, and the beginning of $360,000,000 in federal assistance started pouring into the city.

Filled with euphoria at the national economic growth and prosperity, the nation came to see the formerly distressed city as a model of social progress — the harbinger of the future for solving urban problems. This was the illusion of the early 1960's.

The weekly *National Observer,* in its July 15, 1963, edition, was typical in its praise of the new Detroit:

> The evidence, both statistical and visual, is everywhere. Retail sales are up dramatically. Earnings are higher. Unemployment is lower. People are putting new aluminum sidings on their homes, new carpets on the floor, and new cars in the garage.
>
> Some people are forsaking the suburbs and returning to the city. Physically, Detroit has acquired freshness and vitality. Acres of slums have been razed, and steel-and-glass apartments—angular and lonely in the vacated landscape—have sprung up in their place. In the central business district, hard by the Detroit River, severely rectangular skyscrapers—none of them more than five years old—jostle uncomfortably with the gilded behemoths of another age.

Accustomed to years of adversity, to decades of drabness and civic immobility, Detroiters are naturally exhilarated. They note with particular pride that Detroit has been removed from the Federal Bureau of Employment Security's classification of an "area with substantial and persistent unemployment."[5]

This rosy outlook extended to the area of racial relations. While outrages against blacks in Selma and Birmingham shocked many people, and Rev. Martin Luther King, Jr., aroused the conscience of the nation to begin the mass civil rights movement, Detroit felt it was an exception because it had what it assumed to be an effective program for racial progress. Detroiters were fond of contrasting the calm in the auto city with the turbulence elsewhere.

Any doubts on this score were dispelled on July 23, 1963, when a massive civil rights demonstration led by Reverend King took place in Detroit. Between 150,000 and 200,000 people participated, about 90 per cent of them black. *Business Week* wrote of the occasion as follows:

Detroit shuddered when it heard plans for Sunday's demonstration—the date (by coincidence, the organizing group says) fell on the 20th anniversary of the nation's worst riot. . . . As it turned out, Detroiters need not have worried about a repetition of the Battle of Belle Isle. The Negro throngs, dressed in their Sunday best, peacefully marched 20 blocks down broad Woodward Avenue to the convention area, where they listened to speeches. There was no untoward incident. The crowd was restrained in action though determined in mood.[6]

Mayor Cavanagh, Governor George Romney, and Walter Reuther were among the prominent whites marching with Reverend King. The size of the march surprised everybody. About 50,000 were expected, and at least triple that number showed up.

Social reform seemed to be working. As a study by

157

the Institute of Labor and Industrial Relations of Wayne State University and the University of Michigan pointed out:

> Long before the enactment of the Federal Civil Rights Act of 1964, and even while the State of Michigan adopted its own Civil Rights Act there was much evidence that the disadvantaged minorities were beginning to break out of their ghetto patterns and establish first class citizenship in many areas.
>
> Unquestionably, this development has its basis in the three year period of relative prosperity affecting to one degree or another all segments of the population, and in the emergence of a broad community leadership from all walks of life, engaged in continuous effort to make social progress, especially for the Negro minority, a reality and not just a promise. The socio-economic premise affords a different social base than the violently explosive patterns of other major metropolitan areas.[7]

The study was carried out as a project for the Detroit Labor-Management Committee on Community Progress, and its conclusions did represent the consensus of experts and prevailing opinion in the city.

Even a skeptical reporter like Stanley H. Brown of *Fortune* magazine was impressed.

> All the diverse elements that make up Detroit's power structure, once divided and pitted against itself, are being welded together in a remarkable synthesis. Every significant accomplishment in such major areas as race relations, urban renewal, and the arts—whether initiated by a single individual or by one special interest—has become the province of a board or committee that includes representatives of the United Autoworkers, one or more of the city's utilities, the clergy, ethnic groups, retailers, the auto companies, real estate interests, finance, the press, political groups and any other relevant interest.[8]

The new attitude in Detroit *was* impressive.

Of all the accomplishments in the recent history of the city, the most significant is the progress Detroit has made

Mayor Cavanagh and the Limits of Reform

in race relations. The grim specter of the 1943 riots never quite fades from the minds of the city leaders. As much as anything else, that specter has enabled the power structure to overcome tenacious prejudice and give the Negro community a role in the consensus probably unparalleled in any major American city. So widespread is Detroit's understanding that the Negro's cry for equality must be heard that in 1963, when Walter Reuther initiated the Citizens Committee for Equal Opportunity to relieve mounting tensions over Negro efforts for civil rights, every business, labor, social, religious, ethnic, financial, and political group of consequence in the city sent its top man. Joseph Ross, president of Federal Department Stores, a chain that finds most of its customers among the city's industrial workers, has been a store executive in New York, Newark, Dallas, Atlanta and Denver, and he says, "Detroit is more sophisticated in race relations than any other city I know."[9]

If the white power structure of the city was different from that of other urban centers, so too were the blacks, as Brown pointed out.

> Negroes in Detroit have deep roots in the community, compared with the more transient population of Negro ghettos in Harlem and elsewhere in the North. Home ownership is high; roughly 65,000 families—more than 40% of the Negro population—own their own houses. Negroes are sufficiently well organized socially and politically to have elected a member of the Detroit common council in a city-wide election. They have also elected three local judges, ten state legislators, and two congressmen (Michigan is the only congressional delegation in Washington with two Negroes).[10]

Most Detroiters implicitly agreed with Brown's evaluation. His assessment of Detroit also carried praise for the stability of industrial relations, and its tension-reducing effect on the community.

The role played by TULC in Detroit's comeback was a major one. In the 1960–1967 period its membership rose

159

at one point to over 9,000, and its achievements led Bayard Rustin, the civil rights leader, to comment, "I wish there was a TULC in every industrial city in the country."[11] The concept of a labor-liberal-Negro coalition seemed to be working. Mayor Cavanagh appointed Negroes to prominent positions. Industry consulted TULC for assistance in hiring people. Even the building trades found it expeditious to talk with TULC about Negro apprentices. When UAW opponents of Sheffield tried to have him removed from the Detroit scene or ousted from his UAW staff job, the daily press and many prominent white and black leaders insisted that Reuther allow him to remain active in the city.

But nothing fails like success, and TULC was soon divided and fragmented by new issues. A congressional seat opened in the predominantly Negro first district, and John Conyers, Jr., the legal counsel of TULC, wanted it. His father, John Conyers, Sr., a long-time UAW activist and staff member, argued in TULC for an endorsement. Sheffield and Battle, however, had their own choice: Richard Austin, an outstanding businessman and civic leader. Conyers won the primary by 32 votes, but the election split TULC deeply.

A rival organization was set up to further fragment the power of black unionists. The Negro church leaders who had sponsored the June 1963 Freedom March in Detroit began exerting independent political pressure, vying with the NAACP, TULC, and other organizations for a dominant role in the city. Meanwhile a dynamic black nationalist spokesman, Rev. Albert Cleage, was drawing larger and larger audiences with his scornful attacks on TULC's "Uncle Tomism." Most white community leaders treated the struggles within the black community as a case of "too many black Napoleons." But this superficial analysis ignored the conflicting pressures building up behind the various black leaders. Whites underestimated the impact of national events on Detroit's black community.

TULC didn't win its fight with the building trades. George Edwards, the police commissioner and a member of TULC, resigned in 1963, and his successor, Ray Girardin, never established the firm control over the police that Edwards had, even though he was well liked in the Negro community and was a "Cavanagh man." The consequence was foreseen by Edwards, now a judge of the United States Court of Appeals for the Sixth Circuit. He wrote in November 1965:

> It is clear that in 1965 no one will make excuses for any city's inability to foresee the possibility of racial trouble. . . . Although local police forces generally regard themselves as public servants with the responsibility of maintaining law and order, they tend to minimize this attitude when they are patrolling areas that are heavily populated with Negro citizens. There, they tend to view each person on the streets as a potential criminal or enemy, and all too often this attitude is reciprocated. Indeed the hostility between Negro communities in our large cities and the police departments is the major problem in law enforcement in this decade. It has been a major cause of all recent race riots.[12]

Nobody listened seriously. In 1965 Mayor Cavanagh won reelection, but on the issue of "law and order" Councilman Mary Beck had attacked Cavanagh for being too friendly with the Negro community. Thomas Poindexter, whom all Negroes considered a racist, defeated a Negro for the council in a special election.

These local events were partly a reflection of the national turmoil. Newspaper reports, TV coverage, and personal accounts of friends and relatives throughout the country kept the Detroit black community in a constant state of agitation. Who could forget the ordeal of James

161

Meredith, or the figure of Bull Connor of Birmingham, Alabama, with his police dogs, fire hoses, and cattle prods? Or the murder of four children in a Negro church by a bomb explosion, the burning of the freedom buses, and the near-murder of Detroiter Walter Bergmann because he had joined the Negroes on the bus? Or the murder of Mrs. Viola Liuzzo, the idealistic Detroit housewife, and the humiliations of Rev. Martin Luther King, Jr., who insisted that Christians practice their religion? Or the riots that kept breaking out in the Eastern cities, in Cleveland and Chicago, and then, like a grand finale, in Watts, California?

Detroit was not an island unto itself. For the black community it was a time of memorial meetings and protest rallies, of shame and anger and despair. In this atmosphere the gains of Detroit blacks—and there were some gains—seemed more like mere tokenism than true social progress.

For closer examination showed that most of the gains benefited the Negro middle class. Economic progress was reflected in the enrollment of more than 2,500 Negro students at Wayne State University—more than in the Big Ten and the Ivy League combined. Ownership of homes rose to over 60 per cent among black dwellers. Yet a survey showed that 90 per cent of the graduates of a Negro high school were unemployed, as compared with only 50 per cent of the dropouts.

The deterioration of the Detroit public school system was another sore point in the Negro community. The increase in the black population from 30 to 40 per cent of the total population created de facto segregation in the schools. The number of children rose by 50,000, adding to the already overcrowded conditions. And the 50 per cent drop-out rate among black youth is hardly surprising when one considers that the white teachers

162

and principals were totally unprepared—either by education or experience—to handle black students. "Baby sitting" rather than education, and discipline rather than influence over youth, became the frequent pattern of work for the frightened or helpless schoolteachers. The contrast with the suburban school system was obvious. In one case, students at the all-Negro Northern High School struck in demand for a better education!

No significant attention was paid to the new mood of dissatisfaction among the black youth. No organization had attracted them in real numbers. No program really involved them as full participants.

The disparity between the poor blacks and the whites increased in this period of prosperity. With all the publicity about housing programs and model cities, only 758 low-income units were built in Detroit in the decade beginning in 1956. Unemployment averaged about 30 per cent for Negro youth. In 1960 the median income in the ghetto was $2,640 for a household, compared to the median family income in Michigan of over $6,000.[13] This was the period when everybody but the poor seemed to make money on the poverty programs.

New programs and massive federal assistance may have changed certain trends in Detroit, but the escalation of the war in Vietnam reduced federal aid at a time when it was most needed. No man knew this better than Mayor Cavanagh. Unless a drastic shift in national priorities took place, Detroit and other urban centers were doomed to failure. Cavanagh decided to run for Senator on a peace and social reform program, but he was ahead of his time. His opponent in the Democratic primary, G. Mennen Williams, proved too strong, with the backing of the labor hierarchy, and he defeated Cavanagh in the primary only to lose to Robert Griffin in the fall of 1965.

The black community was upset by Cavanagh's decision to seek a higher office so soon after his reelection as mayor. They had a fondness for "Soapy" Williams, and they were concerned over a possible successor to Cavanagh. The frank dialogue and rapport between the mayor and the black community were somewhat strained at the time each needed the other most.

In the fall of 1966, Detroit barely avoided a race riot. A handful of black nationalists clashed with police on the east side, but the populace didn't join with the youths. Neighborhood and community leaders convinced the blacks to stay at home, and the scuffle was confined to a minor incident.

However, the storm signals appeared in the spring of 1966, and no one recognized them more clearly than Mayor Cavanagh. The killing of a young Negro war veteran by a gang of white youths infuriated the Negroes. The police arrested only one of the gang. In the slum area on Twelfth Street, a prostitute was killed—by a pimp, according to police; by the police, according to Negroes. Friction between the police and the blacks was visible everywhere. In private sessions Cavanagh met with both Negro and white leaders to find ways of alleviating the tension, but their efforts were fruitless. In May 1967, the mayor and I discussed the situation and concluded that it would be a miracle if Detroit escaped what already appeared inevitable in other cities: a major riot.

The disintegration of cohesive social and political forces suggested events were getting out of hand.

In June the Detroit Police Officers Association, led by Carl Parsell, staged a blue-flu strike in which hundreds of Detroit policemen, for the first time since the Boston police strike of 1919, walked off their jobs for five days to support demands for higher pay.[14]

The city was a keg of social dynamite. Yet a public

warning by Cavanagh that Detroit had not eliminated any of the causes of a potential riot was not taken seriously. The people were too busy with business-as-usual, politics-as-usual, and unionism-as-usual, to listen. The illusion that Detroit was different was too strong to dispel.

Only two days before disaster struck Detroit, the highly respected Negro councilman, Rev. Nicholas Hood, reflected the views of most Detroiters when he denounced "the long hot summer mongers." Reassuring the white community, he added, "I haven't heard any Negroes talk about the possible violence this summer—only white people are talking about it."[15]

And this is not the least of the reasons why the riot in July 1967 shattered Detroit like a terrible earthquake. The shock was to prove painful indeed.

A City Besieged: The Riot of '67   11

A NATION MADE tense by the daily TV visions of violence from Vietnam, and stunned by the impact of Watts and Newark, could not be expected to imagine anything but the worst when the reports came that "Detroit is having IT" in July 1967.

For America, the Detroit scene seemed to be described accurately by the journalist who wrote ". . . whole sections of the nation's fifth largest city lay in charred, smoking ruins. From Gratiot Avenue six miles to the east, tongues of flames licked at the night sky, illuminating the angular skeletons of gutted homes, shops, supermarkets. Looters and arsonists danced in the eerie shadows, stripping a store clean, then setting it to the torch. Mourned Mayor Jerome Cavanagh, 'It looks like Berlin in 1945.'

"In the violent summer of 1967, Detroit became the scene of the bloodiest uprising in a half century and the costliest in terms of property damage in U.S. history. At the week's end, there were 41 known dead, 347 injured, 3,800 arrested. Some 5,000 people were homeless (the vast majority Negro), while 1,300 buildings had been reduced to mounds of ashes and bricks, and 2,700 businesses sacked. Damage estimates reached $500 million."[1]

For most of Detroit's citizens, black and white, the week was a nightmare of fear, hysteria, and terror, heightened by the spread of fantastic rumors. These gained credence because news of the "trouble on Twelfth Street" was withheld from the general public most of Sunday, while excited people phoned horror stories to each other.

Only after the riot was over, and then thanks to the brilliant investigative work of three *Detroit Free Press* reporters, did an understanding of what had happened begin to penetrate the public mind.[2] It was then too late to repair the emotional damage, the scars of hatred and violence which became the legacy of the city.

The miracle was that the week's rioting had not become a bloody uprising; fewer than 10 per cent of Detroit's 500,000 blacks were involved in any way—most arrests were for curfew violations, not looting, arson, or sniping. Most Negroes stayed home, hoping the police and National Guard wouldn't go crazy and do more wild shooting than they did. All Negro leaders tried to prevent the outbreak. There was no black revolution, as the suburbs feared, with thousands of ghetto residents storming into the stores and mansions of Grosse Pointe and Birmingham.

There was no race riot—although some members of the press and radio referred to the events as such—as there had been in 1943, with thousands of whites battling or beating up blacks on the streets. Looting was done by both blacks and whites. Property damage turned out to be around $50 million and not $500 million—most of the city and the ghetto were intact. The majority of the 43 riot victims need not have died. Their deaths could have been—and should have been—prevented.

Instead, it was a new sort of disorder: a social riot. "It was mostly a rebellion of people who have no stake in society, people in both races. You put up with the status

167

quo as long as it works for you. If you are going nowhere
and there is no end in sight, then the hostility grows," a
spokesman for Mayor Cavanagh told the press soon after
the outbreak, but no one paid attention or accepted such
an analysis.[3]

In the shock of the events, most Detroiters succumbed
to old fears and prejudices. Panic and ignorance, mixed
with hate and disbelief, gripped the city. Only a full
display of federal power—combat veterans—could confine the riot. The mayor and many citizens knew it, but
until this was recognized nationally, the time lag in
calling out federal troops would take its toll. Meanwhile,
Mayor Cavanagh and many others watched his hopes
for a progressive Detroit go up in flames.

The mistakes began with the decision to make a police
raid in the midst of the ghetto, Detroit's tough and turbulent Twelfth Street, early one Sunday morning—a
time when the police force is at its weakest and the streets
are filled with the resentful, the alienated, the "don't-
give-a-damn-for-anything" residents. Probably another
incident elsewhere in Detroit would have set off some
social explosion, but if a Machiavelli had wanted to
provoke a confrontation between the police and the
blacks, he couldn't have chosen a better time and place
than Twelfth Street on that Sunday morning. A "blind
pig" (illegal bar) was raided, dozens of its occupants,
drunk and sober, herded into the street, and many arrested. A crowd gathered and the first bottle or stone
was thrown after the inevitable rumor—perhaps based
on fact—that the cops were abusing a screaming woman.

By mid-morning Twelfth Street was in shambles. The
street had been one of the worst in the ghetto. On it, as
Detroit reporter Barbara Stanton discovered, there were
buildings owned by whites from the suburbs who called
the second-story apartments vacant, then took a cut
from the earnings of the prostitutes who worked there.

There were those who despised their Negro customers, and showed it by the filth that lay in their grocery aisles, the sour smell of clotted milk and rotting meat that rose from their counters.

There were others who greeted the Negroes as friends, hired them, befriended them, and were warned by them when the looting began—although it did them little good.

On Twelfth Street, holdups were so common, they went unreported daily, numbers slips passed hands, small children stole, pawn shops did a thriving business, the streets were clogged with cars and scattered with litter.[4]

Detroit's police, under a humanitarian commissioner, Ray Girardin, did have a plan in the event that a riot broke out in the city. In theory, police would seal off the troubled area, slowly sweep through it, picking up rioters and looters, and herd them into buses. The prisoners would be taken to temporary detention centers for speedy arraignment, and the whole operation would be handled bloodlessly and without shooting.

The police tried it and failed because the crowds were simply too big. There was no shooting, and despite an undercurrent of tension, a kind of carnival atmosphere prevailed.

There was some suspicion at this point that the police reaction to the large crowds was partly based not on fear, but on resignation. The city police felt overworked, underpaid, neglected, and certainly understaffed, and perhaps there was some feeling that Detroit had to learn its lesson the hard way. In any event, on the first day, most police kept their "cool."

The next major effort to dampen the riot came from Detroit's top Negro leaders, working with Mayor Cavanagh.

This, too, failed. Young John Conyers, Jr., went into his congressional district, the focal point of the rising storm. He was booed and stoned when he tried to talk. "You try to talk to these people and they'll knock you into the middle of next year," he reported later.[5] This was the reception given a Negro leader whom many fellow Democrats often viewed as "too chauvinistic."

"Buddy" Battle of TULC—another black leader often criticized for being "too aggressive"—was on the streets for a while. He reported, "You couldn't use dialect speech, Swahili or anything else. You couldn't speak to those kids. This was not 'hate the man,' just looting."[6]

When Mayor Cavanagh met Sunday afternoon with over 100 Negro leaders, the meaning of the riot had become increasingly clear and the powerlessness of the Negro leadership too obvious to belabor. Curbing the rioters would take much more force than the city police could possibly muster. The difficulty was, as Mayor Cavanagh pointed out, that calling for state police and the National Guard contained an element of risk, "because they're all white—we're leery of that." The troubled Negro leaders were divided in their recommendations, and Mayor Cavanagh decided to ask Governor Romney for state assistance. This decision made Governor Romney the new man in charge until Monday midnight, when Cyrus R. Vance took over for the President of the United States with federal troops.

Meanwhile, at 3:30 P.M. on Sunday the FBI had alerted the President of the United States about the riot in Detroit, and preliminary steps were taken to have federal troops available. Behind the scenes Mayor Cavanagh was already seeking help from Washington, for he was convinced it would take a show of federal force to bring the situation under control. But with Governor Romney, a potential candidate to the presidency, the involvement of federal troops became a complicated issue with heavy political overtones. The unmistakable impression grew that while Detroit was burning, the politicians with a national stake were fiddling around. Nothing that occurred in the next 24 hours lessened the suspicion.

The Michigan National Guard were readily available since their summer encampment was going on, and 200 of them were in training in Detroit that Sunday. By 7 P.M. the first contingents were on the streets, and this only added fuel to the fire. Neither by experience, temperament, nor training were the Guardsmen prepared to cope with the situation, and as a result, both officers and men panicked at times. As the *Detroit Free Press* study pointed out:

> One major critical observation must be made. Both city and army authorities acted to try to keep the death toll at a minimum, though they did so in different ways. In both cases, their efforts were not successful and permitted unnecessary death.
>
> At 11:20 Monday night, within hours after the National Guard came under federal control, Lt. General John Throckmorton, the commanding officer, issued a general order commanding all troops under this control to unload their weapons and to fire only on the command of any officer.
>
> Throckmorton's regular army troops obeyed that order; only one person was killed in paratrooper territory in the five days that followed.
>
> *The National Guard did not obey, in many cases because the order was improperly disseminated and was never made clear to the men on the street. As a result, the Guard was involved in a total of eleven deaths in which nine innocent people died.*
>
> Military discipline and attention to Throckmorton's order could have avoided those deaths.[7]

But few persons knew or cared about that during the week. Most citizens, black and white, gripped by fear and the general panic, wanted social order at any cost.

But not everyone. The most effective looters had come in cars and hauled away an amazing amount of goods and furniture—in most cases they were not the havenots; they were both black and white, and they sometimes aided each other. However, it was the poor who took the rap for the looting. They were the ones who were caught or shot.

Burning credit records in stores, and then the stores themselves, soon turned parts of Twelfth Street into a holocaust, with city firemen helpless in the face of the mob's antagonism. Governor Romney flew over the scene Sunday night and reported, "It looks like the city has been bombed on the west side and there was an area two and a half miles by three and a half miles with major fires, with entire blocks in flames."[8]

Neither Mayor Cavanagh's 9 P.M. curfew edict nor Governor Romney's state of emergency declaration had any effect in quelling the riot, which by now had spread to another and smaller black ghetto on the east side of Detroit.

The hysteria in the city continued to mount, until, in the judgment of the army commander, the city was saturated with fear; the National Guardsmen were afraid, the residents were afraid, and the police were afraid.[9] And numerous persons, the majority of them Negroes, were being injured by gunshots of "undetermined origin."

A specter haunted Detroit. It was first referred to as "them," and soon became "snipers" or "organized conspirators." In the circumstances it was easy to visualize an armed insurrection in the city, and too many law enforcement officials and some reporters did just that.

A majority of Detroit's police were convinced that the riot was organized. The defense for the policemen accused of the sensational slaughter of three Negro youths would claim that "the riot was a war, and Detroit a battleground. There were four separate armies fighting the enemy—the Detroit police, the Michigan state police, the Michigan National Guard, and the soldiers of the 101st Airborne Division."[10]

Mass arrests ensued, with bond set as high as $200,000

for suspected snipers.) One judge remarked to a defendant, "You're nothing but a lousy, thieving looter. It's too bad they didn't shoot you."[11]

The National Guardsmen looked nervous and frightened even on TV. One officer instructed his men as follows: "If you find a sniper, don't stand back and shoot at him. Use fire and movement to get into that building and turn it upside down and find what's in there. I don't want to hear of 30 soldiers pinned down by one sniper."[12]

Totally inexperienced, and poorly commanded, the Guardsmen did not know whether or not they were fighting an organized enemy, but they assumed, to be safe, that they were; a black man was automatically suspected of being one of "them."

The headlines and some of the stories in Detroit's daily papers added to the general fear and hysteria. Monday most of downtown was deserted and factories closed. Readers of the morning *Free Press* saw the headline "Police and 4,000 Guardsmen Move Against Looting and Burning Mobs."[13] The *Detroit News,* the afternoon paper, informed its readers that "7,000 Troops Guard Detroit: Riot Loss Nears $100 Million," and its lead story began, "Detroit is in a declared state of emergency today as arson, looting and gunfire from a major racial outbreak left three persons dead, almost 500 injured or wounded and a property damage toll that may exceed $100 million for the city."[14]

On Tuesday, the *News* bannered, "Snipers Prolong Emergency: Death Toll Climbs to 23."[15] The crescendo grew. On Wednesday, the *News* headlined, "Tanks, Troops Battle Snipers on West Side: 12 More Die." A sub-story said a woman was killed watching a sniper duel.

Anyone not anxiety-ridden by Wednesday had only to read the *News* feature story entitled, "Guerrilla War Erupts on Riot-Scarred 12th." The story ran as follows:

173

Backed by tanks and armored personnel carriers, national guardsmen and police last night and early today fought house-to-house war on 12th Street.

The scene was incredible.

It was as though the Viet Cong had infiltrated the riot-blacked streets.

Snipers in what sounded like at least two dozen locations snapped off rounds as police and riflemen slid past the dingy houses.

They were answered by quick volleys from M-1 carbines, blasts from machine guns and bursts from submachine guns.[16]

The *Detroit Free Press* picked up the sniper play on Thursday with the headline, "Snipers Stage Daylight Attacks; West Side Sealed Off by Guard. U.S. Aide Predicts More Deaths." The story which followed bristled with Vietnam-type reporting.

Negro riflemen raked Detroit's still smoldering ghetto on the West Side with sniper fire Wednesday in a daring and apparently organized daylight outbreak.

National Guardsmen rushed tanks to the area and opened up with .50 caliber machine gun fire as the nation's worst racial explosion in recent history continued.

Police said the sporadic sniper fire that broke out over the entire 12th and Clairmont area about 4 P.M. led them to believe the attack had been planned.

"It looks organized, in groups of five or six," said one policeman.[17]

TV viewers nightly saw the glow of fires, the marching of troops and the mobs, and the sound track carried the crack of gunfire. Within Detroit, a glance out of the darkened windows seemed to verify the vision of a city under siege. Unfortunately, the scenes of whites and blacks standing guard together in neighborhoods and the young people helping the firemen were obscured by the dramatic pictures and stories suggesting a battleground.

Nothing in George Romney's experience prepared him

for the role thrust upon him by the riot. Nor was he responsible for the poor performance of the National Guard. And he was no match for the politicians in the White House in the byplay over the use of federal troops.

From 6 A.M. Monday morning, when Mayor Cavanagh and Governor Romney met with Vance, the President's representative, until midnight Monday, Detroiters cursed at the arguments and delays in letting the federal troops take over. At one point Congressman Charles Diggs, the black moderate, threatened to buy nationwide TV to denounce President Johnson unless the White House rushed the troops to Detroit. Mayor Cavanagh kept insisting on this from the moment Vance stepped off the plane from Washington.

Governor Romney was given conflicting counsel by his advisers, whose inexperience was the equal of his, and didn't send the "right" kind of telegram for federal intervention until Monday night. But then, Vance had toured the city around suppertime Monday and had stated he didn't think the troops needed to be deployed. For most Detroiters, Monday's procrastination was a disgraceful display of petty politics. An editorial in the *New York Times* sharply criticized the President for his role in the delay.

> . . . Because he holds the highest office and therefore bears the highest responsibility both to act and to set an example, President Johnson offended most conspicuously in his pussy-footing response to the debacle in Detroit. He shilly-shallied for several hours in ordering Army units into action in the city despite pleas of local officials that troops were urgently needed. And when he did act, Mr. Johnson issued a proclamation and a personal statement both of which were clearly designed to place the entire political responsibility on Governor Romney.
>
> It is no disgrace to either the Governor, a Republican, or to Mayor Cavanagh, a Democrat, that the situation

slipped out of local and state control. The fact that Governor Romney may be the Republican Presidential candidate next year may explain but cannot excuse President Johnson's nervous posturing at this critical time.[18]

A Republican political statement blaming only President Johnson was also censured by the *Times*.

(The arrival of federal troops, including the 101st Airborne Division, brought cheers on the streets of the east side where the paratroopers were concentrated. Black and white citizens were very friendly, and peace came quickly to this part of Detroit.) Yet there was a puzzle about the deployment of the federal forces. "Detroit policemen have asked military commanders why the paratroopers had been kept on the relatively quiet East Side while the bulk of the fighting was being done by tired and less well-trained guardsmen on the West Side."[19] No satisfactory answer was ever given, but Detroit "knew." The rumored explanation—firmly believed by many people—was that President Johnson had ordered this to protect Henry Ford and the Grosse Pointe residents farther out on the east side. Whatever the reason, the unbalanced deployment of federal forces was responsible for many unnecessary deaths, for the Guardsmen simply couldn't handle themselves like professional soldiers.)

The *Christian Science Monitor* was the first to point this out.

It must be reported there is some evidence had President Johnson permitted federal troops to arrive earlier the death toll and the number of injuries would have been far lower. These confident and cool-headed troops, many of them recently returned from Vietnam, had no deaths charged to them. Yet their section of the city was the most orderly.

They had been dispatched to Detroit's East Side, where the gun play had been heaviest on Monday night, with national guardsmen spraying buildings with bullets. On

176

Tuesday and Wednesday nights, there was nearly total calm in the area. The gunfire had shifted to the western section, where the guardsmen were assigned.[20]

How many of the tragedies in Detroit might have been prevented by the quick and total deployment of federal troops everywhere can never be fully appraised.) But the contrast was vivid between the conduct and effectiveness of General Throckmorton's soldiers and that of the inexperienced Guardsmen. Obsessed by a fear of "snipers," whose number and actions were grossly exaggerated, the Guardsmen involved were in many cases reacting to their own gunfire . . . and frightened citizens kept phoning reports of sniper fire to the police stations any time the crack of rifle fire was heard.

General Throckmorton's orders for all soldiers to unload their rifles was an attempt to control the acts of military hysteria. The evidence before the U.S. Riot Commission supported the wisdom of Throckmorton's decision. It also described some of the unnecessary tragedies.

A Detroit newspaper reporter who spent the night riding a command jeep (national guard) told a Commission investigator of machine guns being fired accidentally, street lights being shot out by rifle fire and buildings being placed under siege on the sketchiest reports of sniping. Troopers would fire, and immediately from the distance there would be answering fire, sometimes consisting of tracer bullets.

In one instance, the newsman related, a report was received on the jeep radio that an army bus was pinned down by sniper fire at an intersection. National Guardsmen and police, arriving from various directions, jumped out and began asking each other, "Where's the sniper fire coming from?" As one Guardsman pointed to a building, everyone rushed about, taking cover. A soldier, alighting from a jeep, accidentally pulled the trigger on his rifle. As the shot reverberated through the darkness, an officer

177

yelled, "What's going on?" "I don't know," came the answer "Sniper, I guess."

Without any clear authorization or direction, someone opened fire upon the suspected building. A tank rolled up and sprayed the building with .50 caliber tracer bullets. Law enforcement officers rushed into the surrounded building and discovered it was empty. "They must be firing one shot and running," was the verdict.[21]

Another report was as follows:

> Employed as a private guard, 55 year old Julius L. Dorsey, a Negro, was standing in front of a market when accosted by two Negro men and a woman. They demanded he permit them to loot the market. He ignored their demands. They began to berate him. He asked a neighbor to call the police. As the argument grew more heated, Dorsey fired three shots from his pistol into the air.
>
> The police radio reported, "Looters, they have rifles." A patrol car driven by a police officer and carrying three National Guardsmen arrived. As the looters fled, the law enforcement officers opened fire. When the firing ceased, one person was dead.
>
> He was Julius L. Dorsey.[22]

More evidence of the incompetence of the National Guard presented to the Commission were the following incidents:

> At 9:15 P.M. Tuesday, July 25, 38 year old Jack Sydnor, a Negro, came home drunk. Taking out his pistol, he fired one shot into an alley. A few minutes later, police arrived. As his common-law wife took refuge in a closet, Sydnor waited, gun in hand, while the police forced open the door. Patrolman Roger Poike, the first to enter, was shot by Sydnor. Although critically injured, the officer managed to get off six shots in return. Police within the building and on the street poured a hail of fire into the apartment. When the shooting ceased, Sydnor's body riddled by the gun fire, was found lying on the ground outside a window.
>
> Nearby, a state police officer and a Negro youth were

struck and seriously injured by stray bullets. As in other cases, where the origin of the shots was not immediately determinable, police reported them as "shot by sniper."

Reports of "heavy sniper fire" poured into police headquarters from the two blocks surrounding the apartment homes where the battle with Jack Sydnor had taken place. National Guardsmen with two tanks were dispatched to help flush out the snipers.

Shots continued to be heard throughout the neighborhood. At approximately midnight—there are discrepancies as to the precise time—a machine gunner on a tank, startled by several shots, asked the assistant gunner where the shots were coming from. The assistant gunner pointed towards a flash in the window of an apartment house from which there had been reports of sniping.

The machine gunner opened fire. As the slugs ripped through the window and the walls of the apartment, they nearly severed the arm of 21 year old Valerie Hood.

Her four year old niece, Tanya Blanding, toppled dead, a .50 caliber bullet hole in her chest.

A few seconds earlier, 19 year old Bill Hood, standing in a window, had lighted a cigarette.[23]

An account appeared in Wednesday's edition of the *News* under the headline "Woman Killed in Motel Watching Sniper Duel." When investigated by the U.S. Riot Commission, it turned out to be a very different story:

> Down the street, a bystander was critically injured by a stray bullet. Simultaneously, the John C. Lodge Freeway, two blocks away, was reported under heavy sniper fire. Tanks and National Guard troops were sent to investigate. At the Harlan House Hotel, ten blocks from where Tanya Blanding had died a short time earlier, Mrs. Helen Hall, a 51 year old white business woman, opened the drapes of the fourth floor hall window. Calling to other guests, she exclaimed, "Look at the tanks." She died seconds later as bullets began to slam into the building.[24]

No one knows—nor was a study ever made—how many police and Guardsmen were actually involved in other and uglier incidents, most of them known to the black community but recognized in the white world only after the *Detroit Free Press* study by the three reporters, and the U.S. Riot Commission's investigation.

The white owner of an expensive three-story house had trouble with some tenants over a period of time and, on the advice of his attorney, took possession of the house. For protection they brought along a .22-caliber rifle, which R. R.'s brother (R. R. was the homeowner) fired into a pillow to test it. This was about 8 P.M. Wednesday night, July 26. R. R. informed his lawyer that the tenants had returned and he had refused to let them enter. The Commission report follows:

Thereupon, R. R. alleged the tenants had threatened to obtain the help of the National Guard. The attorney relates that he was not particularily concerned. He told R. R. that if the National Guard did appear he should have the officer in charge call him (the attorney).

At approximately the same time the National Guard claims it received information to the effect that several [men] had evicted legal occupants of the house, and intended to start sniping after dark.

A National Guard column was dispatched to the scene. Shortly after 9 P.M. in the half light of the dusk, the column of approximately 30 men surrounded the house. A tank took a position on a lawn across the street. The captain commanding the column placed in front of the house an explosive device similar to a fire cracker. After setting this off in order to draw attention to the presence of the column, he called for them to come out of the house. No attempt was made to verify the truth or falsehood of the allegations regarding snipers.

When the Captain received no reply from the house, he began counting to 10. As he was counting, he said, he heard a shot, the origin of which he could not determine. A few seconds later he heard another shot and saw a "fire streak" coming from an upstairs window. He thereupon gave the order to fire.

According to the three young men, they were on the second floor of the house and completely bewildered by the barrage of fire that was unleashed against it. As hundreds of bullets crashed through the first and second story windows and ricocheted off the wall, they dashed to the third floor. Protected by a large chimney, they huddled in a closet until, during a lull in the firing, they were able to wave an item of clothing as a sign of surrender. They were arrested as snipers.[25]

But their troubles had just begun, for they soon received the treatment hundreds of Negroes were to complain about to Congressman Conyers. The Commission report continues:

Jailed at the 10th Precinct Station sometime Wednesday night, R. R. and his two companions were taken from their cell to an "alley court"—police slang for an unlawful attempt to make prisoners confess. A police officer, who has resigned from the force, allegedly administered such a severe beating to R. R. that the bruises were still visible two weeks later.

R. R.'s 17 year old brother had his skull cracked open, and was thrown back into the cell. He was taken to a hospital only when other arrestees complained that he was bleeding to death.

At a preliminary hearing 12 days later the prosecution presented only one witness, the National Guard Captain who had given the order to fire. The police officer who had signed the original complaint was asked to take the stand. The charges against all three of the young men were dismissed.[26]

A wire service sent out the following story on this event:

"Two National Guard tanks ripped a snipers' nest with machine guns Wednesday night and flushed out three shaggy-haired white youths. . . ."[27]

There were two conflicting versions of why police began to take off their bright badges and cover their license plates so they could not be identified. The police claimed it was because of sniper danger, while blacks argued it was to protect the police from being identified for brutality. The Commission report states that ". . . as hundreds of arrestees were brought into the 10th precinct, officers took it upon themselves to carry on investigations and to attempt to extract confessions. Dozens of charges of police brutality emanated from the station as prisoners were brought in uninjured but later had to be taken to the hospital. In the absence of the precinct commander, who had transferred his headquarters to the riot command post in a nearby hospital, discipline vanished."[28]

Seared in the memory of Detroit's black population was this breakdown of law and order—a police department unable to control its own men and pretending otherwise. It was as if a counter-riot arose from the original one. Two other events deepened the animosity between the young blacks and the police. The first was the shooting to death of a black youth by an officer. Again there were two versions of the story.

According to the officers' version, police and National Guardsmen were questioning a youth suspected of arson, when he attempted to escape. As he vaulted over the hood of a car, an officer fired his shotgun. Without checking, the police and Guardsmen drove off.

The other version was that of several witnesses, who claimed the youth had been shot by police after he had been told to run.

The reliability of the official version was questioned because, despite the fact that an autopsy disclosed the youth had been killed by five shotgun pellets, only a cursory investigation was made, and the death was attributed to "sniper fire."

After a Detroit newspaper editor presented the statements of several witnesses, the police investigated, and one policeman identified himself as firing the shot. The prosecutor's office declined to press charges, citing the conflicting testimony.[29]

As the violence expended itself and "normalcy" began to return by the end of the week, the Negro community heard a story calculated to increase "cop hatred." Rumors were that city police had caught three young blacks with two white girls at a party in a motel, had killed the men in cold blood, beat up the girls, and worked over other people to keep them quiet about what happened.

The initial police report in these deaths was that three snipers had been killed at the Algiers Motel on Woodward Avenue.

Joseph Strickland, a Negro staff writer on the *Detroit News,* investigated the rumors and came up with a solid witness, Robert L. Greene, a former staff sergeant and veteran of Vietnam. Strickland, like many other reporters, had wondered why the first report of the dead men in a motel came from motel personnel, and not the individuals responsible for the killing.

With this exposure, the inevitable investigations began, and soon the world learned about the killing of the three blacks. The full horror of the case later became the subject of novelist John Hersey's best seller, *The Algiers Motel Incident.*

In their own book, *Nightmare in Detroit,* two newsmen, Van Gordon Sauter and Burleigh Hines, summarized the cold facts in one paragraph:

> The events of the next hour left a stain on the Detroit police department that will not be erased for decades. Pollard, Cooper and Temple—unarmed and outnumbered—were shotgunned to death. Each was shot more than once at a range of fifteen feet or less by twelve gauge double 0 buckshot. Temple and Pollard were apparently shot while lying or kneeling. The two girls were mauled and beaten. The others were threatened and terrorized, and a few beaten up.[30]

The Vietnam veteran wasn't frightened into silence. He talked, and official investigations resulted. One and a half years later, three suspended Detroit policemen, Ronald August, David Senak, and Robert Paille, and a private guard, Melvin Dismukes, a Negro, were tried on charges of conspiracy against the civil rights of the three dead men and seven other individuals. An all-white jury found them not guilty.

But what the Negro community "knew" in August 1967 was confirmed by events: No white policeman would ever be tried and found guilty of murdering a black man caught with a white woman. Charges of murder were made and dismissed against two of the policemen. There was also the unforgettable scene of over 50 police officers demonstrating their support of the accused men.

Out of the ashes and debris came a new mood of militancy and bitterness among young blacks. When H. Rap Brown came to the city an overflow crowd of 3,000 cheered his denunciations of the "system" in the flamboyant rhetoric of the extreme Left. A large number of the total of 7,200 arrested during the week never forgot the treatment they received or saw others receive in jail. A federal judge was moved to criticize the incredible performance of the local courts in the crisis.

In the bitter aftermath of the disastrous July days, Detroit's black middle class and labor moderates found themselves scorned by the new generation of young militants as "Uncle Toms," and shunted aside by the white power structure as failures.

The extremists of both Right and Left found new listeners and Detroit resounded with their inflammatory speeches.

The most prominent victim of the black-white hostility—or polarization, as it is politely called—was the

184

symbol of Detroit's social progress: Mayor Jerome P. Cavanagh. His decision not to seek reelection in 1969 was almost inevitable in view of Detroit's post-riot experiences and its failure to heal the wounds of that terrible week.

Post-Riot Reconstruction: The Failure of the Power Elite

12

THE AFTERMATH of the July 1967 riot was a backlash of black rage and white fear, the extent of which was seldom comprehended. Prestigious industrial and business leadership floundered in its efforts to reconstruct the city whenever these polarized reactions were provoked by specific events. For a while, however, Detroit appeared to be living under new illusions of progress, mistaking good intentions for concrete results. The auto industry cutbacks and layoffs in the winter of 1969–1970 deflated many of those illusions.

Detroit entered the 1970's with only a token improvement in its economic and social conditions. It was still a city in deep trouble.

Immediately after the riot, Mayor Cavanagh and Governor Romney called upon the important decision-makers in the Detroit area to help rebuild the city, and the subsequent rally of these leaders was described by the press as an "upheaval of human spirit."

Walter Reuther was cheered by the captains of industry when he pledged the volunteer help of 600,000 unionists to clean up the city. It was the first of many mirages of social unity and "city-effort." Soon the auto workers were preoccupied with national contract negotiations and a strike at Ford—an event which caused barely a ripple in the city plagued by larger problems.

The riot fires were still smoldering when Henry Ford II joined in the efforts to rebuild the city. Among other measures, he summoned Levi Jackson, the black former all-American football star and Yale scholar who had been languishing in the Ford personnel department, and sought his help in studying the causes of the riot.

John P. Roche, president of General Motors, also learned something from the events of that week in July. "I stood on the roof of the G.M. building [G.M.'s main offices are within easy sight of the notorious Twelfth Street]. I never thought I would see anything like that in the city of Detroit. I went to sleep and heard gun shots. I never thought I would hear that in the city of Detroit."[1]

Lynn Townsend, president of Chrysler, reacted similarly. The big three tycoons personally joined a 39-man committee to be known as the New Detroit Committee. It was endorsed and supported by downtown business, labor, and the churches.

Success in coping with Detroit's problems seemed assured when a young and talented executive agreed to direct the New Detroit Committee. He was Joseph L. Hudson, Jr., president of Detroit's very successful department store which bears his name.

Not only were the important members of the power elite going to participate in the work of the New Detroit Committee—and this was to be the key to its success—but the committee was determined to listen to and work with the new leaders in the Negro community: the black militants.

The challenge to the New Detroit Committee and the city was outlined by Joseph L. Hudson, Jr., before the opening luncheon of the United Foundation, the charity fund-raising organization.

Negroes must be encouraged to play a larger role in determining how their problems are to be solved . . . the problems which demand immediate solution are primarily in the area of jobs, housing, schools and public order. The riots themselves were clearly and thoroughly wrong. But behind them lie such fundamental causes as high unemployment among Negroes, mistreatment by some policemen, profiteering by some stores and landlords, substandard housing and the frustration of so many of the benefits of American life which they don't have.[2]

But most of white Detroit wasn't listening. They were debating the question of why police didn't shoot earlier. State police director Frederick Davids blamed the escalation of the riot on the tardy recognition that the so-called "soft approach" to controlling the situation had failed. No public official or the New Detroit Committee had convinced citizens otherwise.

No less a liberal than Ralph McGill, columnist and publisher of the *Atlanta Constitution,* fed the fears of Detroit's whites. In a sensational article in the *Detroit News* he stated flatly that, "There is now evidence that the sniping against police, firemen and individuals was organized,"[3] although, to quote the report of the New Detroit Committee, "the Kerner Commission, the City of Detroit administration and others have concluded that there is no evidence available that the July disturbances were planned or directed by any group, local, national, or international. No official agency has concluded that an organized conspiracy was behind the looting, burning or sniping that occurred in Detroit."[4]

Governor Romney and state police officials also had concluded that there was no conspiracy behind the riot.

For good measure, the *Detroit News* printed in large type a document of the Student Nonviolent Coordinating Committee with the headline, "Document Calls for a Black Revolution." The revolutionary rhetoric received more publicity from the *News* than all the efforts of all the militants put together could have accomplished in a year of hard work. Frightened whites had their worst fears "confirmed."

"We must first gain Black Power here in America. Living inside the camp of the leaders of enemy forces, it is our duty to revolt against the system and create our own system so that we can live as MEN," the manifesto proclaimed.[5]

The white suburbanites would also hear the words of Reverend Cleage at the memorial service for those killed in the riot. With both Mayor Cavanagh and Governor Romney in the audience, Reverend Cleage declared, "We are engaged in a nation-wide rebellion, seeking to become what God intended that we should be—free men with control of our own destiny, the destiny of black men."[6]

In reaction to such statements of a new black militancy America was soon treated to the TV spectacle of suburban housewives practicing pistol shooting, getting ready for the black invasion. Detroit's police joined the National Rifle Association by the hundreds, and through their membership over 300 of them purchased carbines for possible riot use.[7] Gun sales to private citizens rose so sharply that Mayor Cavanagh felt compelled to broadcast a plea for calm and a rejection of the flood of rumors engulfing the community. The mayor's efforts were fruitless. The white community was listening to a more exciting individual.

Donald Lobsinger, a city employee and organizer of Breakthrough, an offshoot of the John Birch society, held rallies all over white Detroit attended by crowds ranging from 400 to 1,000 persons. The slogan of Breakthrough was "SASO" standing for "Study, Arm, Store Provisions, and Organize." Literature was distributed by TACT

(Truth About Civil Turmoil), a front group created by the Birch society.[8]

For Lobsinger, an extreme right-winger, the civil war was only a matter of time.

> What I anticipate—I don't like to use dates, as I don't think they have a timetable, a specific year or anything like that—what I anticipate is that in this country there will be guerrilla type warfare such as is being waged in Vietnam and was waged in Algeria.
>
> Within two years we will have a block-to-block defense system over vast areas of Detroit. The block-to-block set-up would make it impossible for terrorists to come in and murder the men and rape the women. They'd never get out alive.[9]

The amazing tolerance for such views and activities of a city employee was reflected in Lobsinger's relative immunity to censure. No one dared fire him even after the following performance, reported in the *Daily Express:*

> Police bodily ejected right-wing extremist Donald Lobsinger from a tumultuous Council hearing Tuesday on a proposed open housing ordinance.
>
> Lobsinger, head of Breakthrough and a virulent opponent of the ordinance, was thrown out midway through the packed, hectic hearing after screaming against a Catholic priest who rose to speak in favor of legislation on behalf of an official city group.
>
> "You are a Judas goat leading your people astray," Lobsinger, who is also a Catholic, screamed at the Reverend James J. Sheehan, chairman of the Housing Commission of the Detroit Commission on Community Relations.
>
> "Rabbi Sheehan," shouted Lobsinger, who had previously expressed anti-Semitic feelings. His screaming denunciation prevented the priest from speaking.[10]

It was a time when it was much more convenient to worry about "black anti-Semitism" and to dismiss Lobsinger as a "crackpot" than to face up to his influence. To its consternation, the New Detroit Committee soon learned what impact the fears Lobsinger aroused could have on its program.

In November 1967, the committee organized an intensive lobbying expedition to Lansing, the state capital, to persuade the legislature to approve a fair housing bill recommended by Governor Romney. (A Detroit open-housing city ordinance, by itself, would have little significance, for the real problem was housing in the suburbs.)

Although the lobbying was inept, the failure was due to something more basic: the lobbyists, who were "heads of powerful corporations and powerful utilities, ministers, educators and politicians" and representatives of the UAW and AFL-CIO, simply didn't know how to counteract the fear of the whites. John P. Roche, GM vice-president; Mayor Cavanagh; Joseph L. Hudson, Jr.; William T. Gossett, former Ford counsel and president-elect of the American Bar Association; and others, were told by many legislators that it would be "political suicide or a violation of principle" to vote for the bill.[11]

The New Detroit Committee suffered another setback when its recommendation for a $5.3 million emergency school aid bill, again recommended by Governor Romney, failed to pass in the legislature, and disorders in Detroit's overcrowded schools continued.

Michigan state legislators in both parties may not have been the smartest politicians, but they did live in the world of political reality. Any proposals that additional school funds come from higher corporation or income taxes would have been considered heresy. Neither the auto industry nor the business interests of Michigan maintain strong lobbies in Lansing to increase their own taxes. As for suggestions to increase other taxes, the legislators knew that such action also carried the risk of political suicide, for it might lead to a revolt of the taxpayers. Nor did the New Detroit Committee understand how strong

191

an undercurrent of racial bias affected the argument over educational funds and the school crisis. Why put out money to educate "them"?

The New Detroit Committee not only lacked political clout, but its policies were often contradicted by individual actions of its members and organizations. The banking and real estate interests were not exactly enthusiastic about any fair housing law. The UAW and other labor unions wanted higher corporation or business taxes to meet the social needs of Detroit and Michigan. Labor endorsed candidates standing for social reform, while most top members of the New Detroit Committee supported Republicans. In 1968 most of them backed Richard Nixon, whose "cure" for inflation assured an auto recession and heavier unemployment in Detroit in 1970.

The political facts of life were recognized belatedly. "In the view of Joseph Hudson, Jr., the millionaire ex-chairman of New Detroit and a somewhat disillusioned man," *Newsweek* reported, "the poor in Detroit and elsewhere are discovering that elected officials really don't have power. The power, he says, resides with the white middle class that keeps turning down school tax proposals, electing somewhat conservative legislators and resisting social change. The Nixon administration, Hudson contends, has tailored its domestic programs accordingly."[12]

As an exercise in white political power the New Detroit Committee was a failure. However, its members did have economic power. Hiring policies were largely a prerogative of management, and the New Detroit Committee supporters did make a serious attempt to hire blacks.

In customary Detroit fashion, both the program and the results were oversold. Henry Ford II announced in October 1967 that his company would set up employment offices in the black community to recruit 5,000 hard-core unemployed. The thousands of Negroes who swamped the offices overwhelmed the facilities.[13] They also astonished the many Detroiters whose anti-Negro bias was expressed in such clichés as "they are too lazy to seek work," "they like welfare," etc. The Ford campaign forgot to mention that those hired would have to meet a minimum health standard, and in thousands of cases this was impossible. General Motors was less ostentatious in its activity. It reported in November 1967 that out of 12,000 newly hired workers in the Detroit area since the riot, about 5,000 were blacks.[14]

Chrysler, in cooperation with the UAW, set up a federal-funded training program which enrolled over 4,000 blacks in a two-year period only to collapse under the budget-cutting ax of the Nixon administration. Chrysler's sales troubles and production cutbacks in the winter of 1969–1970 added to the unemployment. Since layoffs are regulated by seniority provisions, the impact was mainly against the newly hired blacks in the auto industry. In desperation, the UAW proposed "inverse seniority," that is, a policy under which workers with higher seniority who are covered by Unemployment Insurance and Supplemental Unemployment Benefits take time off and the young are retained.[15]

This expedient was rejected by the auto firms on grounds that older employees were more disciplined and more experienced, so that keeping the young on instead would increase labor costs. What disturbed UAW leaders about the layoffs, as Douglas Fraser, director of the UAW's Chrysler department, pointed out, was that "the resulting sense of frustration and despair could lead to new flare-ups of violence, for hopes raised and then destroyed are the most dangerous kind of social tinder."[16]

193

As a matter of fact, it can be argued that Negro gains in employment in the 1960's were due more to labor market shortages in the period of economic growth than to a significant improvement in discriminatory policies.[17] Conversely, the loss of jobs in 1970 would not be primarily a function of overt discrimination, but the result of adverse sales and production cutbacks. The unemployment rate among young blacks in Detroit rose above the national average of 25 per cent, as economic growth was deliberately retarded by the Nixon administration's fiscal and monetary policies for slowing down the rate of inflation.

Another major economic activity of the New Detroit Committee was mistaken at first for support of Black Power, revolutionary style. "Financing the man who says 'burn whitey' isn't common sense," declared Horace Sheffield when the NDC offered a $100,000 grant to a coalition of militants, the Federation for Self-determination, headed by Reverend Cleage.[18] The NDC also gave $100,000 to a moderate coalition, the Detroit Council of Organizations, chaired by Rev. Roy Allen. In both cases the committee's aim was to placate the blacks and to provide seed money for developing "black capitalism," the new catchword in business circles. Taking into account the trends of economic ownership in the nation, however, the amounts involved, as well as further NDC programs of assistance, could only have a token effect on the financial status of the blacks.

Even discounting the negative effects of the Nixon administration's anti-inflationary policies in slowing down the economy and increasing black unemployment significantly, the prospects of black capitalism appeared dim, according to a major study by Andrew F. Brimmer, member of the Board of Governors of the Federal Reserve System, and Henry S. Terrell, the economist.

They concluded:

> The low income, high levels of unemployment, relatively large debts and relatively small holdings of financial assets of urban Negro families constitute a poor economic environment for business investment. Moreover, economic advancement within the Negro community may not improve profit prospects of Negro-owned businesses. Instead, it may accelerate the competition from national firms seeking to serve the expanding Negro market.
>
> Negro businesses tend to be small-scale operations, heavily concentrated in the provision of personal services and neighborhood retailing, with slender profit margins. While their small size is an obstacle to efficiency, economies of scale do appear to prevail: it is estimated that profits increase roughly $10.00 per worker with each increase of $1,000 in sales.
>
> The attempt to expand small-scale, Negro-owned businesses is running against a strong national trend. In retailing (in which most Negro businessmen are engaged), the trend is toward large units in which efficiency is rising rapidly.[19]

The limitations of black capitalism were especially visible in the city of Detroit, where in 1966, 65 per cent of the inner-city population was black, but only 38 per cent of the businesses were owned by blacks. Of these —mostly small retail and service operations—60 per cent had an annual net income of less than $8,000. Urban renewal programs have hurt black business. Fifty-seven per cent of the Negro-owned businesses failed to survive urban renewal compared with only 35 per cent of white businesses. Thus federal or private programs to foster black capitalism are offset by the impact of urban renewal developments.[20]

Lumping all the funds for the New Detroit Committee projects together, the total of $3,000,000 made only a small dent in the economic life of the blacks compared to the $14,000,000 received by black workers from a wage increase of 10 cents an hour won by the' auto workers union.

A sympathetic appraisal of Detroit's efforts, which appeared in *Fortune* magazine in February 1970, stated:

> Detroit's corporations have evolved a sophisticated structure for assuring black capitalism. But it is still too early to judge its success. . . . Many of Detroit's major corporations, tired of years of talking and worrying about an urban crisis, are becoming apathetic about the whole effort. Max Fisher, the city's leading fund raiser, believes that "volunteer fatigue will be our biggest problem over the next few years."[21]

In this context, the debates between the New Detroit Committee, the black militants, and the moderates were more useful as an outlet for grievances than in actual problem-solving. The NDC also channeled many bright young militants into "on-the-job-training" executive programs in the black community.

Perhaps inadvertently it also drew attention away from a more basic failure: the lack of progress in integrating higher staff levels or in breaking the skilled trades bottleneck in the auto industry and elsewhere. The NDC report does admit its failure in 1968 to get building trades unions to accept Negro apprentices, in spite of verbal commitments and union convention resolutions. But the report somehow manages to avoid an analysis of the reasons why the auto industry hasn't done much better.[22]

An important symptom of the frustration among black workers over the lack of progress within plants was the momentary success of a handful of black militants who organized themselves into the Dodge Revolutionary Union Movement (DRUM) and the Eldon Revolutionary Union Movement (ELDRUM). They took credit for two wildcat strikes in Chrysler plants over "racist policies and working conditions." One of the leaders, John Watson, was a student at Wayne State University, where he had become editor of *South End,* the university daily paper. During his year in office, *South End* proudly proclaimed the revolutionary goals of the organizations, printing manifestos against the auto companies and the UAW. Although Wayne State President William Keast was under heavy pressure to suppress the paper, he refused to do so. While this gave DRUM and other militant groups publicity, it also allowed social steam to blow off harmlessly. *South End's* slogan, "One Class-Conscious Worker Is Worth 100 Students," assured its organizational isolation on the campus, and its failure to win recruits in the auto plants doomed its attempt to win local union offices.

However, the panicky reaction of some top UAW officials gave DRUM and its affiliates a moment in the center of the stage. Emil Mazey, secretary-treasurer of the UAW, insisted in the public press that the violence of black militants in Detroit's auto factories posed a greater threat now than communist infiltration did in the 1930's, thereby giving the tiny handful of black radicals exactly the kind of boost they needed.[23] However, their revolutionary rhetoric and hostile tactics—plus two unsuccessful wildcat strikes—ensured the defeat of DRUM-endorsed candidates in UAW elections, while UAW black activists won easily in major local unions, and now have a power base which portends much for future relations in the black and white communities of Detroit.

Wiser union leaders in the UAW, like Douglas Fraser and Shelton Tappes, director of the Fair Employment Practices Department, met with the revolutionary dissidents and urged them to become active in the union. Neither Mazey's misreading of early UAW history nor

197

his hostility to the young militants has kept other UAW leaders from enlisting some of them by candidly admitting that blacks do have many legitimate grievances. Present estimates are that, out of 1,700,000 UAW members, about 250,000 are black. Two are members of the policy-making international executive board of 27. Over 80 are staff representatives, and soon blacks will be a majority in most plants in the Detroit area, which will give them control of most local unions—a power base they have never had before in American union history.[24]

The turmoil within the auto plants was caused as much by outside unrest as by conditions within the factories. 1968 and 1969 were years in which the city lived on a razor's edge. City government seemed paralyzed, and Mayor Cavanagh became the popular scapegoat for the city's ills. The *New York Times* published what was in effect a political obituary of the mayor—and few persons in Detroit disagreed.

> Cavanagh's fall from grace is more than a personal tragedy of a bright young man; it is a major factor in the lives of the four million people in metropolitan Detroit. Fifteen months after the Detroit riot, the most costly Negro riot in American history, the city has been unable to effect even the beginnings of meaningful reconstruction. Urban renewal and the war on poverty go badly; New Detroit, Inc., the committee set up to guide Detroit's rebuilding, has made little real progress; race relations are abysmal. Cavanagh himself, bitter over his defeat in the Democratic senatorial primary in 1966, and still dazed by the 1967 riot, appears sullen and defensive, unwilling to grasp the levers of government.[25]

With Detroit's daily papers shut down by a strike from November 1967 to June 1968, tension in the city was maintained by rumors and the impressionistic reports on television and radio. Mayor Cavanagh at one point appeared on television to urge the citizens to ignore rumors and remain calm. But his influence was negligible, since neither he nor the New Detroit Committee were able to cope with a persistent source of trouble: the conduct of the police department.

Reports that Police Commissioner Ray Girardin was resigning as soon as a successor was found made Girardin a "lame duck," and to all intents and purposes the police department ran itself until Johannes F. Spreen, a former high police official from New York, took the job in June 1968.

Meanwhile, the policy of the department was dominated by the Detroit Police Officers Association under the shrewd leadership of Carl Parsell, an aggressive and outspoken individual who symbolized the "law and order" approach. Under Parsell the DPOA emerged as an influential political machine which openly resisted any changes it didn't like and ignored civilian control.

Mayor Cavanagh's proposal to strengthen the department by adding 1,000 officers, and his recommendation to raise wages to $10,000, failed to win him friends among the police, any more than his statement, "We will not tolerate lawlessness or violence from any segment of society," endeared him to the Negro community. The police received their raise, but the mayor and the new commissioner had a difficult time disciplining them, and their hostile actions against blacks became a city scandal. Passage of a "stop-and-frisk" ordinance with Cavanagh's support pleased police but chagrined black leaders.

On the night of April 4, 1968, the news that Rev. Martin Luther King, Jr., had been assassinated sent Detroiters scurrying home, again expecting the worst. The governor mobilized 9,000 National Guardsmen and sent 3,000 to Detroit. Mayor Cavanagh declared a curfew; schools were closed either by black militants or fire

199

alarms. At Wayne State University, black youth took over the cafeteria and barred all whites, to mourn Reverend King by themselves. No major violence occurred; blacks seemed too stunned and bitter to react. The murder was a heavy blow to the voices of moderation and non-violence.

Less than two months later, mounted police charged into the march of the Poor People's Campaign in downtown Detroit, a sight visible to TV viewers. Several months later, two officers were disciplined by Spreen, but only after they had been identified by officials from the Justice Department who witnessed the assault. During the fall election campaign, police assailed a picket line protesting the appearance of Gov. George Wallace, and a number of demonstrators were injured. In November the black community was aroused by the beating of several well-dressed middle-class Negro youth who had left a high school affair and were met by some off-duty policemen leaving a DPOA dance. In defense the policemen argued that the youths had insulted their wives, but the evidence to the contrary was so strong that Commissioner Spreen suspended nine officers, one of whom was charged with assault and battery and another with felonious assault. A few weeks later one policeman was suspended for being involved in pistol-whipping a young black.[26]

Oblivious to the feelings of the black community, the Detroit Police Officers Association interpreted all these events quite differently. In its official paper the DPOA declared:

> The charges of police brutality are part of a nefarious plot by those who would like our form of government overthrown. The blue print for anarchy calls for the destruction of the effectiveness of the police. Certainly, it must be obvious that every incident is magnified and exploited with only one purpose. A lot of well meaning

people, without realizing their real role, are doing the job for the anarchists.[27]

Among the targets of this attack was the New Detroit Committee, which had proposed a $367,000 study of the functioning of the police department—a proposal Parsell denounced as an investigation. Eventually the School of Police Administration of Michigan State University received the grant, with no assurance of police cooperation. In a discussion of the proposal, the contempt with which the New Detroit Committee and black people were viewed by high echelon police officers was openly stated to a *Detroit Free Press* reporter: "The big guys are on the niggers' side."[28]

Passions reached a post-riot high in April 1969 after a white policeman was killed and his partner wounded by a black man. The event opened every wound which had been festering since the 1967 riot. Pretensions that Detroit was "on its way back to racial harmony" were punctured by the repercussions of the death of Patrolman Michael Czapski and the wounding of Patrolman Richard Worobec.

What happened, according to the earliest versions in the daily press, was that two policemen were ambushed while making a check of black men seen carrying arms near the New Bethel Baptist church. The church had been hired for a rally of the Republic of New Africa, a black separatist organization. Police reenforcements responding to the cry for help engaged in a gun battle with black revolutionists hiding inside the church. Police firepower subdued the enemy, and 143 persons at the church rally were arrested for questioning. Then, to the shock and dismay of the police and over the protests of Wayne County Prosecutor William L. Cahalan, a highly controversial black judge released the prisoners. The judge was George C. Crockett.

Later the *Detroit Free Press* editorially apologized for

erroneous reporting in its early story. The *Detroit News* reacted differently. Its major follow-up story declared, "Police blame Crockett for the fact that they have not arrested the murderer of Patrolman Michael Czapski. Forced by Crockett to release prime suspects, the police say the trail has gone cold."[29]

White fear became outrage as the news media spread the first version of the events. The public outcry against Crockett reached hysterical proportions when his record as a defense lawyer for the Communist party in the Smith Act trials of 1948 and 1949 was called to public attention. Crockett had been convicted of contempt by Judge Harold P. Medina for his trial conduct and had served four months in a federal prison. Yet when Crockett ran for the office of recorder's judge in 1966 this information failed to defeat him, although it was widely disseminated by his opposition.

Public opinion was inflamed when it read a *News* full-page feature story and interview with Crockett which led to a campaign for his removal. The following is an excerpt from that article:

> In a host of other episodes, Crockett was accused of being soft on criminals, of browbeating policemen and prosecution witnesses in his courtroom and of stretching the law to the advantage of the accused and the disadvantage of the forces of law and order.
>
> But the most serious charges against Crockett are that he is: (a) a Communist or (b) a Communist sympathizer.
>
> In reply Crockett says simply and disarmingly, "I am not a Communist and I never have been."
>
> Nevertheless, the charges hound Crockett's existence.
>
> Breakthrough, one of Detroit's ultra right-wing political organizations, campaigned against Crockett's election to the bench in 1966.
>
> Breakthrough alleged that Crockett was an "enemy sympathizer" an "enemy collaborator" and a vice-presi-

dent of the National Lawyers Guild, named as a Communist front group by two congressional committees.

Crockett has never denied his affinity and admiration for the Communist Party's public stance on behalf of Negro rights and equality. But to attempt to translate this admiration into unquestioned subservience to, and membership in, the Communist Party is intelluctually indefensible, says Crockett.

After serving as defense lawyer in the Smith Act trial in 1948 and 1949 Crockett said this:

"The Communist Party, greatest champion of Negro rights, does not have to take off their hats to anyone when it comes to fighting on that issue and naturally, it would select a Negro attorney."

Curiously, that quote was excerpted from the *Daily Worker,* Communist Party newspaper of January 29, 1950.

Copies were distributed without comment by the FBI in Washington this week.[30]

Police picketed Crockett's court, demanding his removal; the state senate passed two resolutions criticizing him; the state judicial tenure committee announced it would review his conduct. The campaign to have him removed seemed well on its way to success. It was a major miscalculation.

Despite efforts of Commissioner Spreen to support the official version, police were unable to produce any evidence that they had been fired on from within the church. They had fired into it, and by some miracle, none of the 143 men, women, or children were hurt. The police arrested everyone, including the children, and held them incommunicado for five hours. As presiding judge, Crockett was called, and with the approval of the prosecutor he released most of them. The sharp dispute between judge and prosecutor, which led Crockett to threaten Cahalan with contempt of court, was over eight men only.

203

As more facts became known, State Supreme Court Justice Thomas E. Brennan made a speech criticizing the Bethel church raid. (Rev. Ralph Abernathy, the successor to Reverend King, had come to Detroit and asked, "Would police dare do this to white people in a white church?") Governor Milliken urged people to withhold judgment on Crockett's conduct; Max Fisher, the influential oil and real estate man who had replaced Hudson, Jr., as chairman of the New Detroit Committee, declared that he thought Crockett had used sound judgment.[31] His release of prisoners on writs of *habeas corpus* was not challenged later in court. The state senate judicial tenure panel quietly dropped the issue. The police did find a suspect who was charged with murder.

The campaign against Crockett found no support in the Negro community, which was solidly behind him. The *Detroit News* had lamented:

> There is a common revulsion for the character and conduct of the militant group involved in the disturbance at the church, for the slaying of a police officer and for the unseemly haste with which Judge Crockett let arrested persons go free.
>
> Unfortunately, there is also a sad failure on the part of the local Negro leaders to express what so many responsible but lesser known black citizens feel about this case. . . .
>
> Where is the black leader who will criticize Crockett's haste?[32]

A devastating reply came from an outstanding Negro leader—a man who had the highest respect of the Establishment, including the *Detroit News,* and whom almost all black leaders wanted as a candidate for mayor in the fall of 1969. He was former councilman William T. Patrick, Jr., now president of New Detroit, Inc.

Declaring that Crockett's conduct was a "beacon light" which may have prevented a riot, Patrick sent a letter to

Crockett. "I view your historic actions . . . as being another peak of achievement for you. . . . Your insistence on full utilization of the law as a servant of the community in a time of great stress was most remarkable. I think you may have saved our community most disastrous consequences as a result of your forthright stand."[33]

A bizarre twist to the "Bethel incident" was the announcement by the leaders of the Republic of New Africa that they would produce Rafael Viera, a New Yorker wanted by police on a charge of murder, and Viera did give himself up. However, Brother Imari (Richard Henry) and Brother Gaidi (Milton Henry), the articulate and talented black leaders, accused the police of a plot to assassinate members of the Republic's Black Legion.[34]

The Detroit Commission on Community Relations issued its study of the entire affair and condemned the killing of the policeman, the response of the police, and the distorted coverage by the press. It pointedly asked the *Detroit News* whether its crime coverage wasn't racially biased and commended the *Detroit Free Press* for correcting its early coverage of the incident.[35]

Richard Marks, the cautious white director of the Community Relations Commission, was so disturbed by the repercussions that he publicly urged more effective leadership from Mayor Cavanagh, the man who had appointed him, and told the police that:

> Whether wittingly or not, the Detroit Police Officers' Association approach has pressed our community's political system to the limit, usurping, in a way which no responsible leadership would permit, the logical role of orderly government.
>
> The DPOA premises of "support law and order" and "remove Recorder Judge George Crockett" have emerged to symbolize the spectre of the police state and para-military government of a colonial people.[36]

As a result of renewed hostility between the police and the black community, race became the dominant issue in the 1969 mayoralty election. The only question was who the black candidate would be.

The outstandingly popular William T. Patrick, Jr. was first choice of many black leaders, including Congressmen John Conyers, Jr. and Charles Diggs. The least likely choice appeared to be Richard Austin—successful businessman, public servant, and Wayne County auditor—who announced early in June he would seek the nomination. Austin had almost defeated Conyers in a congressional primary a few years before.

Mayor Cavanagh was the choice of many leaders of the auto workers union, and he had an early endorsement from TULC. He was assured of heavy competition from Ed Carey, president of the Common Council, who had considerable popular appeal. Likewise Councilwoman Mary Beck, a persistent critic of Mayor Cavanagh, declared her intentions to run and her demands for "law and order." Some politicians were maneuvering to get Roman Gribbs, Wayne County sheriff, in the race. Cavanagh bowed out, Carey had a heart attack, and Gribbs was induced to run. Austin and Gribbs won the highest number of votes in the "nonpartisan" primary, and faced each other in November. Mary Beck ran a poor third.

Austin received a political boost when four UAW regional directors endorsed him in the primary—an unusually bold action—and later he was supported by some Teamsters Union liberals.

Five days before the election about sixty prominent liberals, including former Governor Williams, published a full-page newspaper advertisement with the challenging headline, "Can You Vote for a Black Mayor?" The ad continued, "If you can, but think the other candidate is superior, we respect that judgment. But if you can't and

206

the reason is color, Detroit is in more serious trouble than most people think."[37]

The narrow victory of Gribbs—the vote was 257,312 to 250,020—reflected the racial polarization. There was jubilation among many whites that "they hadn't taken over," while in the black community there was disappointment, but not despair. Black political power had made an impressive showing. Since both candidates were Democrats, and Hubert Humphrey had carried the city by 70 per cent in 1968 through the efforts of a labor-liberal-black coalition, party politics were not really involved; the election results confirmed the finding of an earlier survey by the *Detroit Free Press,* that "Among all Detroiters interviewed, race and race-related topics— mainly the schools and the police—form the overriding issue in the campaign."[38]

Gribbs, the winner, although supported by the police, white extremists, real estate and business interests, was not a "Wallace man"; he didn't need to be. As sheriff he automatically symbolized "law and order." His other assets as a vote-getter were the fact that he was white, Polish Catholic, and had a black for an opponent.

The *Detroit Free Press* endorsed Austin; the *Detroit News,* Gribbs. The contest itself was conducted with great restraint; the situation was too explosive and the issue too clear to permit otherwise. Nothing was more innocuous than the final television debate between Gribbs and Austin. Clichés about stopping crime, making the city safe, treating everyone as equal abounded. Nevertheless, the total vote was an astonishingly high figure, particularly for a rainy election day. In many districts over 70 per cent of the voters registered—both Negro and white—went to the polls, when ordinarily an off-national election year would make 50 to 60 per cent participation good. The unfortunate reason for Austin's defeat was the inability of the city's liberal forces and the union leaders who had endorsed him to win the support of enough white blue-collar workers (Austin needed a 20 per cent white vote to win). The AFL-CIO council's ambiguous position, and the building trades unions' support of Gribbs, didn't help the cause. Walter Reuther's personal letter to over 100,000 auto workers living in the city, 60 per cent of whom were white, failed to achieve significant results. Austin had only 17 per cent of the white vote, and much of that was in middle-class areas.

Unquestionably, the liberal-union slate had some impact on the Common Council races—a small consolation in the circumstances. Mel Ravitz, a sociologist at Wayne State University, was reelected to a third term with 315,-259 votes, which made him the next president of the Common Council. Rev. Nicholas Hood, the Negro incumbent, was second with 265,665 votes—the first black ever to receive a majority vote. The reelection of Robert Tindal and the election of a newcomer, Ernest C. Browne, Jr., made a total of three seats now held by blacks. Two other newcomers, Carl M. Levin and David Eberhard, also won on the liberal slate and three conservatives (William Rogell, the ex-Tiger star; Philip Van Antwerp, the ex-police inspector; and Anthony Wierzbicki) were returned to office.[39]

As the 1960's ended, Detroit was floundering in economic uncertainty and social instability—its business leadership unable to guide it to recovery and its union movement splintered into political factions. Only the black community had a sense of social cohesion and political purpose. What this portended remained to be seen.

Detroit–
Black Metropolis
of the Future

13

DETROIT in the 1970's is a startlingly different city from the factory complex associated in modern times with the auto industry, the UAW, and the late Walter Reuther. It no longer has the appearance of a swarming beehive of auto workers rushing to and from the huge industrial plants on the east and west sides. Now the major traffic consists of white middle-class suburbanites driving early in the morning into the city's downtown commercial center and inching their way out of the city before darkness sets in. The bright, newly built commercial buildings in downtown Detroit stick out like shining thumbs amid parking lots, expressways, and vacant land —less than 30 per cent of downtown Detroit is being used for active commercial and industrial purposes. There are large areas of wasteland within the city limits proper.

All the auto companies have decentralized their production, partly by expanding into the undeveloped sections of the vast metropolitan area surrounding the city— an area in which almost half of Michigan's 8,000,000 population resides—and partly by developing plant capacities in other states, like Ohio.

Where giant auto plants once stood on the east side, there is nothing. The deterioration of the city is visible everywhere, not just on Twelfth Street, where the physical scars of the 1967 riot remain untouched by any reconstruction.

For every new business moving into the city, two more move out. There are over 7,000 vacant store fronts.[1] Thousands of other small stores look like tiny military posts under siege because of their wire or steel fronts and closed doors. Symbolic of the city's new look is the *Detroit News* building downtown, with its surrounding brick wall reminiscent of a medieval fortress.

These are only a few surface manifestations of the many physical, economic, and demographic changes which are transforming the city into a black metropolis, surrounded by a growing white-dominated suburban area. Racial and class tensions in the 1970's are bound to occur within this framework.

The city lacks a rapid transit system to facilitate spending by potential suburbanite consumers, and public fear due to racial tension and a much publicized "high crime rate" also keeps buyers away. The city seldom looks busy, even during the day. Downtown shoppers are predominantly black—and with a lower income level than their white counterparts who flock to Northland, Eastland, or the other thriving shopping centers away from the central city.

At night only a handful of whites can be seen in the downtown theaters. The restaurants which are busy during the day do a minimum of business at night, with few exceptions; many are quietly folding, as are the nightclubs. Detroit streets are so deserted after dusk that the city appears to be a ghost town—like Washington, D.C., the nation's capital.

The city continues to shrink physically and demographically. There has been a net loss in the total supply of dwellings each year since 1960, when 553,000 units were available. By 1970 the number of dwelling units had declined to 530,770. How this occurred is explained by the Department of Planning and Building Studies of the Detroit Board of Education:

> The net loss is the result of demolitions for both public and private purposes. In the public sector there have been 5,000 units removed for freeway construction, 9,700 units for various urban renewal programs, 3,300 for school sites, and 1,000 for recreation and other public uses. In the private sector there has been clearance for gasoline stations, for parking lots, and some demolitions with no other objective than reducing value for tax assessment purposes. The number of dwelling units demolished by the city as a result of abandonment and vandalization is on the scale of 1,500.[2]

The decrease in the number of housing units available has not, however, worsened the problems of space for the city's inhabitants. A decline in population has offset the decline in dwelling units. Detroit in 1970 was still the fifth largest city in America, but its population of 1,-492,507 represented a drop of 190,000 from the 1960 figure. Meanwhile, the population of metropolitan Detroit grew from 3.7 million to 4.2 million.

Even more important was the change in the social composition of the city. Another 345,000 whites fled to the suburbs in the decade 1960–1970, causing a 29.2 per cent decrease in the white population. An increase in the black population did not make up for the exodus of the whites; hence the city is smaller. The overall result of these trends is that blacks now constitute 43.7 per cent of the city's population and are on the way to becoming a clear majority.[3] The city is also left, in these circumstances, with more than a normal percentage of aged, very young, and poor—both black and white. Since there is little middle- or lower-income housing in downtown Detroit and upper-income housing is at a premium, the trend toward suburban living continues unchecked.[4] As for low-cost housing, the ambitious plans of Walter Reuther to develop assembly-line construction techniques failed to get off the ground after three years of valiant effort, even though the big three auto firms and other business interests joined him to create the Metropolitan Detroit Citizens Development Authority. Jack Wood, executive director of the Detroit Building Trades Council and a critic of factory-built housing, stated, "Some of the most powerful people in the world sit with me on the MDCDA board. They are in a trap and don't know how to get out of it."[5]

Thus the city becomes more and more of a ghetto. What is evolving is a unique black metropolis, with distinct economic, social, and political characteristics not found in other major American cities. It is a society whose links to white society are constantly strained and remolded by the force of events.

The *de facto* segregation which overwhelms metropolitan Detroit is reflected in two hard facts revealed by the 1970 census data:

1. With all the rise in suburban population, the percentage of blacks who lived anywhere in metropolitan Detroit only inched from 3.6 to 3.7 per cent.

2. A survey of the number of blacks living outside the city limits shows an all-white pattern in major suburbs which can scarcely be duplicated in any racist area in the United States. To mention a few examples: Warren, Michigan, has doubled its population to 180,000 in the past decade; it has five black families. Dearborn, home of the Ford Motor Company, with over 100,000 people, lists one black family. Grosse Pointe has two, Harper Woods one, Hazel Park one, Birmingham five.[6]

How violently Detroit's white suburbs will continue to resist any change in the status quo was illustrated in the summer of 1970 when George Romney, former governor of Michigan, and now the Secretary of Housing and Urban Development, tried to allay the fear of integration in housing. A series of articles in the *Detroit News* provoked the situation.

The *News* reported: "The Federal Government intends to use its vast power to force integration of America's white suburbs—and it is using the Detroit suburbs as a key starting point."

The article quoted a HUD memorandum which described the Detroit suburbs as "an unparalleled opportunity for the application of a fair-housing strategy" with the aim of loosening "the 'white noose' surrounding the central city" of Detroit. At a public meeting in Warren, Michigan, irate homeowners gave the former governor a difficult time when he tried to explain that "there is no such policy."[7] He was booed roundly, and his wife, Lenore Romney, running for senator against Philip Hart that fall, lost many votes over this issue.

Since about 80 per cent of the houses in Warren are owner-occupied and their median value is $23,400 in contrast to the median value of $15,600 of houses in the city, the concern over a possible devaluation of property was great among the suburbanites.[8]

Anxiety permeates the social climate of Detroit. An astonishing number of citizens—both black and white —have armed themselves out of fear and rage. Detroiters possess over 500,000 handguns, more than 400,000 of them unregistered, according to Mayor Roman S. Gribbs.[9] The city seldom has a moment of respite from incidents reflecting the racial tension. In the spring of 1971, R. Wiley Brownlee, principal of the Willow Run High School, was tarred and feathered by masked men because he was considered an integrationist. In the fall of 1970, there was a shoot-out between

213

black militants and Detroit police in which one patrol-man was killed. Only the brave intervention of a black woman leader, Nadine Brown, assisted by city officials, kept the city from exploding again, as she arranged for a truce and peaceful surrender. Fifteen Black Panthers were indicted on murder charges after the death of Patrolman Glenn Smith, and later acquitted.

The self-arming of Detroiters reflects the lack of con-fidence in the Police Department, whose image was tarnished during the 1967 riots. For the whites, there is the memory of police incompetence and helplessness in handling major troubles. For the black community, there is the legacy of the Algiers Motel killing of three young blacks. No police were convicted in that situation, although newspaper accounts and two brilliant studies exposed the truth.

For a brief year, a New York policeman, Patrick Murphy, acted as police commissioner and did provide the city with a breather because of his effective control of the police, but then Murphy returned to Manhattan, where he became police commissioner. Meanwhile, an-other police scandal broke out. Inspector Alex Wierz-bicki, three lieutenants, and twelve other policemen were indicted in April 1971 on graft charges, confirming what most blacks think about "white police."

The *Detroit News'* persistent campaign against "crime waves" helps keep the city in a state of fear. Perhaps in consequence, an April 1971 survey showed that people of metropolitan Detroit think that crime is their most important problem.[10] This at a time when one out of eight persons in the city of Detroit is on welfare, unemployment rates are 50 per cent among black youth and 25 per cent among black adults, and the general city unemployment rate is 14 per cent.[11]

The city's school system is a disaster, according to most authoritative studies, and a constant source of

214

turmoil. "Our high schools are appallingly inadequate —a disgrace to the community and a tragedy to the thousands of young men and women whom we compel and cajole to sit in them," stated the Detroit High School Study Commission.

Edward L. Cushman, executive vice-president of Wayne State University, and Federal Judge Damon J. Keith, who co-chaired the study, added: "This is not a hasty verdict. It is the conclusion of two years of work by some 350 dedicated citizens—professionals and laymen alike—who examined our high schools from every point of view." The schools are "outmoded and overcrowded," and the "teachers overburdened."[12] The school system no longer attracts people to Detroit; it is a reason for their *not* coming to the city.

The schools are also a hotbed of racial frictions. Since the 1967 riot, they have been the scene of constant skirmishes between black and white students, of turbulent community meetings and racist gatherings. In March 1971, for example, the meeting of the parents of Osborn Heights High School, to quiet down the fighting between students, turned into a hate session. The school has about 600 black and over 3,000 white students. As one observer at the meeting put it, "Whites fear that blacks have too much power and can get away with anything, while blacks fear they are second-class underdogs."[13] Policy-making in the school system became a shambles after the liberal majority of the Board of Education was recalled in the fall of 1970, a victim of the conflicts between black and white groups, Catholic and upstate interests, the argument over centralization versus decentralization, and the financial crisis. As usual, the *Detroit News* has a conspiratorial theory to explain the chaos in the schools. In a major story which appeared in March 1971, the *News* gave the following analysis:

"Seven teachers interviewed said a deliberate well-

215

financed effort was being made by outside agitators to cripple the schools in the hope of toppling the system."[14]

An indication of the gravity of Detroit's school crisis was the announcement by the Detroit Archdiocese that at the end of the spring 1971 school term, 56 of the 269 Roman Catholic schools would be closed. Moveover, the outlook for 26 schools was uncertain, and 30 would reduce enrollments in the fall of 1971, according to John Cardinal Dearden, the archbishop. There are currently 140,000 students in the Catholic school system; 18,000 of them will be seeking new schools because of closings, 5,000 others will be affected by the enrollment reductions, and 11,000 are in the 26 schools whose fate has not yet been decided. Among other things, this means a heavier burden on the already overcrowded public school system.[15]

In view of the changes in the city of Detroit, its tax base and its income level are far below those of the suburbs (white median income in 1969 was $8,760; black median income was $5,290), so there is little likelihood that the city can pull itself up by its bootstraps in terms of social or educational needs.

Detroit has witnessed two major attempts to reverse these trends. In February 1970, the Central Business Association, supported by the newspapers, launched a "Talk Up Detroit" campaign with a plea to "invest in attitudes." Edwin O. George, president of the Detroit Edison Company and leader of this newest attempt to revive the city, declared: "Idle chatter which downgrades Detroit hits us all in the pocketbook. The entire economy is sagging because the whole town has a chip on its shoulder.[16] This explanation, however, is hardly satisfactory. Any economist or reader of the daily press could have informed the committee that the Nixon administration's monetary and fiscal policies to curb inflation at the cost of increasing unemployment were largely responsible for the auto industry's cutbacks and the decline in Detroit's, as well as the nation's, economy. Furthermore, the optimism of the downtown businessmen about Detroit's future was based on the more favorable statistics for the total metropolitan area—statistics which greatly distort the picture of the inner city's economic woes. The white suburbs and metropolitan business and industrial areas have grown, while the city has deteriorated. And as we shall indicate, this trend will be accelerated in the 1970's.

Easily the most prestigious effort to revitalize a major city was the widely proclaimed New Detroit Committee —the city's version of the Urban Coalition—which was created after the 1967 riot. According to its own report, New Detroit's efforts were "hopelessly inadequate."[17] The committee failed to get the state legislature to pass an open housing bill or to get emergency aid for the city's schools, but spent $3,000,000 largely in token gestures aiding black capitalism, while a recession racked the city.

The power structure in the New Detroit Committee fell apart for another reason also. Class tension destroyed the accommodations being worked out between labor and management. In 1970 the UAW began negotiating a new contract with the big three, which led to a nine-week General Motors strike. Both the auto industry executives and the UAW leadership were too busy coping with more immediate problems to participate seriously in the New Detroit Committee.

Long before the GM strike, both sides recognized the inevitability of a major walkout, because of general discontent over shop conditions. (There were over 250,000 written grievances in GM in 1969—one for every two workers.) The impact of inflation on real wages was considerable, as UAW members were no longer fully covered by an "escalator" clause. Furthermore, a "new working class" had emerged in the auto industry. Neither the life style nor other characteristics of the young workers in the plants resembled those of the complacent, crabgrass-worried middle-class worker described by conventional wisdom. Instead, this is how management and the union saw the workers of the 1970's:

> Employees in the 1970's are (1) even less concerned about losing a job or staying with an employer; (2) even less willing to put up with dirty and uncomfortable working conditions; (3) even less likely to accept the unvarying pace and functions on moving lines; and (4) even less willing to conform to rules or be amenable to higher authority.
>
> The traditional American work ethic—the concept that hard work is a virtue and a duty—will undergo additional erosion.
>
> There are two basic causes of the new situation in industrial plants. On the one hand, we have on the hourly employment rolls more of the kind of persons that carry the label "problem employees." These are the people who almost habitually violate our plant rules. Although some of them do so with an open attitude of rebellion and defiance, in a great many other cases it is just a matter of the problem employee bringing with him into the plant the mores of his own background. He continues to follow his own way of life—to live by the loose code he grew up with—and he is generally indifferent to the standards of someone else's society.
>
> While some of the problem employees have come to us through our efforts to hire the so-called hard-core unemployables, most of them are simply a reflection of the labor market we've been drawing from our normal hiring during recent years.
>
> The other root cause of our present difficulties with the work force might be termed a general lowering of employees' frustration tolerance. Many employees, particularly the younger ones, are increasingly reluctant to put up with factory conditions, despite the significant improvements we've made in the physical environment of

our plants. Because they are unfamiliar with the harsh economic facts of earlier years, they have little regard for the consequences if they take a day or two off.

For many, the traditional motivations of job security, money rewards, and opportunity for personal advancement are proving insufficient. Large numbers of those we hire find factory life so distasteful they quit after only brief exposure to it. The general increase in real wage levels in our economy has afforded more alternatives for satisfying economic needs.

There is also, again especially among the younger employees, a growing reluctance to accept shop discipline. This not just a shop phenomenon; rather, it is a manifestation in our shops of a trend we see all about us among today's youth.[18]

How this kind of youthful work force affects collective bargaining was summarized accurately in the 1970 Ford Foundation labor report.

As with the young elsewhere, their attitude toward their union and the leaders is characterized by colossal irreverence. Like the blacks, they demand to be heard, to question and challenge the leadership which, not unlike institutional leadership generally, has not been prepared for this wave of disrespect and revolt.

Union leaders and university presidents (indeed the President of the United States) are beginning to learn the meaning of words such as "flexibility," "responsiveness," "participation" and "accommodation." To the extent that leadership lags in this painful process of adjustment, one can only predict a continuing swell of revolts, rejections and disruption.[19]

Since the UAW remains far more democratic than most unions, and its leaders far more responsive to social moods and changes than most union leaders, the 1970 GM strike was inevitable. It was also successful, although the financial strain on the union left its mark. The UAW spent $176,000,000 in strike benefits and other costs. But it retained the loyalties of the younger generation—something management seems unable to achieve.

Perhaps the unique feature of the GM strike was its failure either to create class cohesiveness in the shops or to impair relations between the union and the company. In fact, as evidence of its willingness to accommodate the union, GM paid $30,000,000 for the cost of the auto strikers' health insurance plans with the UAW's verbal assurance that the union would repay GM after the strike. The Teamsters union also loaned $25,000,000 to the auto workers at standard rates of 8 per cent but required as security a mortgage on UAW property.

The GM strike turned out to be a form of controlled social protest, which had little effect on the consciousness of either the auto workers or the people of the city of Detroit.

As a matter of fact, on three different occasions, through intensive interviewing at the plant where I spent 15 years as a union official and plant worker, I discovered, to my surprise, drug addiction and racial tension, not class strife.

The execution of seven young men and women in June 1971 dramatized the city's drug problem. It was the latest horror in a bloody war between two black gangs seeking to monopolize the highly profitable heroin trade. Between 25 and 50 persons had already been killed in the dispute. But until the *New York Times* reported the concern of auto management over the use of hard drugs in the auto plants,[20] little attention was paid to this aspect of industrial problems.

The *Times'* report was published about a week after I visited an auto plant, where I talked to plant and local union officials and to one of the UAW's international staff members who functions as a "troubleshooter." These are findings I did not expect, and they are buttressed by the *Times'* survey of GM plants, which is not covered in this study.

Sam Bellomo, the vice-president of Local 7 who has been elected to office either in the plant or the large local union for almost 30 years, described the situation this way:

> The boredom on the job? The speed-up? That's routine. What the workers fear most is the drug addict in the plant, both in terms of safety of operations and in the dread of knowing that pushers operate in the plants, and their victims work there. It's not confined to any one group of people. It's the young mainly, both black and white. They don't give a damn about anything.[21]

I checked this with other officials whom I have known for years. They confirmed this viewpoint, as did the international union that staff members interviewed. Nor could this be attributed to the returning Vietnam veterans, they insisted. There weren't that many of them. It was a general problem. On wages of $35 a day, not counting fringe benefits, an assembly-line worker is far more likely to have the "loot" to buy expensive fixes than the unemployed or welfare client. Pushers of hard drugs have found a new marketplace in the auto shop, and a new victim in the young blue-collar worker.

To my dismay, I learned that the drug scene is so frightening that it is one of two reasons why many local union officials—like so many Detroiters—carry guns.

The other reason has to do with racial relations. At best, the black and white workers in the plants tolerate each other. The UAW, once known for its class solidarity, is now homogeneous in the attributes and views of its members. Jesse Cundiff, a former local union president who is currently a staff man, described the situation as follows:

> Among skilled workers, the old-timers, the ethnic groups nothing has changed. They are still anti-Negro. They hate the colored man's guts but can't do anything

221

about it. As for the blacks, they are aggressive and taking over wherever and whenever they can—in many cases this is long overdue, after what they have taken.[22]

Today, local union elections follow a general pattern. When the blacks are a majority, they take the big spots, and give a white man a token job. Men like Sam Bellomo are now the exception. He's executive vice-president in a local where all other officers, including the president, William Gilbert, are black. When whites are a majority, they keep as much control of offices as possible, and have a token black officer. It's a power relationship based primarily on race. Election contests are intense, with few holds barred.[23] Yet each year, as the social composition of the plants changes, the blacks gain more and more power on the local union levels—and are currently represented in the international union by a vice-president and a regional director. And this is only the beginning. Eleven local union presidents in the Detroit area are now black.

Between the high turnover among young workers— over 30 per cent annually in spite of the recession— and the new auto industry policy of hiring blacks, the auto industry now has over 250,000 black blue-collar workers: GM about 25 per cent, Ford 35 per cent, and Chrysler about 25 per cent. They are concentrated in the Detroit area. In many plants the blacks are either a majority or close to it, and this has vast significance for the future of black unionism, in which the UAW continues to play an important role.

The shift in power is a painful process for both blacks and whites, and sporadic incidents heighten the tension. A major topic of conversation in the auto plants in June 1971 was the acquittal of a black worker who killed a white skilled worker and two foremen—a white and a black—in the Chrysler Eldon Avenue plant last year—

hence the other reason for carrying a gun in the shops. The case attracted much attention, for the black worker was a veteran, James Johnson, Jr., and his attorneys were Kenneth Cockrel, of the League of Revolutionary Black Workers, and Justin Ravitz. They argued that Johnson was temporarily insane, that he suffered severe mental illness resulting from his days as a sharecropper in Mississippi, and that unsafe working conditions coupled with harsh treatment by Chrysler foremen drove him to a point where he could not control his impulse to kill the three men. Johnson had been transferred from his job, over his protest. He went home, got his M-I carbine, and returned to the plant on a killing rampage. A jury of eight blacks and four whites acquitted him.[24]

Reaction to the verdict was largely along racial lines, with ugly overtones among white workers. Soon afterward, twelve members of Detroit's Black Panther party were acquitted of murder charges in the death of Patrolman Smith, who was killed in October 1970. Again the reaction was divided. Blacks accepted the decision and whites viewed it with chagrin.

The extent to which these events affect attitudes in the plants and relationships between union members was illustrated by the election at the Eldon plant in May 1971. A *Detroit Free Press* article described the situation:

> A candidate supported by black militant auto workers was narrowly defeated Friday in a runoff election for president of UAW Local 961 at the troubled Chrysler Corp. Eldon Ave. gear and axle plant.
>
> Jordon Sims, fired by Chrysler May 1, 1970, for allegedly provoking a wildcat strike, was defeated by Frank McKinnon, chief steward on the third shift, by a vote of 1,178 to 1,142.
>
> Sims planned to protest the vote and appeal the election results because, he said, armed private guards pa-

trolled the union hall corridors and intimidated voters.

Sims also said about 250 votes were invalidated and he was unable to get from election authorities an adequate explanation for the invalidation.

Local 961 represents 4,000 production workers at the plant, scene of a triple slaying last summer. The plant has also been plagued by wildcat strikes, demonstrations and other violence.

McKinnon, who is white, and Sims, who is black, were pitted in the runoff after leading four candidates in a hotly contested previous contest earlier this month.

Sims, whose opponents identified him with militants, led the four candidates in the first round of balloting. He had 806 votes to 739 for McKinnon.

Elroy Richardson, the incumbent president, finished third and was eliminated from the runoff.

McKinnon and Sims became runoff candidates because neither had a majority as required by union by-laws.

Sims has denied he is a member of any radical group. But Richardson said Sims was endorsed in leaflets distributed by the Eldon Revolutionary Union Movement (ELDRUM), an affiliate of the militant League of Revolutionary Black Workers.

The armed guards were hired by the incumbent president Elroy Richardson. He defended the decision saying that it assured a fair election.

He said the guards prevented "extremists and outsiders from disrupting the election process."[25]

The friction and outbreaks of violence in the city and the plants in the early 1970's indicated that color-consciousness was prevailing over class-consciousness. This was due, above all, to the new awareness and growing power of the blacks. Forty years of strikes had not made Detroit workers class-conscious, only union-conscious, and this loyalty was being strained by the emergence of black unionism. But the last forty years of struggle by the blacks, and their hard-won acceptance in industry, have created a different black community with a different population, both middle class and blue collar. Middle-class Negroes may have almost the income levels of white middle-class individuals but they are much tougher, shrewder, and more ambitious. Most of them earned their money against enormous odds. Just to survive in the ghetto was an accomplishment; to lift oneself up into another income bracket was truly an achievement.

The thousands of black blue-collar workers and their leaders are also different from the stereotypes of the white working class. They have created vital social and institutional bases in society.

In 1971 this growing black working class had an annual income of $7,500 per person, providing a socioeconomic base unlike any in the nation. Since many of these workers have to drive out into the suburbs to the new plants and then return to the city at night, they have a daily reminder of the living restrictions placed on them in metropolitan Detroit.

The high concentration of blacks in the auto industry has made the UAW a pioneer in the development of black unionism, since its elective processes, more democratic than those of many unions, have given Negroes access to political power in the union. Among the union officials elected with their support were Nelson "Jack" Edwards, an international vice-president; Marcellius Ivory, a Detroit regional director; and eleven local union presidents in the Detroit area. There are also hundreds of black local union officers, shop committeemen, and chief stewards. Many of these belong to a new generation of ambitious unionists—men who have no more in common with the members of the discriminatory building trades unions than the early CIO militants had with the old guard of the AFL craft unions.

Almost half of Detroit's teacher's union is black; other city unions have a similar composition. Symbolic of the new power of the black unionists was the election

225

Detroit: City of Race and Class Violence

of Tom Turner, a black steelworker, to the presidency of the AFL-CIO council—an unprecedented event which clearly indicates the unique nature of the movement. For this kind of unionism and its expansion of influence, Detroit in the 1970's may well be what the city was for the CIO in the 1930's: a major forerunner and an example for other black unionists, still chafing under benevolent white union paternalism. Although there are more than 2,500,000 black workers in the AFL-CIO, they are somewhat less than adequately represented in most AFL-CIO unions, or in the top leadership of the AFL-CIO. Unionism as an institution has been a most useful vehicle for black aspirations in this auto center.

The city of Detroit had also become a major base for black political power, as demonstrated in the mayoralty campaign in 1969. The black candidate, Richard Austin, did not disappear into oblivion after his defeat. He was elected secretary of state in the 1970 election, thus joining a growing group of black leaders on the state level (Senate and House) who are important figures in Michigan's Democratic party. Coleman Young is both a spokesman in the legislature and the national committeeman from Michigan in the Democratic party.

The black community also had an articulate national voice in the two Democratic but independent-minded Congressmen, John Conyers, Jr., and Charles Diggs. And two outstanding federal judges in the midwest, Wade McCree, Jr., and Damon Keith, are from Detroit.

The expansion of these various forms of black power —economic, union, and political—suggests that more effective struggles, based on institutional forms of power, will gradually replace the primitive battles of Detroit's past. But there are many formidable obstacles to the fulfillment of black aspirations and to social stability. The erosion of the city's economic base indicates that the trend toward economic and racial separation between city and suburbs will continue.

Three major developments in recent times warn of the pitfalls ahead. The first serious blow was William Clay Ford's announcement that he was taking the Detroit Lions out of the city to Pontiac. In prestige and money, Detroit lost.

More important, in the long run, was the announcement by Henry Ford II that he had approved the construction of a $750,000,000 housing-commercial project in Dearborn, the all-white community. The drain from Detroit is obvious. Even if some token integration were to occur—and there is no sign of this yet in the plans—the remaining middle class in Detroit has another place to run. And Max Fisher, the oil and real estate millionaire who recently chaired the New Detroit Committee, is also spending millions on a new housing development in the suburbs beyond the reach of the blacks.[26] Even General Motors management, which won the approval of the black press for adding Rev. Leon Sullivan to its Board of Directors, shows little interest in the city's troubles, although Twelfth Street's ruins are near GM's main headquarters on Grand Boulevard.

Still, it is too soon to accept former Mayor Jerome P. Cavanagh's projection of Detroit's place in the future: "Detroit twin cities—Nagasaki and Pompeii."[27]

Nor should it be assumed that the city of Detroit is similar to Newark or Chicago. On the economic scale, Newark is far below Detroit. Its industry is not of the same magnitude as the rich auto industry. Newark's pay scales seem paltry in comparison to Detroit's blue-collar wages. In Detroit, the unions and the blacks within them are a powerful socio-economic force. Newark's unions are of secondary importance; a teacher's strike was lucky to survive the squeeze of racial pressures. A black mayor

227

in Detroit, with all the handicaps mentioned above, would nevertheless have an economic base far superior to that of Newark: for needed funds, its mayor, Henry Gibson, is almost totally at the mercy of the state and federal governments. In Chicago, blacks have been held back largely by the power of the Daley machine in politics, by the strength of white-dominated unions under the building trades' influence, and by social rigidities.

In contrast, Detroit has become a city with enormous potential for blacks, since its industrial makeup enables them to push forward on several fronts. This black social mobility and relative economic power is building the city into a black metropolis with a strong middle class, a strong working class, and a young generation of leaders who are emerging in every institution. These factors also tend to prevent any real revolutionary crisis, the kind loudly proclaimed in the rhetoric of the Left, both black and white. With the frustration caused by the sharp contrast in living standards, unequal job opportunities, and other forms of racial discrimination, it was unavoidable that Detroit should have its share of black radicalism in the 1970's. In both periods, the singular role of the radicals was to articulate and to make more visible the deeply rooted causes of social unrest. Only in a totalitarian society are the voices of protest muted or silenced completely—and a very large degree of freedom still exists in this country.

In both periods of Detroit's history, radicalism was often mistaken for the cause of discontents, rather than a reflection of them. In each case, only when the radicals worked within the framework of viable institutions did they obtain the social leverage or power to effect changes in those institutions. The sitdowns of the 1930's turned out to be a demand for a voice and a share in the system rather than a prelude to revolution—as its antagonists feared and some of its proponents hoped.

228

For most blacks, the industrial and public-sector unions and the political organizations are an effective vehicle for protest. In many instances, a sense of outrage as well as aspiration motivates social action. At other times, the angry voices of the Left spur the leaders of various organizations and unions to greater effort. What is unmistakable in this broad context of social change, affecting all aspects of city life, is the increasingly important position of the blacks in Detroit.

Many setbacks are ahead. Detroit may explode again. The national economic and political climate always affects the city deeply. Certainly the police, the firemen, the building trades, and other white-dominated and white-based organizations may be expected to continue their resistance to the expansion of black power. But this resistance is essentially a rearguard action. The next municipal election offers the black community another chance to elect its mayor, and the opportunity is awaited eagerly. Bit by bit, Detroit is becoming the largest black metropolis in the world; although separated from its white suburbs both physically and economically, it is an important base of power which the rest of American society can no longer ignore.

As before, the severest strains are most likely to occur in the plants, in the unions, and in the political and social institutions where the blacks have had the biggest impact. Only recently a black caucus was formed in the Michigan Democratic party—a sign of power and independence. In the UAW, it is only a matter of time before all four regional directors in Detroit are black. The city unions are moving in a similar direction. This trend poses an acute dilemma and a challenge to white politicians and white unionists. The growing separation of blacks portends a drastic decline in white political and union power. But courting the large black vote carries with it the risk of losing the white suburban and plant vote. The chal-

229

Detroit: City of Race and Class Violence

lenge is to form a coalition of equals—an integrated coalition. Otherwise the current growth of separatism may turn out to be not just a detour on the road toward an integrated society, but another move in the direction of the total polarization which has proved so dangerous in Detroit and elsewhere. A society torn by hatred and racial strife cannot be reformed through the tepid measures so often prescribed in the past. The blacks have too much power to accept the once acceptable tokenism.

Epilogue:
Detroit—A Reexamination

TWO DECADES after Detroit's devastating 1967 riot, the city's destiny remains in the grip of two powerful forces —social and economic—that victimize its shrinking population and make living a nightmare and the future bleak. One social force, like an incurable cancer, is the persistence of racism, manifested in black frustration and rage and white fears, which prevents healthy race relations.

In 1985, David Adamany, president of Detroit's Wayne State University stated without fear of contradiction that "everybody talks about the race issue, but not for public consumption. You can't go anywhere in the metropolitan area without having the issue of race relations opened up. And it's much worse now than when I came here two summers ago."[1] Bob Talbert, a popular Detroit columnist, expressed the anxieties of many white residents when he wrote in the fall of 1986: "I hate to feel nervous driving around city streets and parking mall lots. For the first time in 18 years I've had this feeling in every street and every lot. I hate the feeling."[2] The dramatic increase in gun violence, random killings, and homicides—and the alarming shooting deaths of teenagers—is behind the heightened anxieties and makes De-

231

troit a city in which many live in fear. In 1967, the homicide toll, including the 41 people killed during the riots, was 281; in 1986 the number rose to 646, though the city had 500,000 fewer residents.[3]

Comparing the city's recent wave of drug-related violence to the bootleg wars of Chicago gangsters during the 1920's, Mayor Coleman Young suggested, "You have the same pattern. The differences being these are young blacks today in Detroit, as opposed to so-called gangsters in the 1920's."[4] Young made the analogy after the weekend killing of three teenagers and the critical wounding of another youth under the age of 17. In an earlier bloody weekend 43 people were shot and 12 killed. With 58.2 murders per 100,000 residents, Detroit had become the murder capital of the nation. Gary, Indiana, with 42.6 murders per 100,000 was a poor second.[5] The city's 635 homicides in 1985 had already produced a per capita rate seven times the national average and at least twice the rate of most big cities, including New York and Los Angeles.[6]

As a cause and a consequence of the social tensions and fear, "Detroiters have armed themselves so extensively that by one estimate there are 400,000 more guns in the city than there are people," the *Wall Street Journal* reported in 1986.[7] The estimate, which few challenged, was the basis for the view that Detroit resembled an armed camp, a situation quite different from the lawlessness in gang-infested Chicago of the 1920's. Gun ownership and the use of firearms affect the entire population, including many youths in Detroit. In 1985, 237 youths were wounded and 31 died from gunfire. The statistics were more dismal in 1986; by the end of the year 343 youths under the age of 16 had been shot, 43 of them fatally.[8]

Parents became increasingly concerned about the

growing number of shootings on or near public school property. Gun and knife control in the schools was argued as passionately as the school drop-out rate and poor educational performance records. One attempted solution was the resumption of periodic gun sweeps under a limiting set of rules that satisfied federal court objections to earlier and broader anti-gun sweeps.

In this context, the debate over local gun control took on a venomous tone. Arguing against local gun control legislation, Mayor Young aroused a storm of controversy with his statement that he would not disarm Detroit "while we are surrounded by hostile suburbs and the whole rest of the state who have guns and where you have vigilantes practicing Ku Klux Klanism in the wilderness with automatic weapons."[9] Leading the critics of Mayor Young was the former Republican candidate for governor, Richard Headlee, who denounced the mayor as "just as evil and mean spirited as the Ku Klux Klan" and "the Number One race baiter in America." Headlee argued that Mayor Young's statement fed "Detroit's terrible boiling pot of youth unemployment, drugs, and crime." He added, "We reap the benefits of that kind of leadership with police killed in line of duty, more drugs, more crime, declining business base."[10]

In this vitriolic political climate, Mayor Young, with misgivings, retreated and signed in December 1986 an ordinance that imposed a 30-day jail sentence and $100 fine for a first offense of carrying a concealed firearm without a permit. Second offenders would get 60 days plus the fine, and repeaters beyond that would get 90 days plus the fine for each offense.

Controversy over the law reflected the wide range of disagreement over its value. The National Rifle Association denounced it as among the most strict in the country and as unfair to otherwise law-abiding citizens.

233

Mayor Young described the law as little more than a fig leaf, covering only the briefest portion of a very complex and very serious problem. The mayor admitted he had changed his mind about a veto because a number of groups and individuals, including some of his supporters, had clamored for him to "do something" about an intolerable situation.

Another manifestation of many Detroiters' desperation over the state of affairs in the city was the effort made in 1986 to contain the lawlessness that had accompanied the celebration of Halloween in recent years. For three nights in 1984—which included Halloween and the preceding night, Devil's Night—the city was plagued by over 810 fires. The blazes reminded everyone of the 1967 riot. Burned out old houses, buildings, and garages were visible evidence of the frightening events.

In 1985, due to massive efforts by police and fire fighters, Devil's Night fires were reduced to 479. To keep the city under control in 1986 Mayor Young mobilized 5,600 police and city employees and another 5,000 citizen volunteers to patrol the city. The mayor also imposed a dawn-to-dusk curfew on youths 17 years of age and under. Even with the city nearly in a state of siege, 343 arson-related fires were reported on Devil's Night, and 494 youths were held for violating the curfew.[11]

All these events occurred during a time of incredibly high unemployment for blacks. In 1965 an adult unemployment rate of 15 percent and an estimated youth unemployment rate of 35 to 40 percent would have been viewed with alarm. Yet in 1985 blacks in metropolitan Detroit had the highest jobless rate—28.9 percent— among those living in the nation's 30 largest metropolitan areas. For black youths 16 to 19 years of age, the unemployment rate was 60 percent.[12] Within Detroit itself the rates were higher because of the high concentration of black population.

Under these conditions, it is understandable why Mayor Young argued in a nationally televised debate: "Welfare is not destroying our economy. It is the lack of jobs, lack of opportunity that has destroyed people."[13] For most Detroit suburbanites, however, a more convincing explanation for continuing high unemployment among blacks was given by the mayor's opponent, Walter Williams, a black conservative economist. He blamed government programs for the rise of welfare dependency among black families. Williams overlooked the loss of over 100,000 manufacturing jobs—mainly related to the auto industry—that wiped out most work opportunities for blacks, still the last to be hired and the first to be fired.

The erosion of Detroit's economic base leaves many blacks with little choice except to starve or go on welfare. Obviously, as long as the conservative outlook expressed by Williams and endorsed by the Reagan administration continues to influence the national mood, there will be no redress to the bleak outlook for the victims of economic dislocations.

In the face of such dire economic conditions, the expansion of an underground drug economy—with its attendant problems of increased crime and murder—is inevitable. Its operation festers on the body politics. The ferment among unemployed youth is visible and new social tensions are building along race and class lines.

The public response to these events is to largely view the crisis as a "crime problem" with an easy answer: more police, more guns for self-protection, and more jails. City Council President Erma Henderson, a leading black politician, supported this short-sighted view of the problem when she declared, "Stricter youth curfews and a tougher law to punish parents whose children commit crimes should be Detroit's top priorities in 1987."[14] Such answers are less tasking than would be an analysis of the reasons why Detroit was transformed from "Dynamic Detroit" or "arsenal of democracy" or "workshop of freedom" into "Murder Capital, USA," a tragic wasteland of human resources.

Above all, there is a reticence to analyze the second powerful force—besides the race issue—which negatively affects Detroit. It is the impact of the decisions of the power structure—the auto industry leaders, the big merchandisers, and the real estate investors—to shift the bulk of its plants, stores, investments, and activities outside the city.

In its search for a bigger bottom line, the auto industry moved its plants or production elsewhere—other states, other countries—and outsourced more of its work. This process wiped out over 100,000 manufacturing jobs in Detroit between 1976 and 1986. For the once-dominant United Auto Workers Union, this signified a loss of 125,000 members in the area—40 percent of its dues payers—between 1979 and 1985.[15]

Merchandisers also moved their operations outside of the city. Sears and Montgomery Wards closed several of their outlets in the city, and Federal Department Stores and Hughes and Hatcher went out of business. The national food chains A & P and Kroger shut down their stores in the city. Perhaps nothing illustrates business's flight from Detroit more than the huge, vacant department store building in downtown Detroit—J.L. Hudson's—a store that once did more business than Macy's in New York. In the suburbs are its replacements— Eastland, Northland, and Westland Hudson's—part of attractive shopping centers that give suburbanites more reasons for avoiding the city.

Thus metropolitan Detroit grew while Detroit proper

shrank. The city was transformed from an industrial complex into a service and commercial center adversely affected by the economic and demographic changes. The captains of industry and business did, however, make one major effort to reverse the plight of the city. It was the corporate initiative spearheaded by Henry Ford II in 1971 to build the 357 million dollar, multi-towered Renaissance Center on the downtown waterfront. From a distance the fortress-like structure resembles huge farm silos rising out of an embankment. Completed in 1977, the center destroyed as much business as it created; three downtown hotels closed and several office buildings were left with vacancies. The Renaissance Center went bankrupt within a few years, however, failing to bring the crowds back into the city for shopping.

The downtown area suffered another setback when William Clay Ford, owner of the Lions, moved his football team to the new Pontiac sports arena. Detroit's basketball team, the Piston's, followed and downtown suffered yet another major economic blow.

During the day, 100,000 people work in the skyscrapers and government offices of downtown Detroit; at night, however, the city is a ghost town. A glance at the areas surrounding the commercial activity reveal vast wastelands. Visible everywhere are burned or dilapidated houses, gutted apartment dwellings, hundreds of boarded up small stores—all testimonies to the plight of the city. The once-famous main arteries—Woodward, Grand River, East Jefferson and Michigan—are now ugly sights. Here and there an empty factory stands as a relic of the city's past glories.

Of course there are a few scattered areas of white and black middle-class residences: lovely Indian Village, Lafayette Park, and sections of northwest Detroit near the city limits. But Detroit's population mostly consists of the old, the indigent, the unskilled, and low-paid service workers. Over 200,000 blacks receive some form of public assistance. In 1983 the city had 97,000 single-parent households, about 75 percent of them black.[16]

The social consequences of this "dying city," as the *Detroit News* described it in a remarkable series of articles published in 1985, are "declining neighborhoods, white flight, crime and economic problems and ever present feelings of racism.[17]

Perhaps the most shocking aspect of Detroit's tragic decline is that it has occurred within one of the richest regions in the United States. With a population of 4,200,000—almost half of Michigan—metropolitan Detroit compares favorably in wealth to any metropolitan region in the nation. In 1983, of the 33 largest metropolitan areas in the United States, only Washington, D.C., and Houston, Texas, had significantly higher average household incomes than Detroit's metropolitan area. The average income in Washington, D.C.'s metropolitan area was $38,629; in Houston it was $36,390. Metropolitan Detroit had an average household income of $33,241, and this figure was deceptively low since it included the average household income within the city of Detroit: $21,556.[18]

Even more revealing of the wealth surrounding the city is the data on property values which are usually assessed at half of the market price. Detroit's valuation dropped from $4,937,375,000 in 1960 to $4,271,216,000 in 1980. Within the same period, Oakland County's valuation rose from $1,351,984,000 to $10,431,731,000; Macomb County's rose from $641,591,000 to $5,443,984,000; and Wayne County's figure climbed from $2,645,862,000 to $5,137,465,000.[19]

Presiding over the explosive black metropolis of Detroit—for the city is about 70 percent black—is Coleman Young, elected in 1973 as the city's first black mayor and reelected three times thereafter. As one of Detroit's ablest black leaders for many decades, Young is a veteran and survivor of the city's race and class struggles since the early CIO days and the triumph of industrial unionism. He was an officer in World War II, and during the notorious McCarthy period he was politically ostracized for his left-wing views. Yet Young bounced back from oblivion and eventually became the majority leader of the democratic party in the Michigan state legislature. He shrewdly combined the machine skills of the late Mayor Richard J. Daley of Chicago with the flamboyance of the late Adam Clayton Powell, New York's famed congressman.

Young is exceedingly controversial, hated in the suburbs, disliked by many white politicians, but he is gifted with at least nine political lives. His administration has withstood scandals, investigations, and a variety of challenges that would dismay a lesser man. He has earned the grudging respect of the white power structure that runs business and industry in Michigan. Young has been criticized frequently by whites for being resentful and belligerent. His response to such charges assure him of political victories among his black constituents:

> I see that the white people are getting tired of me talking about race. Well, I'm sorry about that. It just happens to be a fact of life. And I think as a person who has been a victim of discrimination and racism—if I can use the word—I'm in a little better position to accurately observe it than people who for the most part unconsciously engage in it, quite oblivious to the impact and the pain that it might have caused others.

> I don't think that I am naturally a vicious person. I'd a helluva lot rather smile than frown. I don't want to get in any arguments with any Goddamn body. But at the same time I don't like to be p_ _ _ _ _ on either.

> And so this is the dilemma. Now for those who say the only kind of black people they can deal with is some sonofabitch that they can p_ _ _ on, and he'll grin, then they've got the wrong nigger in me.[20]

Young's reelection in 1985 was a foregone conclusion. The white power structure and most black leaders supported Young, and Civic Searchlight, a non-partisan organization that evaluates public officials, had given Mayor Young its highest rating. Opposed by an unknown black businessman, Thomas Barrow, the 67-year-old incumbent won with 60.89 percent of the vote. However, only 10 percent of the whites who voted supported Young. Most whites in the city shared the suburbanites' dislike for him. Nor did Mayor Young's acceptance of a 44 percent pay increase in 1986 endear him to the white population. At $115,000 a year, Young earned more than the governor of Michigan and became the highest paid chief executive in the nation's ten largest cities.

Since black political power has replaced labor clout as the major force in this unionized town, Mayor Young has become the predominant political figure, overshadowing many other civic leaders, such as Erma Henderson and Reverend Nicholas Hood. Young also towers over several influential black labor leaders: Tom Turner, head of the AFL-CIO council; Marc Stepp, UAW vice president; and Horace Sheffield. In the 1984 presidential primary Young further demonstrated his political importance by delivering the votes that assured Walter Mondale's victory in the Michigan Democratic primary. In the past this role was played by the United Auto Workers Union. Now the black members of the UAW are far more influenced by Mayor Young and in the 1988 presidential primaries by Reverend Jesse Jackson than by the largely white leadership of the auto workers union.

Young's performance is particularly noteworthy in community-police relations. According to Young, the Detroit police force, "which was predominantly white and racist and lived in the suburbs, acted like a foreign army of occupation."[21] By assuming some control over the department through the appointment of a black police officer, William Hart, as chief of police and by increasing the number of black policemen, Mayor Young eased a sore point in black-white relations: police behavior. The resultant change in the social composition of the police force is remarkable. In 1967 only 244 police were black; in 1987 nearly half of the force was black. Under Mayor Young a concerted effort also was made to recruit more women to the force. Their numbers increased from two percent in 1967 to nearly 20 percent in 1987 and included three female commanders and Deputy Chief Mary Jarrett-Jackson.[22]

Given his successes, one would think that Mayor Young has fulfilled the beautiful dream for Detroit which he expressed in his 1973 campaign for mayor: "I will lead a business resurgence that will produce jobs by the thousands, revitalize our downtown, and our entire city. I will move Detroit forward on a program that includes new port facilities, a stadium, rapid transit, recreational facilities, and housing."[23] The cruel irony is that Young's ideas are an impossible dream, given that the city of Detroit is not metropolitan Detroit basking in its recent richness. There is little appreciation in the suburbs for Mayor Young's accomplishments. His administration has been able to keep a modicum of social peace, even in explosive situations as in the riot of 1975. In addition, Mayor Young has given many blacks hope and pride.

Although Young has gained political power, he has learned that political promises cannot be fulfilled without economic power. This economic power still rests with the white power structure whose "sound" business decisions have turned metropolitan Detroit into the kind of place Young thought Detroit would be. The metropolitan area's resurgence is primarily a white community gain, whereas the blacks are still on the periphery.

Nevertheless, the black community keeps making herculean efforts to survive. In 1981 Young persuaded General Motors to plan the construction of a $600,000,000 Cadillac plant in Detroit and in a section of Hamtramck —known as "Poletown"—which had been ravaged in 1980 by the closing of Dodge Main, its chief employer. As stated in *Working Detroit,* "The cost of persuading GM to build its new Cadillac plant seemed especially high to many. The $200,000,000 in taxpayers' money the city spent to condemn and clear the 500-acre plant site would not bring a single new job to Detroit."[24]

The new "Poletown" plant was expected to replace General Motors' aging Clark Avenue assembly and the Fleetwood body plants on the city's west side. The houses and businesses of Poletown were razed, and television viewers across the country witnessed the agony of displaced residents as well as the controversial destruction of a Polish Catholic church. Both General Motors and Mayor Young shared heaps of criticism for the cost of the new Cadillac plant. The project was a tribute to the triumph of the philosophy once espoused by C. E. Wilson, a former General Motors president: "What's good for General Motors is good for the country, and vice versa." This viewpoint, once highly challenged, seems to have gained credence as a national philosophy in recent years, as evidenced by the fierce competition among several states for GM's much-publicized Saturn car project. In neither the Poletown nor the Saturn projects did the resulting production or employment pros-

242

pects live up to earlier claims by GM executives.

The people of Detroit went through yet another painful time between 1978 and 1980. Michigan's largest employer—the auto industry—reeled under the impact of the national recession, high interest rates that lowered car sales, successful Japanese imports, and bad management marketing and product policies. The industry suffered a 4.2 billion dollar loss in 1980. Chrysler was the worst off. With its plants centered in and around Detroit, the prospect of bankruptcy and extinction haunted Detroiters, for Chrysler was the largest employer and taxpayer in the city. In jeopardy were the jobs of thousands of autoworkers, white collar employees, and small merchants whose livelihoods depended on the automaker.

For two leading Detroiters in particular the situation was intolerable. Douglas Fraser, president of the UAW, had already seen his union shrink by 500,000 members, half of whom had little prospect of ever seeing the inside of an auto plant again. The UAW had been blamed for the auto industry's plight, and if Chrsyler collapsed, another 100,000 employees might be added to the unemployment lines, with the UAW taking further blame. The other Detroiter was Mayor Young, presiding over a city wracked by every possible urban problem. The future of the city and his own destiny were endangered. What could be done? There was little confidence that Chrysler management had any satisfactory answers.

Through a fortuitous act Henry Ford II provided the anwer. He fired Lee Iacocca, his talented and ambitious president, who reportedly had been Ford's rival for control of the Ford empire. Iacocca, therefore, was searching for a chance to redeem himself and to prove Henry Ford had been wrong to fire him. The chairmanship of Chrysler was a God-send opportunity for Iacocca. Before he accepted the challenge, however, Iacocca had insisted on getting a commitment from Fraser that the UAW would do its share in sacrifices to save the company. Iacocca had another key ally in Mayor Young, since Young had close personal and political ties with then-President Jimmy Carter.

Assured of that invaluable backing, Iacocca was able to mount a successful campaign for federal government intervention—a bailout. Iacocca's performance was dazzling. He juggled the company's finances to keep it from bleeding to death, reorganized the company's structure, and squeezed bargaining concessions from the UAW. He had to surmount the formidable opposition of important bankers, high-level federal officials, and outraged conservatives who demanded that the market be allowed to settle the problem. If Chrysler failed, they argued, it deserved it. Despite claims that the free enterprise system was being subverted or betrayed—and Iacocca had frequently proclaimed the virtues of free enterprise—the Carter administration worked out a loan guarantee program that nourished Chrysler with cash. The Chrysler bailout was a classic case of corporate welfare.

Chrysler was saved and Detroit was relieved of at least one major anxiety. Iacocca became a national celebrity: he was cheered at union and business meetings alike and his 1984 autobiography became a best-seller. In 1986 Chairman Lee Iacocca received compensation worth more than 20 million dollars, making him one of the highest paid executives in U. S. history. There were other winners, too. The federal government made 311 million dollars on its loan guarantees and bankers and other creditors hit a bonanza when Chrysler preferred stock and warrants rose from $3.50 to $18 in one year.

But not everyone was a winner. As Robert Reich

wrote in *New Deals: The Chrysler Revival and the American Dream:*

> Nor did the intervention defend the most vulnerable of Chrysler's constituents. It was not the blue-collar employees but stockholder, managers, lenders, consultants, lawyers, and lobbyists—all relatively wealthy—who benefited the most from the bailout. Chrysler workers as a whole fared poorly, compared to these groups. Despite the company's stunning revival, in 1984 its American work force was still smaller by a third than it had been in 1979.[25]

The losers were the cast-off autoworkers and the 20,000 white-collar employees eliminated at Chrysler. Their numbers swelled the ranks of the unemployed. These kinds of permanent cutbacks help to explain why in 1987 40 percent of the city's residents lived below the poverty line and about 25 percent of Detroiters were unemployed.[26]

An important factor that contributed to Michigan's high unemployment rate was the policy of the auto industry during its recovery to impose compulsory overtime—ten-hour days and six-day weeks—rather than rehire its unemployed. The UAW estimated that the equivalent of 95,000 jobs were "lost" in 1984 due to overtime. The policy also created tensions between the employed and unemployed autoworkers. For the 200,000 employed autoworkers in Michigan and the Detroit metropolitan area it was a period of unprecedented prosperity: those who already earned an average of $28,900 a year brought home an additional $5,000 to $10,000 in overtime pay.[27]

The boom times in metropolitan Detroit were a reflection of that extra cash flow. Of course this was only a part of the money that poured into Michigan and the Detroit area when the auto industry went from a loss of 4.2 billion dollars in 1980 to the fabulous 8.9 billion dollar net profit in 1984. Stockholders, top executives, and middle managers received pay increases and bonuses. For the employed on all levels, happy days were here again.

The optimism about Detroit's progress was evident in *Crain's Detroit Business,* a biweekly business paper that boosts Detroit. The headlines of an August 1985 story read, "Detroit Poised for Big Building Boom," but a close reading of its survey on economic prospects indicated that the "booming" meant the Detroit area. In the first half of 1985, nonresidential building was up 75 percent in Oakland County, 41 percent in Macomb County, and 69 percent in Washtenaw county. Wayne County—including Detroit—had no upward movement.[28]

Observing Detroit in 1985 and 1986 gave one an inescapable sense of déjà vu. The extravagant publicity surrounding plans to rebuild the city was reminiscent of 1968 when the Renaissance Center was touted as the city's hope. Once again the Renaissance Center became the centerpiece of a downtown revitalization plan and was expanded to include two twenty-one story office towers to supplement the original four 39-story office towers and the 70-story hotel. The center, which had to be reorganized in 1983 after losing 103 million dollars in three years,[29] remained in the red in 1985 and 1986.

Nevertheless, real estate boosters created illusions of a successful city by combining already existing developments such as Millender Apartments and Hotel, Trappers Alley, Harbortown, River Place, and the expanded Cobo Hall with projected plans to portray a dazzling picture of future success. Even if most of the plans were to fall into place—a questionable assumption—developments such as Rivertown Detroit might in the early 1990's have living room for about 5,000 residents, provided they can afford middle-class and upper middle-

246

class rents. This hardly offsets the 20,000 annual decline in the city's population in the late 1980's.

Rivertown also bypasses the mainstream of Detroit's residents. Rather, such downtown developments might be "new, attractive and alive for a select band of suburbanites, downtown Detroiters, visitors and conventioneers," to quote city councilman Mel Ravitz, a veteran white liberal leader. Ravitz added that the developments will be "a new playground for the well-to-do."[30]

One of the most ambitious projects designed to draw people downtown was the construction of the "People Mover," a 2.9 mile overhead rail system connecting various points in the downtown enclave of buildings and hotels. It was supposed to attract 15,000 passengers daily, but in early 1987 it was averaging only 10,000 riders a day. Financed by federal, state, and local government money, the project cost over 210 million dollars including a 72 million dollar cost overrun. It had been plagued by financial sourcing problems, scandalous construction flaws, and a dispute over management competency and control before it was completed in December 1986. Under Mayor Young's urging, its management was taken away from the Southeastern Michigan Transportation Authority (SEMTA), which had lost the confidence of important public officials, and was placed under the direction of the Detroit Transportation Corporation set up for that purpose. It began operating in the fall of 1987.

The success of the People Mover depends on its overcoming several obstacles, perhaps the most difficult being its image in the suburbs where it has been dubbed "The Mugger Mover." Another factor militates against the success of any mass transit system in Detroit. Michiganders grow up in a car-minded culture. Owning and driving a car is viewed as one of the basic necessities of life.

While there are many problems in Detroit, perhaps none are as tragic as the lives and fate of the children growing in the midst of turbulent changes and a deteriorating school system. As the white middle class fled the city or shifted their children to private schools, Detroit's school population fell and the birth rate dropped from 40,000 to 20,000 annually, from about 300,000 to less than 200,000.[31] Consequently, many schools have been closed or reorganized. And in spite of federal court desegregation orders and supervision, Detroit schools were more segregated in 1985 than they were in the previous 25 years. Only three of its 22 high schools had a mixed student population; the majority of students were black. The retention rate dropped from a "high" of 50 percent in 1965–66 to 34.6 percent in 1980. While the rich suburbs spent over $4,000 per pupil, the city schools, with the greatest needs in staff, teachers, and training programs, only had $2,670 per pupil.[32]

In *Brown vs. the Topeka Board of Education,* the U.S. Supreme Court ruled in 1954 that state-sponsored segregation of public education was unconstitutional. Separate but equal educational systems were outlawed. In the Detroit area—as if to mock the constitution—schools are still separate, segregated, and inferior within the city of Detroit despite years of federal court jurisdiction and supervision.

Even worse, between 1985 and 1987 Detroit students were subjected to police searches and sweeps that never would have been tolerated in Grosse Pointe or Birmingham. In the 1960s Detroiters had rejected police programs of mass sweeps and arrests in the black community, whereas most of the public approved of the more recent actions, humilitating as it was to the students and schools.

The failure of the white-controlled school system over

248

the decades was at last being recognized by some educational experts as a major cause of the schools' deterioration. "The fact of the matter is, despite all these educational schools we run, we don't have the vaguest notion of how to reach the black low-income population—to convince them that the route to all things important in life is through education," stated Professor Harvey Brazer of the University of Michigan, a scholar who has studied the Detroit system for many years.[33]

In this context, shifting the control in 1975 of the city schools to black educators—the superintendent of schools and many teachers and staff were black—seemed to be equivalent to giving an experienced sailor the captaincy of the Titanic after it had crashed into the icebergs and was sinking. Furthermore, providing grants to a select few schools was like giving lifeboats to only a few when most were drowning in despair.

Perhaps the saddest commentary on the state of education in Detroit was the report that one out of every four high school graduates from the class of 1985 did not pass a proficiency exam which tested minimum reading, writing and math skills.[34]

Occasionally, a voice of bitter protest rises from the social cauldron called Detroit and breaks through the thin veneer of social harmony and progress so firmly believed by a self-deceiving and myopic conservative public. Such warnings of impending trouble are largely ignored by complacent white and black leaders, just as they had been prior to the 1967 riot. For example, little attention was paid to the grim conclusions contained in the report, "The State of Black Michigan 1985," which was produced by the Michigan Council of Urban League Executive and Urban Affairs Program of Michigan State University. The report found that "political power is precarious for blacks, housing is often segregated, education unequal, family life besieged, and economic status poor. The levels of segregation are escalating and the outlook grim."[35] In the conservative climate of 1985, few public officials or pundits are willing or able to estimate how a conservative America will affect the frustrated black population.

Yet some black leaders—though they are largely ignored—continue to air black frustrations. Consider the startling speech delivered at a college graduation in Detroit in May 1985. The speaker made many statements that shocked most whites. He claimed that President Reagan's popularity is due to racism and that America is in a "totalitarian, fascist phase" of its history. He supported the latter statement by citing what he called the six signs of fascism: (1) A blind patriotism. (2) An overemphasis on law and order at the expense of civil liberties and justice. (3) Alignment of government with big business at the expense of . . . the consumer. (4) Persuading the working class and the middle class to work against their own best interests. (5) A narrow . . . religiosity. (6) The exploitation of racial phobias.[36] The speaker was not Louis Farrakhan. It was the Reverend Charles Adams, pastor of the Hartford Memorial Baptist Church, who holds a doctorate from Harvard Divinity School and is a past president of the Detroit Chapter of the NAACP.

Nor is enough attention paid to the voice of another distinguished black Detroiter, a man with impeccable credentials. Damon Keith, circuit judge of the U.S. Court of Appeals for the 6th Circuit wrote in the *Detroit Free Press* in August 1985:

> There are people in America, in spite of these statistics, who say that blacks should be pulling themselves up by their own bootstraps and that race is not a factor in the upward mobility of blacks in America today.

Let's face it. We live in a racist society. We have
been enslaved, segregated, rejected, excluded, mis-
treated, locked out, exploited, despised, disenfran-
chised, and discouraged for one reason only, and that
is the fact that we are black. If the society that we live
in has damaged us because we are black, and it has,
then the society must now remedy the situation.

More blacks were poorer in 1985 than were in 1975.
The black middle class is disappearing. Three times
more blacks are unemployed than whites. There are
fewer blacks in medical school and law school in 1985
than in 1975. There are fewer than 10,000 black doc-
tors in America. There is one doctor for every 3,000
black persons while there is one white doctor for every
500 white persons. Eighty percent of black teenagers
are unemployed, and 50 percent of black teens are high
school dropouts. Black enrollment in colleges is declining nationwide. There are more blacks of college age in
prison than in college, although it costs more than
twice as much to keep a person in prison for a year—
$40,000—than to send a person to the best college—
$12,000.[37]

Of course, the Reagan administration and most conservative pundits reject this portrait of the plight of
blacks in Detroit and other urban centers. For them per-
sonifications of the black community come in successful
individuals like William Lucas, the former Wayne
County executive, who switched from the Democratic to
the Republican party in 1985. Lucas was a former F.B.I.
agent and was elected Wayne County sheriff and Wayne
County executive with the aid of Coleman Young and
the labor movement. Republican party leaders convinced Lucas to run against the incumbent governor,
Democrat James J. Blanchard in the 1986 gubernatorial
race. Next to Mayor Young, Lucas was the best-known
black politician in Michigan, excluding Richard Austin
who as secretary of state held a non-controversial and
essentially administrative position.

The Republicans' strategy was obvious: use a black to defeat a popular white governor and offset Mayor Young's political clout in the black community. Lucas even met with President Ronald Reagan. The strategy almost fell apart before the GOP primary, however, when an unknown Republican businessman, Dick Chrysler, challenged Lucas. Chrysler poured nearly $3,000,000 into his campaign and appeared to be on the road to victory until a damaging series of articles in the *Detroit News* raised some disturbing questions about Chrysler's employment and business practices and his personal record. Lucas won the primary.

Living in their own dream world, Republican strategists convinced Lucas to bolster his ticket with a woman for lieutenant governor. Lucas selected right-wing state representative, Colleen Engler, who had finished a poor third in the GOP primary. Although President Reagan campaigned for Lucas in Michigan, the polls showed that the visit actually hurt Lucas' campaign. In the end, Lucas was slaughtered in the November election, losing to Governor Blanchard by a 63–31 margin. It was a political disaster for the Republican party.

It was also an uneasy triumph for the Democrats. Post-election analysis verified what many other political observers saw from the beginning: Lucas' bid for governor was foredoomed because of his race. Jack Casey, a veteran Detroit political consultant and analyst who works with Democratic candidates, summarized the campaign—and Michigan politics—quite plainly when he declared voters mask their feelings when asked sensitive social and racial questions. Casey stated bluntly that race played a major role in the campaign. Illustrative of this is an exit poll in which 73 percent of the voters claimed they would not allow race to be a factor in their selection, though they thought their neighbors would be so influenced.[38]

Lucas and the Republican leaders, then, started out with a cynical plan to capture the black vote and it backfired. Blacks voted their party and their interests; it was a racial election by design. The blacks didn't fall for the Republican strategy, and the whites—Republicans and Democrats—voted by race and chose the white male, Blanchard.[39] GOP national committeeman Peter Secchia seemed to confirm this view when he stated that part of the reason for the magnitude of Lucas' defeat was that out-state voters thought Lucas was like Mayor Young.[42]

The taste of victory for Governor Blanchard and Mayor Young was further soured a few days after the election. General Motors shocked Michigan when it announced its plans to close in 1987 nine plants, five of them in the state. It was a disquieting portent of the future.

For Detroit, the shutdown of the Clark assembly and nearby Fleetwood plants in 1987 further reduced the city's small industrial base. It permanently laid off 6,600 autoworkers—most of whom were black—thereby increasing the city's already high unemployment rate of 25 percent. For Michigan, the closing of major plants in Flint and Pontiac would add to the burden these auto towns already had from earlier cutbacks. An estimated 17,450 high-paying jobs would be lost to the state.

A disturbing portent of the economic future of Michigan and the Detroit area in particular is arising from the auto industry's incessant drive to modernize and remain competitive. An estimated 195,000 out of 650,000 auto-related jobs are expected to be eliminated by 1990. In Michigan, "losing only 30 percent of the state's auto-related jobs is good news," delcared one auto expert, "because the state will have to trim its work force by that much to stay competitive in the auto industry."[40] It was scarcely good news for the autoworkers.

In addition, while public attention has been focused on the new Mazda plant in Flat Rock near Detroit with its 5,000 new jobs, about 25,000 Michigan auto plant jobs have been exported by Ford, Chrysler, and General Motors to cheaper labor in Mexican plants—a continuing trend in the last five years.

The outcome of the 1987 major contract negotiations between the UAW and Ford and General Motors did not alter the trend of declining jobs within the auto industry. The basic bargaining pattern had already been presaged by the 1986 negotiations between the UAW and Chrysler, which involved the Jefferson plant on the east side of Detroit. The union signed a seven-year contract assuring Chrysler of flexible work rule and other changes. In turn the company agreed to construct a new plant on a city site adjacent to the Jefferson plant which was earmarked for demolition. While the new plant was being built, auto workers at the old Jefferson plant could expect periodic layoffs. The new plant was also designed to use fewer workers.

Just as Chrysler's financial recovery had once dazzled the country while overshadowing the human costs involved, Ford's soaring profits in 1986 obscured the social costs of success. Ford's net income of over 3.3 billion dollars plus the accumulation of 8 billion dollars in cash reserves was an incredible record.

In 1987 the fabulous recovery of auto industry profits continued. The Big Three posted a $9.1 billion net profit, and that did not include the increase in cash reserves. However, the gains have not been shared by the thousands of white- and blue-collar workers whose jobs have been eliminated in recent years.

American auto industry prosperity no longer automatically signifies economic health for Detroit and other

Michigan auto cities where plants have closed down. At a January 1987 conference, members of the Southeast Michigan Council of Governments emphasized that point in a public statement: "Detroit area economy should continue to chug along with moderate growth, but the city of Detroit and certain manufacturing businesses will not share the wealth."[41] Obviously, any recession in the foreseeable future would vitiate this forecast and result in a further decline.

Given this economic prognosis, continuing race polarization, and increasing anxieties about drugs and crime, the most recent responses to the city's crises are less than reassuring, if not dismaying. The white power structure, whose decisions have deindustrialized Detroit, have joined Mayor Young to form a new super committee to develop a "strategic plan" to rescue the city. The very need for such a committee is a commentary on the record of earlier widely publicized committees. The kindest evaluation of previous efforts was made by Walter Douglas, who retired in late 1986 after serving for seven years as chief executive of the New Detroit committee. "I thought we could accomplish more than we have . . . I would have thought that our city would be further along."[42]

The newly assembled blue-ribbon group includes a big name from the auto industry: Roger Smith, chairman of General Motors. His participation, however, did not lead General Motors to reverse its decision to close down two major plants in the city. The gung ho leader of the new committee is Alan Schwartz, millionaire corporate lawyer. He is one of the movers who helped Henry Ford put together the unlucky Renaissance Center project. A *Detroit Free Press* article reminded the public that "Schwartz has been involved in efforts to repair the city for at least thirty years, ever since Mayor Louis Miriani named him chairman of a committee to rehabilitate the old Michigan Avenue skid row in the 1950's. Since then the area in need of rejuvenation has spread from Michigan Avenue almost to the city limits. But Schwartz rejects suggestions that such efforts, past or present, have been fruitless."[43] Few motorists driving down desolate Michigan Avenue would be inclined to share Schwartz's appraisal.

Co-chairman of the new committee is Walter McCarthy, chairman of Detroit Edison, the company immersed in solving its long-standing nuclear plant problems. Another member, the influential real estate developer Max Fisher, has been on every committee since the 1967 riot.

Ostensibly, the new factor on the committee is the official presence of Mayor Young, one of the originators of the group. Of course, he has been doing business with the power elite since his first election in 1973. What makes the alliance unusual is its fusion of the most powerful black Democratic politician with rich Republican supporters of William Lucas and president Ronald Reagan—Mayor Young's political enemies. The strains within the alliance are difficult to conceal, given that most of the white power structure and Mayor Young serve different constituencies, and have different political philosophies as well as conflicting political agendas.

Two months after its formation, the committee adopted an imposing name: "Detroit Strategic Planning Project." Since its inception it has gathered more top level names: Michael Blumenthal of Unisys; Gerald Greenwald, president of Chrysler; Donald Petersen, chairman of Ford; and labor leaders Douglas Fraser, the former UAW president, and Marc Stepp, a UAW vice president. Excluded are some executives who are not on Mayor Young's favorite list.

The prestigious makeup of the committee, however, did not exempt it from receiving stinging criticism from Detroit City Council members. When committee co-chairman McCarthy outlined the committee's objectives for tackling the problems of crime, unemployment, education, transportation, race relations, and the city's poor image, council member Clyde Cleveland responded angrily: "For the people on this committee to be talking about the problems of Detroit and what we can do about it—when these are the folks who created the problem—that is the height of racism."[44]

The real difficulty with the committee's final report, released in November 1987, is that it sounded too much like a replay of the power elite's pronunciations of 20 years earlier. Most of its ideas could be found in the plethora of master plans, blue prints, studies, recommendations and proposals for curing Detroit's ills that are abundantly available in the public and university libraries and in the archives of the city planning commission.

Additionally, the committee somehow managed to avoid taking a position on the hotly debated issue affecting Detroit's future in the spring of 1988: the question of legalizing casino gambling. Although Detroit voters rejected the idea in referendums in 1976 and 1981, the mayor appointed a 64-member commission to review the proposition. By a vote of 45 to 15, the Young commission recommended voters approve casino gambling in a special referendum on August 2, 1988. Aside from the expected negative public reaction and bitter opposition from church and civic leaders, the casino gambling proposition came under attack from unexpected sources. The Greater Detroit Chamber of Commerce, not waiting for the commission's report, publicly opposed casino gambling, arguing that casinos would hurt the city's image and discourage businesses from locating or expanding in Detroit. Another shock came when metropolitan Detroit's top three officials announced their opposition: Wayne County executive Edward McNamara, Oakland County Executive Daniel T. Murphy, and Macomb County Commission Chairman Mark A. Steenbergh.[45]

Joe H. Stroud, editor of the *Detroit Free Press,* added his voice to the opposition, declaring, "There is something unspeakably sad about the headlong rush to plunge Detroit into the casino gambling business." Stroud added, "What is wrong is that this is a campaign inspired by a mirage. The notion that Detroit could, with the simple catalyst of casino gambling, convert itself into the spa of the middle part of the country defies common sense."[46]

If casino gambling is rejected, its proponents may argue that this will be a setback for Detroit's economic future. A negative vote would certainly be a setback for Mayor Young. However, a greater tragedy might well be turning Detroit into another Atlantic City, as far as the well-being of its residents is concerned. The point is well made in a *New York Times* assessment of Atlantic City:

> Ten years after the first of a dozen casino hotels opened in Atlantic City, it is clear that they have failed to be the "unique tool of urban redevelopment" the New Jersey Legislature envisioned. The casinos have made fortunes and have transformed the Boardwalk into a glittering strip of towers; they provide thousands of jobs and pay hundreds of millions of dollars in taxes. But much of Atlantic City is still blighted, with dilapidated housing, boarded-up businesses and unkempt vacant lots where buildings were razed for development that hasn't occurred.[47]

The leaders of the white power structure—many of whom have sat on such planning committees—face a dilemma arising from their own successes. By moving their businesses to the suburbs, the movers and shakers have helped to make metropolitan Detroit one of the richest areas in the nation. However, much of this achievement has turned out to be at the expense of the city. So many businesses have left Detroit it is hard to imagine what will lure the white middle class back into the city. The black middle class is also trying to leave.

The advantages of living outside the city are well stated by a suburbanite in an editorial in the *Detroit Free Press*:

> The main reason why I live where I do is that I can shop at Twelve Oaks Mall, Westland Mall, Livonia Mall and Tel-Twelve Mall. I can shop at these malls with relative safety. Also the suburbs provide careful zoning of land that allows for easements connected to property and neighborhoods for the use of parks.
>
> What does Detroit offer to the common people living day-to-day? The Renaissance Center, Trappers Alley and Joe Louis Arena are fine for out-of-town travelers and once-a-week Saturday night entertainment, if you can afford the prices and the parking. Detroit has nothing to offer in the way of everyday downright living.[48]

Other formidable challenges to Detroit's revitalization remain. How can a poor school system with a drop-out rate of 41 percent be transformed into an educational system attractive enough to bring families back into the city? How can the white population's fear of living next to "Them" be overcome? Indeed, racism is still evident throughout metropolitan Detroit. When it comes to black residency in the white suburbs, tokenism is still the name of the game. Only a handful of middle-class and rich blacks have quietly moved into communities noted for good living. The Grosse Pointes, Birmingham,

Bloomfield Hills, Dearborn, Dearborn Heights, St. Clair Shores, Royal Oak, Warren, Troy, Harper Woods, and East Detroit are white enclaves in the 1980's, as they were in the 1960's. They were 99 percent pure when it came to color as late as 1983.

Only Southfield and Oak Park, where Jewish people formerly from Detroit have settled, are exceptions. About 7,000 of Southfield's 75,568 residents are black, most of them middle class. In Oak Park about 12 percent of the 31,537 middle-class residents are black.[49]

Of course, the crude racism of former Dearborn mayor Orville Hubbard, reelected 18 times until he retired in 1978 after 36 years in office, was no longer vocalized in the suburbs. Mayor Hubbard had at one time openly declared, "I have nothing against Negroes. I just don't believe in integration. When that happens, along comes socializing with whites, and then mongrelization."[50]

However, a Dearborn referendum passed in 1985 sent word to the blacks in a more subtle fashion by restricting park use to residents only. Dearborn parks were sometimes used by blacks. Sensitized by events in South Africa and disturbed by any manifestations of "apartheid" in public law, Detroit black leaders were outraged by the Dearborn action. A coalition of white religious leaders of all faiths and black leaders formed to challenge the ordinance. An economic boycott was organized, since blacks did shop in Dearborn. It sobered up some of the suburban community. Court suits by the NAACP and the American Civil Liberties Union stymied the park law. The issue was defused but the raw tensions remained. Ironically, Dearborn residents had argued they had been picked on unfairly. After all, they had pointed out, the Grosse Pointes and St. Clair Shores, among other communities, excluded non-residents from some of their parks.

As 1987 began, it became clear that most Detroiters viewed crime as the number one issue. The sense of growing despair in the city was illustrated in a *Detroit Free Press* editorial: "Detroiters have begun looking to the heavens for a solution to crime. Detroit Mayor Coleman Young has declared this week a time of prayer and an end to crime, and City Councilman John Peoples wants Detroit churches to ask God's help in conquering Motor City lawlessness. The Rev. Peoples has asked Metro Detroit churches to join a prayer/fasting vigil during Lent."[51]

In January of 1987, the mayor stirred controversy with a declaration that he would not be willing to unveil any plan to fight criminals in Detroit until he found more space in which to jail them. Young said, "We know of 300 to 500 kids that if they were removed from the streets, that would reduce the shootings to almost zero."[52] The Mayor proposed to Governor Blanchard that unused air bases in Michigan's Upper Peninsula be turned into detention facilities. Keeping the kids "in the frigid zones of the North would help cool them hotshots out," the Mayor insisted.[53] Critics scorned the mayor for trying to create a Siberian Gulag. Residents of the Upper Peninsula objected strongly to having "black penal colonies" among them.

In an attempt to mute the argument, Gary Owen, the House Speaker in the legislature, suggested the state consider youth work camps all over the state: "We (the state) own thousands and thousands of acres . . . and we can use them for isolated camps. We can put them (youths) so far in that you'll have to pipe sunshine in."[54] However, creating "Work and Learn" camps, somewhat modeled after the New Deal Civilian Conservation Camps of the Great Depression, had become entangled with the persistent issue—"Who wants THEM around?"

An unfortunate side effect of the Mayor's remarks was the resulting public perception that the police had a list of 300 to 500 identifiable trouble makers. The picture of hundreds of criminal black youths roaming the city streets was hardly reassuring and unfairly stereotyped the vast majority of black youths as undersirables.

The raw nerves festered by the status of many blacks in Michigan surfaced after Governor Blanchard's 1987 state of the state message. His optimistic tone concerning the state's future drew praise from most Democratic and Republican legislators. But it received a stinging rejoiner from the leader of the 14-member black Democratic caucus. Representative Alma Stallworth of Detroit, chairperson of the caucus, issued an eight-page critique pointing out that "The economic improvements cited by the governor have not yet reached the majority of black Michiganians. The failure to develop an urban strategy, when combined with structural unemployment and racism, spells disaster for Michigan's black community."[55] Mayor Young echoed those opinions a few days later.[56]

An unusual twist in federal litigation kept the racial pot simmering on another front. In 1986 the Civil Rights Division of the U.S. Department of Justice began a series of investigations and law suits over alleged racial discrimination in municipal hiring by more than a dozen Detroit suburbs. Dearborn with 966 employees Warren with 924 employees—none of whom were black —were conspicuous among the suburbs facing lawsuits that were based on a March 1986 U.S. District Court decision involving Cicero, Illinois, hiring practices.

Joyce Garrett, Detroit's personnel director, blasted the federal actions, claiming they were politically motivated and were intended to create racial tensions: "I don't think (the Justice Department) is motivated for the welfare of women and minorities, but to form interracial strife and create a situation in which minority groups become the object of increased hostility among largely lower-middle-class, well-paid, blue-collar, white people." She added that investigations were a diversionary tactic by the Reagan administration to distract the public from America's disastrous foreign policy.[57]

Partisan politics reached a further extreme when the most influential Republican spokesman in the state legislature, Senator majority leader John Engler, compared Detroit to Beirut, "where nobody would seriously think of going to invest." He added, "You simply can not create jobs in a combat zone." As for prayer week, Engler said, "I think it will take a lot more than prayers to solve the problems of Detroit." He further stated, "The prayer they're suggesting for the victims of violence, while important, is not a substitute for action by the Legislature. There is no unified commitment on the part of the mayor and the City Council and police agencies or the neighborhood groups that I can see."[58] The senator's ugly analogy was neither ridiculed nor challenged by any influential voice in the state. The public appeared not to mind, as they were already saturated by media coverage of savagery in the Middle East and crime stories from Detroit.

Engler's rebuke came from residents of the large Lebanese-American community. They resented his comparison and one Lebanese declared, "Detroit streets are worse than Beirut because in Beirut you don't have rape and killing of children.[59] A Lebanese journalist said that war had made Beirut a horrible place to live. One Detroit legislator did ask the senator for an apology. Senator Engler later replied that he did not mean to offend Detroit or Beirut residents. It is unlikely that the exchange will put the senator in disfavor with most white voters in the state; there are no signs that Detroit bashing is unpopular in the state.

Similarly, although the Detroit area in and near Dearborn does have the largest concentration of Middle Easterners in the United States—ranging from an estimated 80,000 to 200,000 people—Arab bashing is also an acceptable political tactic. It was a factor in the election of the mayor of Dearborn, who promised to keep the Arabs in their place.[60]

In reviewing the city's history since the 1967 riot, one thing became increasingly clear to me: I had been overly optimistic in my 1972 prognosis, although at that time many considered my views as too negative. In my original study I concluded:

> All trends suggest that Detroit, the city, is destined to become a black metropolis—not just a slum or a ghetto, though these do exist, but a municipality with a strong black middle class and, perhaps more significantly, a powerful black unionized working class. This black community has already demonstrated its strength, viability, and leadership on both political and union fronts. It is moving toward domination of the city and challenging the white suburbs in every area of public controversy.[61]

Only Wilbur Thompson, the distinguished Wayne State University urban economist, suggested it might be too optimistic. In terms of the economic projections, Professor Thompson turned out to be right. Blacks have achieved political power, symbolized by the triumph of Mayor Young. They are visible in every city institution, in the courts, and in governmental agencies. They have two unbeatable congressmen—John Conyers, Jr. and George W. Crockett—a majority in the city council, and seats in the state legislature. But political power has not been matched by economic power. It is still in the hands of the white elite and the suburbanites. Labor, from which so many leaders have emerged, has lost its powerful industrial base, and unions now rest largely on the government and service sector.

Within this framework, however, is a hopeful sign for the future. It is the emergence of a new and ambitious strata of black women and men observable in every aspect of city life: city and school institutions, the churches, the court system, and the unions. Unburdened by the weight of the past, they walk in pride and show every indication of just beginning to demand respect and their rights.

So what is the future of Detroit, a city plagued with a poor image, suburban-city racial tensions, and the turmoil of economic change? While the Beirut analogy did catch the public eye and further damage the city's image, it is an absurd comparison. The city is like a cauldron but it isn't a war zone.

The ever-ebullient mayor paints a rosy scenario. "The city was poised for a great leap forward," declared Mayor Young in his 1986 state of the city message. "The outlook was more positive than it has been in any of my previous ten years as mayor," he asserted.[62] For its residents, however, the litmus test was in the question, "Was Detroit a better place to live in 1986?" Were the streets a safer place to walk, day or night? The painful truth was that there was little evidence to support an affirmative reply. Rather, Detroit is a city of angry, anxious, and concerned citizens, outraged at the youth killings, the homicide rate, and joblessness.

Each positive move forward has had negative sides: destruction, human cost, and failure. Assuming an optimistic prognosis that most of the razzle-dazzle schemes and plans will succeed, the basic trends of the past twenty years remain. Those who stand to profit from building investments, hotel and commercial activities, and conventions, and those who hold most of the good jobs are still the suburbanites. Neither the white power elite nor the thousands of day commuters give any indication of wanting to return to the city.

As for the city's residents, most of the prosperity will bypass them as it has in the past. The city's population will remain a mixture of the elderly, the welfare clients, and the working poor employed in low-paying service jobs. The middle-class enclaves—mostly black—will stand out as a reminder of a growing two-tier economy. But most blacks and poor whites will be stuck in the lower half of the tier.

Unquestionably, one of Mayor Young's accomplishments has been his contribution to instilling pride in the black people of Detroit. If ever a man went from defeat to victory, it is the mayor. He has been a major force in the establishment of black political power in the city. Nor can it be denied that his presence and position have been decisive factors in keeping social peace—avoiding riots on at least two occasions—during his tenure.

Yet on St. Valentine's Day 1987 there was a massacre in Detroit. It was not a replica of Chicago in the 1920's. Rather, it was a mockery of the Reverend Martin Luther King's dream. The occasion was a $300-a-ticket fund-raising party for the mayor. Three thousand tickets were sold and 2,000 contributors came to enjoy caviar, shrimp, and roast beef as part of a cocktail party. It was the 14th annual benefit for the mayor's war chest, which already had a balance of about 2 million dollars. The affair was more in the style of an Emperor Jones than a man presiding over a city in which most of the residents live bleak lives, and are buffeted by forces beyond their control. An admirer of Mayor Young explained that no doubt the mayor would run for reelection in 1989, and with the fund-raisers, "He's making the price of running against him so high, no one will try it."[63]

Yet the mayor's achilles heel may well be the arrogance of power he displayed at the gathering: "I think this is bigger than last year's crowd. It seems that the more the newspapers and TV and radio stations knock this administration, the more and more people show up and show support. . . . As long as people like you continue to support this administration, frankly, I don't give a damn what the newspapers and TV say."[64] Who knows what young Cassius or "Corey" lurks in the background? Who knows how long the influential Republicans in the white power structure will support a Democratic mayor?

The crude media-bashing in the mayor's scornful remarks sounds more like the last hurrah of an old-line politician rather than the needed rallying cry to save the city. "I have overcome" may be personally satisfying, but it is a poor substitute for the clarion call "We Shall Overcome." Democratic politicians in the city and state were reminded of the power of ideas when Reverend Jesse Jackson gained a stunning victory in the 1988 Michigan presidential primaries. The Jackson triumph forced the national media and pundits to quit asking what Jesse wanted, and to recognize him as the most eloquent spokesmen for a restive political constituency no longer willing to remain quiet about politics-as-usual.

According to a report issued in 1988 by the Commission of Minority in Education and American Life, "America is moving backward—not forward—in its effort to achieve the full participation of minority citizens in the life and prosperity of the nation. In education, employment, income, health, longevity and other basic measures of individual and social being, gaps persist—and in some cases are widening—between members of minority groups and the majority population."[65]

It is a painful summary of the heart of the Detroit story—and many other urban centers—since the 1967 riot. This is the challenge America still has to face.

Notes

Chapter 1: The Legacy of the KKK

1. Kenneth Jackson, *The Ku Klux Klan in the City, 1915–1930* (New York, Oxford University Press, 1967), p. 141. An excellent source book and penetrating analysis of the KKK. See "Detroit," Chapter 9.
2. Cited in Irving Stone, *Clarence Darrow for the Defense* (Garden City, N.Y., Garden City Publishing Co., 1941), p. 472.
3. Arthur Garfield Hays, *Let Freedom Ring* (New York, Boni and Liveright, 1928), p. 202.
4. Cited in Arthur Weinberg, ed., *Attorney for the Damned* (New York, Simon and Schuster, 1957), pp. 223–224.
5. Hays, *op. cit.,* p. 199.
6. *Detroit Free Press,* July 12, 1925.
7. *Detroit News,* August 15, 1965, interview with Otis Sweet.
8. Transcript of first trial (Sweet case).
9. *Detroit News,* August 15, 1965, Otis Sweet interview.
10. *Ibid.*
11. *Detroit Free Press,* November 20, 1925.
12. Transcript (Sweet case).
13. Cited in Weinberg, *op. cit.,* pp. 241–242.
14. *Detroit News,* August 15, 1965.

Chapter 2: The Twenties

1. Ulysses W. Boykin, *A Hand Book on the Detroit Negro* (New York, The Minority Study Associates, 1943), p. 12.
2. *Ibid.,* p. 14.
3. John G. Van Deusen, *The Black Man in White America* (Washington, D.C., Associated Publishers, 1944), p. 30.
4. Horace Cayton and George Mitchell, *Black Workers and the New Unions* (Chapel Hill, N.C., University of North Carolina Press, 1939), p. 6.

5. Van Deusen, *op. cit.,* p. 60.
6. "The Life Story of Joe Louis," *New York Times,* November 5–12, 1948.
7. Van Deusen, *op. cit.,* p. 62.
8. Irving Howe and B. J. Widick, *The UAW and Walter Reuther* (New York, Random House, 1949), p. 12.
9. Arthur Wood, *Hamtramck* (New York, Bookman Associates, 1955), p. 27.
10. Allan Nevins and Frank Ernest Hill, *Ford: Expansion and Challenge: 1915–1933* (New York, Charles Scribner's Sons, 1957), p. 311.
11. Personal experiences in Detroit schools.
12. *New York Times,* October 12, 1969.
13. *The Negro in Detroit* (Detroit, Mayor's Interracial Committee, 1926).
14. Howe and Widick, *op. cit.,* p. 216.
15. Lloyd Bailer, "Negro Labor in the Automobile Industry" (Doctoral dissertation, University of Michigan, 1943).
16. Boykin, *op. cit.,* p. 94.
17. *Ibid.,* p. 110.
18. Nevins and Hill, *op. cit.,* p. 589.
19. *We Work at Ford,* pamphlet (Detroit, UAW National–Ford Department, 1961), p. 19.
20. *Detroit News,* March 16, 1931.
21. Henry Ford, *Moving Forward* (Garden City, N.Y., Doubleday, 1930).
22. Nevins and Hill, *op. cit.,* pp. 514–18.
23. *Ibid.*
24. *We Work at Ford,* p. 24.
25. *Ibid.,* p. 35.
26. *Ibid.,* p. 36.
27. Booton Herndon, *Ford* (New York, Weybright and Talley, 1969), p. 185.
28. Irving Bernstein, *The Lean Years* (Boston, Houghton Mifflin, 1960), pp. 509–10.
29. Notes from conversations with Emil Mazey, 1948.
30. Robert Dunn, *Labor and Automobiles* (New York, International publishers, 1929).
31. William Z. Foster, *American Trade Unionism* (New York, International Publishers, 1947).
32. "The Communist," report of Jack Stachel to Sixth Convention, Communist Party of the U.S.A., May 1929.
33. *Ibid.*
34. *Ibid.,* April 1929.
35. *Ibid.,* May 1929.
36. *Ibid.*

Chapter 3: The Depression and the Growth of Radicalism

1. Sidney Fine, *The Automobile Worker Under the Blue Eagle* (Ann Arbor, University of Michigan Press, 1963), p. 4.

2. Richard D. Lunt, *High Ministry of Government: The Political Career of Frank Murphy* (Detroit, Wayne State University Press, 1965), p. 36.
3. *Business Week*, February 8, 1933.
4. Raymond C. Miller, *Kilowatts at Work: A History of the Detroit Edison Co.* (Detroit, Wayne State University Press, 1957), p. 330.
5. Edmund Wilson, *The American Jitters* (New York, Charles Scribner's Sons, 1932), pp. 66–67.
6. Miller, *op. cit.*, p. 332.
7. *Ibid.*, p. 333.
8. Louis Adamic, "Straws in the Wind," *Scribner's*, February 1932.
9. Mary Heaton Vorse, "Rebellion of the Prairie Farmers," *Harper's*, December 1932.
10. Lunt, *op. cit.*, p. 125.
11. See *Detroit News*, March 7, 1932, for coverage of speech.
12. *Detroit News*, March 8, 1932.
13. *Detroit Mirror* and *Detroit News*, March 8, 1932.
14. *Ibid.*
15. *Detroit Times*, March 19, 1932.
16. Keith Sward, *The Legend of Henry Ford* (New York, Rinehart, 1948), p. 240.
17. *Ibid.*
18. Matthew Josephson, *Infidel in the Temple* (New York, Knopf, 1967), p. 186.
19. Fine, *op. cit.*
20. *Detroit News*, February 6, 1933.
21. *Detroit Herald*, February 1933.
22. *Detroit Tribune*, July, August 1933.

Chapter 4: CIO Sitdowns

1. *New York Times*, June 17, 1933.
2. *New York Times*, February 11, 1934.
3. Henderson Report for the National Recovery Administration, January 23, 1935.
4. Samuel Romer, "That Automobile Strike," *Nation*, February 6, 1935.
5. *Ibid.*
6. Art Preis, *Labor's Giant Step* (New York, Pioneer Publishers, 1964), p. 22.
7. Associated Press, May 24, 1934.
8. Charles Rumford Walker, *American City* (New York, Farrar and Rinehart, 1937), pp. 192–99.
9. Richard D. Lunt, *The High Ministry of Government: The Political Career of Frank Murphy* (Detroit, Wayne State University Press, 1965), p. 125.
10. Forrest Davis, "Labor Spies and the Black Legion," *New Republic*, June 17, 1936.
11. *Business Week*, April 10, 1937.
12. *New York Times*, January 22, 1937.

13. Excerpts from John L. Lewis' speech to the UAW convention at St. Louis, 1940.
14. *Fifteenth Anniversary Celebration of the Chrysler Sit-Down Strike by Local 7, UAW-CIO*, March 1952.

Chapter 5: Labor's Triumph

1. Personal interviews with early participants in UAW history form the basis of this chapter. They are contained in an unpublished report done by the author for the Fair Employment Practices Department of the UAW in 1956.
2. *Michigan Chronicle*, November 27, 1939.
3. *Ibid.*
4. Irving Howe and B. J. Widick, *The UAW and Walter Reuther* (New York, Random House, 1949), Chapter 4, "The Fall of Ford." This section was heavily documented by government and other official sources since the event was so controversial. The UAW pamphlet "We Work at Ford" contains comparable material on pp. 85–106.
5. *New York Times*, January 12, 1969.

Chapter 6: Unionism—A New Foothold for Negroes

1. Cited in Alfred McClung Lee and Norman Daymond Humphrey, *Race Riot* (New York, Dryden Press, 1943), p. 63.
2. Robert Shogan and Tom Craig, *The Detroit Race Riot* (Philadelphia and New York, Chilton Books, 1964), p. 1.
3. Bette Smith Jenkins, "The Racial Policies of the Detroit Housing Commission and Their Administration" (Master's thesis, Wayne State University, 1950). Other material in this chapter was developed from this excellent study.
4. Lowell J. Carr and James E. Stermer, *Willow Run: A Study of Industrialization and Cultural Inadequacy* (New York, Harper & Brothers, 1952), p. 11.
5. *Detroit Free Press*, July 5, 1940.
6. Roi Ottley, *New World a-Coming* (Boston, Houghton Mifflin, 1943), p. 266.
7. John G. Van Deusen, *The Black Man in White America* (Washington, D.C., Associated Publishers, 1944), p. 62.
8. Herbert Garfinkel, *When Negroes March* (Glencoe, Illinois, The Free Press, 1959), p. 144.
9. Irving Howe and B. J. Widick, *The UAW and Walter Reuther* (New York, Random House, 1949), p. 221.
10. Cited in Lloyd Bailer, "The Negro Automobile Worker," *Journal of Political Economy*, October 1943.
11. *Life*, August 3, 1942.
12. Jenkins, *op. cit.*
13. Ottley, *op. cit.*, p. 267.
14. Jenkins, *op. cit.*
15. *New York Times*, March 2, 1942.
16. Jenkins, *op. cit.*

17. *Detroit News,* April 12, 1943.
18. Walter White and Thurgood Marshall, *What Caused the Detroit Riot* (NAACP publication, July 1943).

Chapter 7: Wartime Detroit

The most authoritative reference to the 1943 Detroit race riot is the succinct study by Alfred McClung Lee, Chairman of the Department of Sociology, Wayne State University, and Norman Daymond Humphrey, Assistant Professor of Sociology, WSU; it was published in 1943 by Dryden Press, New York.

Another major report is the book *The Detroit Race Riot* by Robert Shogan and Tom Craig, two former Detroit newspapermen, published in 1964 by Chilton Books, Philadelphia and New York.

A valuable analysis in retrospect is the pamphlet "Detroit—Ten Years After" by Charles J. Wartman, executive editor of the *Michigan Chronicle,* the Negro newspaper; it was printed by the newspaper in cooperation with the Wayne County CIO in 1953. The pamphlet contains a series of feature articles which appeared in the *Michigan Chronicle* (February 21 to March 28, 1953).

1. *Detroit Free Press,* June 28, 1943.
2. *The Wage Earner,* June 1943.
3. Cited in *Michigan Chronicle,* June 7, 1943.
4. Lee and Humphrey, *op. cit.,* pp. 20–21.
5. Shogan and Craig, *op. cit.,* p. 43.
6. Malcolm Bingay, *Of Me I Sing* (New York, Bobbs Merrill, 1949), p. 121.
7. *Detroit Tribune,* July 3, 1943.
8. Shogan and Craig, *op. cit.,* p. 46.
9. *Detroit News,* June 22, 1967.
10. *Detroit News,* June 23, 1967.
11. *Racial Digest,* June 1967).
12. Cited in Shogan and Craig, *op. cit.,* p. 87.
13. *Ibid.,* p. 88.
14. Lee and Humphrey, *op cit.,* p. 46.
15. *Detroit Times,* July 27, 1943.
16. *Fact Finding Committee Report* on the Detroit riots, August 11, 1943.
17. *Detroit Free Fress,* August 12, 1943.
18. *Ibid.*
19. Louis E. Martin, *Michigan Chronicle,* editorial, August 13, 1943.

Chapter 8: McCarthyism and Vigilante Democracy, Detroit Style

1. Irving Howe and B. J. Widick, *The UAW and Walter Reuther* (New York, Random House, 1949), pp. 126–148.
2. *Ibid.*
3. Daniel Bell, "The Treaty of Detroit," *Fortune,* July, 1950.
4. Ralph C. and Estelle D. James, *Hoffa and the Teamsters* (New York, D. Van Nostrand, 1965), p. 86.

5. *Labor Action,* February 11, 1951.
6. *Detroit Free Press,* July 2, 1948.
7. *Detroit Free Press,* August 7, 1948.
8. *Detroit Free Press,* April 15, 1950.
9. Personal experiences, UAW Local 7.
10. *Ibid.*
11. *Labor Action,* March 7, 1952.
12. *Labor Action,* March 14, 1952.

Chapter 9: Postwar Reconstruction in Reutherland

1. *Facts About Michigan,* Research report, Democratic Party, 1960.
2. B. J. Widick, "Detroit: More Plants, Fewer Jobs," *The New Republic,* March 15, 1954.
3. Report on School Population and Employment Trends, 1960; Division of Planning and Housing, Detroit Board of Education.
4. Charles Abrams, *Forbidden Neighbors* (New York, Harper & Brothers, 1955), pp. 100–101.
5. Statement of Robert M. Frehse to the United States Commission on Civil Rights, Hearing on Housing and Job Discrimination Against Negroes, December 14, 1960, p. 36.
6. Guy Nunn, radio broadcast, April 1957.
7. Civil Rights Commission Hearing, p. 87.
8. Civil Rights Commission Hearing, p. 88.
9. *The Vanguard,* publication of Trade Union Leadership Council, April 1965.

Chapter 10: Mayor Cavanagh and the Limits of Reform

1. Irving Howe and B. J. Widick, *The UAW and Walter Reuther* (New York, Random House, 1949), p. 275.
2. J. David Greenstone, *Labor in American Politics* (New York, Alfred A. Knopf, 1969), p. 122.
3. *New America,* November 24, 1961.
4. George Edwards, speech before TULC meeting, April 1962.
5. *National Observer,* July 15, 1963.
6. *Business Week,* July 30, 1963.
7. E. J. Forsythe, *A Profile of Detroit and Michigan Economy,* Reprint series 32, University of Michigan–Wayne State University Institute of Labor and Industrial Relations, March 1965. As research director of the project, the writer bears much of the responsibility for the optimistic conclusions, which seemed reasonable at the time.
8. Stanley H. Brown, "Slow Healing of a City," *Fortune,* June 1965.
9. *Ibid.*
10. *Ibid.*
11. *The Vanguard,* Trade Union Leadership Council, November 1963.
12. *New York Times,* December 6, 1965.
13. *U.S. Riot Commission Report,* March 1968, pp. 131-142.
14. *Detroit Free Press,* April 20, 1969.
15. Cited in *Detroit Free Press,* July 23, 1967.

Chapter 11: A City Besieged

On September 3, 1967, the *Detroit Free Press* published a five-page report entitled "The 43 Who Died," an investigation of how and why Detroit's riot victims were slain. For five weeks, three top-notch newspaper reporters with unusual credentials interviewed over 300 persons including policemen, National Guardsmen, witnesses, and families, and studied hundreds of documents to produce a study which earned them a Pulitzer prize. The team consisted of Barbara Stanton, a graduate of the Columbia School of Journalism with a master's degree and six years' experience as a reporter; William Serrin, a former Army officer and experienced newspaperman; and Gene Goltz, a previous winner of a Pulitzer prize, with nine years' background as a newspaperman in Texas and New York. They had also covered the actual riot. Most of the findings of the *United States Riot Commission Report,* prepared by the National Advisory Commission on Civil Disorders, were based on the facts dug up by the *Detroit Free Press* team.

My own personal research was small indeed compared to the outstanding job done by the *Detroit Free Press* team, and I gratefully acknowledge the debt.

The report of the National Advisory Commission on Civil Disorders provided excellent documentation for what was known but, until it was published in March 1968, lacked confirmation.

Anthony Ripley, now of the *New York Times,* who was a close friend and assistant to Mayor Jerome P. Cavanagh until after the riots, was a most useful source of information, and the mayor himself was very cooperative. Merle Henrickson, a most knowledgeable Detroiter and director of the Detroit Board of Education, Housing and Planning Division, was extremely helpful in providing and analyzing material, as were many other individuals in Detroit.

1. *Time,* August 4, 1967.
2. *Detroit Free Press Report, op. cit.*
3. Anthony Ripley statement, *Detroit Free Press,* July 26, 1967.
4. *Detroit Free Press,* July 28, 1967.
5. *Detroit Free Press,* July 24, 1967.
6. *New York Times,* July 26, 1967.
7. *Detroit Free Press Report, op. cit.*
8. *Detroit News,* July 24, 1967.
9. *U.S. Riot Commission Report,* p. 99.
10. *New York Times,* January 31, 1970.
11. *Time,* August 4, 1967.
12. *Detroit Free Press,* July 30, 1967.
13. *Detroit Free Press,* July 24, 1967.
14. *Detroit News,* July 24, 1967.
15. *Detroit News,* July 25, 1967.
16. *Detroit News,* July 26, 1967.
17. *Detroit Free Press,* July 27, 1967.
18. *New York Times,* July 26, 1967.
19. *New York Times,* July 27, 1967.
20. *Christian Science Monitor,* July 28, 1967.
21. *U.S. Riot Commission Report,* p. 97.

22. *Ibid.,* p. 98.
23. *Ibid.,* pp. 101–102.
24. *Ibid.,* p. 102.
25. *Ibid.,* p. 103.
26. *Ibid., p. 104.*
27. *Ibid.*
28. *Ibid.,* p. 105.
29. *Ibid.*
30. Van Gordon Sauter and Burleigh Hines, *Nightmare in Detroit* (Chicago, Henry Regnery Co., 1968), p. 163.

Chapter 12: Post-Riot Reconstruction

1. *New York Times,* November 10, 1967.
2. *Detroit News,* November 2, 1967.
3. *Detroit News,* August 1, 1967.
4. *New Detroit Committee Progress Report,* April 1968.
5. *Detroit News,* August 1, 1967.
6. *Detroit Free Press,* August 7, 1967.
7. *Detroit Free Press,* November 9, 1967.
8. *Detroit Free Press,* September 28, 1967.
9. *Ibid.*
10. *Daily Express,* Detroit, November 22, 1967.
11. *Detroit Free Press,* November 15, 1967.
12. *Newsweek,* June 2, 1969.
13. *Detroit News,* October 31, 1967.
14. *New York Times,* November 10, 1967.
15. *New York Times,* February 14, 1970.
16. *Ibid.*
17. *New York Times,* March 24, 1968. Its survey indicated that
    (1) job creation by private industry amounts to filling vacancies caused by business growth and employee turnover;
    (2) though there were 28,000 more people at work in Detroit in February than a year ago, this reflected "normal growth."
18. *Business Week,* February 3, 1967.
19. Andrew F. Brimmer and Henry S Terrell, "The Economic Potential of Black Capitalism," Paper delivered at American Economic Association meeting, December 29, 1969.
20. *Ibid.*
21. Ann Scott, "Report from Detroit," *Fortune,* February 1970.
22. *New Detroit Committee Report.*
23. *Detroit News,* March 16, 1969.
24. Thomas R. Brooks, "Workers, White & Black," *Dissent,* January-February 1970.
25. William Serrin, "How One Big City Defeated Its Mayor," *New York Times Magazine,* October 27, 1968.
26. William Serrin, "God Help Our City," *Atlantic,* March 1969.
27. Editorial in *Tuebor,* Detroit Police Officers Association, April 1969.
28. Serrin, *op. cit.*

29. *Detroit Free Press,* April 6, 1969.
30. *Detroit News,* April 6, 1969.
31. *Detroit News,* April 3, 1969.
32. "The Crucifixion of George Crockett," *The Metro,* April 8, 1969.
33. *Ibid.*
34. *Detroit News,* April 19, 1969.
35. *Detroit Free Press,* May 19, 1969.
36. *Detroit Free Press,* April 17, 1969.
37. *Detroit Free Press,* October 31, 1969.
38. Michael Maidenberg, "Mayor's Race a Close One," *Detroit Free Press,* October 26, 1969.
39. *Detroit News,* November 5, 1969.

Chapter 13: Detroit—Black Metropolis of the Future

1. *Detroit News,* February 13, 1970.
2. Merle Henrickson, "Population Trends Which Have Affected School Enrollments," Department of Planning and Building Studies Report, January 14, 1971.
3. U.S. Census Report, U.S. Department of Commerce, Bureau of the Census, February 1971.
4. UDA Research Project Document DOX-USA-A60, Detroit Edison Company–Wayne State University–Doxiadis Associates, January 1969.
5. *Wall Street Journal,* February 26, 1971.
6. 1970 Census of Housing, U.S. Department of Commerce, Bureau of the Census, February 1971.
7. "Furor over a Drive to Integrate the Suburbs," *U.S. News and World Report,* August 10, 1970.
8. Housing Census, *op. cit.*
9. *Detroit News,* April 11, 1971.
10. *Detroit News,* March 20, 1971.
11. *Detroit Free Press,* March 29, 1971.
12. *New York Times,* June 25, 1968.
13. *Detroit News,* March 22, 1971.
14. *Detroit News,* March 21, 1971.
15. *New York Times,* April 19, 1971.
16. *Detroit News,* February 13, 1970.
17. *New Detroit Committee Progress Report,* 1968.
18. Off-the-record report of a personnel director of an auto company.
19. Mitchell Sviridoff, *Ford Foundation Report on Labor,* 1970.
20. *New York Times,* June 21, 1971.
21. Personal interview, June 15, 1971.
22. Personal interview, June 16, 1971.
23. *Ibid.*
24. *Detroit Free Press,* May 22, 1971.
25. *Detroit Free Press,* May 29, 1971.
26. *New York Times,* April 20, 1971.
27. *Time,* April 26, 1971.

Notes to Epilogue

Epilogue: Detroit—A Reexamination

1. Quoted in "Metro Detroit: A Look Ahead," reprint of a 15-part *Detroit News* Special Report, January 6, 1985 to January 20, 1985, written by Andrew W. McGill, business editor.
2. Bob Talbert, *Detroit Free Press*, September 27, 1986.
3. *Detroit Free Press*, January 1, 1987.
4. *Detroit Free Press*, November 15, 1986.
5. *Detroit News*, September 28, 1986.
6. Ibid.
7. *Wall Street Journal*, September 12, 1986.
8. *Detroit Free Press*, January 1, 1987.
9. Coleman Young, interview by Barbara From, September 26, 1986, Canadian Broadcasting System.
10. *Detroit Free Press*, October 14, 1986.
11. *Detroit News*, November 1, 1986.
12. *Detroit Free Press*, September 6, 1986.
13. *Detroit Free Press*, January 27, 1986.
14. *Detroit Free Press*, January 7, 1987.
15. UAW letter to author, May 22, 1985.
16. *County and City Data Book*, U.S. Department of Commerce, Bureau of Labor Statistics, 1983, pp. 730–735.
17. "Metro Detroit: A Look Ahead," p. 1.
18. Ibid., p. 2.
19. Ibid., p. 8.
20. Ibid., p. 5.
21. *Current Biography Yearbook*, H. W. Wilson, 1977, p. 454.
22. *Detroit Free Press*, January 22, 1987.
23. Dan Georgakes and Marvin Serkin, *Detroit, I Do Mind Dying, A Study in Urban Revolution*, St. Martin's (New York), 1975, p. 222.
24. Steve Babson with Ron Alpern, David Elsila and John Revitte, *Working Detroit*, Adama Books, New York, 1984, p. 229.
25. Robert B. Reich and John D. Donahue, *New Deals: The Chrysler Revival and the American Dream*, New York Times Books, 1985, p. 269.
26. *Ann Arbor News*, December 27, 1987.
27. *Solidarity*, UAW publication, September, 1985.
28. *Crain's Detroit Business*, August 5, 1985.
29. *Detroit Free Press*, September 1, 1985.
30. *Crain's Detroit Business*, April 15, 1985.
31. Memoranda from Merle Henrickson, director of the Detroit Board of Education, Housing and Planning Division, to Arthur Jefferson, general superintendent of schools, December 13, 1982, May 11, 1983 and March 5, 1985. Personal interview with Henrickson, August 15, 1985.
32. Ibid.
33. "Metro Detroit: A Look Ahead," p. 21.
34. *Detroit Free Press*, May 6, 1985.

278

35. *Second Annual Report,* Michigan Council of Urban League Executives and Urban Affairs Programs of Michigan State University, July, 1985.
36. *Detroit Free Press,* August 9, 1985.
37. Ibid.
38. *Detroit News,* November 6, 1986.
39. *Detroit Free Press,* November 6, 1986.
40. *Ann Arbor News,* November 19, 1985.
41. *Detroit Free Press,* January 15, 1987.
42. *Detroit News,* November 8, 1985.
43. *Detroit Free Press,* November 17, 1986.
44. *Detroit News,* May 28, 1987.
45. *Detroit News,* June 4, 1988.
46. *Detroit Free Press,* June 5, 1988.
47. *New York Times,* June 5, 1988.
48. *Detroit Free Press,* January 30, 1987.
49. *County and City Data Book,* U. S. Department of Commerce, Bureau of the Census, 1983, pp. 854–55.
50. *Detroit Free Press,* November 11, 1985.
51. *Detroit Free Press,* February 3, 1987.
52. *Detroit Free Press,* January 17, 1987.
53. Ibid.
54. *Detroit Free Press,* January 21, 1987.
55. *Detroit Free Press,* February 5, 1987.
56. *Detroit Free Press,* February 11, 1987.
57. *Detroit Free Press,* February 12, 1987.
58. *Detroit Free Press,* February 7, 1987.
59. Ibid.
60. *Detroit Free Press,* November, 1985.
61. B.J. Widick, preface, *Detroit: City of Race and Class Violence,* New York, Quadrangle Books, 1972.
62. *Detroit Free Press,* January 23, 1986.
63. *Detroit Free Press,* February 14, 1987.
64. Ibid.
65. *New York Times,* May 24, 1988.

Index

281

Index

Index

Index

Index

288

Index

B. J. WIDICK, formerly a professor of industrial relations at Columbia University's Graduate School of Business, has long been involved in the Detroit trade unions. He served as research director for the United Rubberworkers Union in the 1930's and was active in the United Autoworkers Union from 1946 to 1961 as a union official and a research economist. Widick taught economics at Wayne State University in the 1960's, and beginning in 1972 served as professor of industrial relations at Columbia University. He has lectured extensively on labor relations both in the United States and abroad, and he was labor correspondent for the *Nation* magazine from 1958 to 1978. His books include *Labor Today: The Triumphs and Failures of Unionism in the United States* and, with Irving Howe, *The UAW and Walter Reuther.*

Manufactured in the United States.